D1249289

"This book represents an essential contribution to scholarship in Indigenous masculinities. As McKegney maps out, we sit at a precarious moment in the field. There have been ruptures of trust and significant questions raised about the efficacy of critical masculinity studies as a viable mode of scholarly inquiry. *Carrying the Burden of Peace* very deliberately engages these questions and persuasively argues for the vital necessity of such work. . . . It is beautifully written, meticulously centered in current critical discourses in Indigenous studies, and offers an important addition to the ongoing scholarly conversations in Indigenous masculinities studies." —LISA TATONETTI, author of *The Queerness of Native American Literature*

# CARRYING THE BURDEN OF PEACE

*Reimagining Indigenous Masculinities Through Story*

## SAM McKEGNEY

THE UNIVERSITY OF
ARIZONA PRESS
TUCSON

The University of Arizona Press
www.uapress.arizona.edu

ISBN-13: 978-0-8165-3703-7 (paper)

Cover and Text design by Duncan Noel Campbell, University of Regina Press
Cover images: "Braided sweetgrass" by Duncan Noel Campbell, and "Braided hair"
by Adobe Stock.

U OF R PRESS
This edition has been published by arrangement with University of Regina Press,
Regina, Saskatchewan, S4S 0A2 Canada. www.uofrpress.ca.

Library of Congress Control Number: 2021931608

Printed in the United States of America
♾ This paper meets the requirements of ANSI/NISO Z39.48-1992 (Permanence of Paper).

*With unending gratitude and respect,*
*this book is dedicated to the memories of*
*Jo-Ann Episkenew,*
*Basil H. Johnston,*
*and*
*Thomas Kimeksun Thrasher,*
*mentors, storyweavers, visionaries.*

# CONTENTS

Burdens and Bundles: An Introduction ix

**1.** Indigenous Masculinities and Story 1

## THE LAND AND THE BODY
**2.** Shame and Deterritorialization 59
**3.** Journeying Back to the Body 89

## THE PEOPLE AND THE GIFT
**4.** De(f/v)iant Generosity: Gender and the Gift 117
**5.** Masculinity and Kinship 147

Naked and Dreaming Forward: A Conclusion 175

*Gratitude* 191
*Acknowledgements* 193
*Notes* 195
*Works Cited* 229
*Permissions* 245
*Index* 247

# BURDENS AND BUNDLES: AN INTRODUCTION

> How do we ensure every Indigenous body, honored and sacred
> knows respect in their bones? —LEANNE BETASAMOSAKE
> SIMPSON (*As We Have Always Done* 51)

Can a critical examination of Indigenous masculinities be an honour song—one that celebrates rather than pathologizes; one that holds people and institutions to account but seeks diversity and strength rather than evidence of victimry; one that struggles to overturn heteropatriarchy without centring settler colonialism; one that validates and affirms without fixing the terms of engagement? Can a critical examination of Indigenous masculinities be an embodied enterprise? Be creative? Be inclusive? Be erotic? Be funny?

Countering the perception that masculinity has been so contaminated by settler heteropatriarchy as to be irredeemable, in this book I examine Indigenous literary art to illuminate the potential generativity of Indigenous masculinities as rubrics for decolonial theorizing. My argument is simple: if we understand "masculinity" as pertaining to qualities connected in some way with maleness, and we recognize that there are individuals within Indigenous families, communities, and nations who identify *as* male (or *with* masculinity regardless of biological sex), then the concession that "masculinity" pertains only to negative characteristics inherited from settler colonialism bears stark consequences. It means that the resources available to affirm those subjectivities will be constrained and perhaps even contaminated by shame, which is why, in the words of enrolled Cherokee scholar Daniel Heath Justice, "literature ought to give us alternatives" ("Fighting" 145). In *Carrying the Burden of Peace*, I pursue imaginings of masculinity that exceed settler colonial logics and can be conscripted in the service of neither heteropatriarchy nor Indigenous dispossession. Ultimately, I contend that masculinities can indeed be included among the resources called upon to help "ensure every Indigenous body . . . knows respect in their bones" (Simpson, *As We* 51)—but only if they are liberated from biological determinism, anthropocentrism, and the putative relationships among gender, race, and power that have come to be naturalized in contemporary North American society.

In *As We Have Always Done: Indigenous Freedom through Radical Resistance*, Michi Saagiig Nishnaabeg theorist Leanne Betasamosake Simpson voices her refusal to concede, in the raising of her children, to coercive gendering practices that serve as instruments of colonial control. Writing within the context of Anishinaabe intelligence, Simpson declares that "my child has a responsibility of figuring out a meaningful way to live in the world that is consistent with her most intimate realities. The job of everyone else is not to direct or control but to support her" (120). Here I will describe the coherence that Simpson champions between "intimate realities" and ways of being "in the world" as integrity: personal, experiential, and embodied knowledge of the self, which enables one to persist in ways that are expressive of one's own truth with neither posturing nor denial; such integrity is cultivated when one's full humanity is honoured and respected by those around them, enabling meaningful integration into the family, community, and nation; it is affirmed through recognition that one is indeed *integral* to those very systems of relation.[1] Knowledge of the self as valued and valuable thus strengthens communities: the more robust the affirmation, the stronger the cultivated sense of personal integrity, the stronger the integration into the community, the more replete the resources available for the affirmation of others. As Kanien'keha:ka writer Beth Brant argues, "a whole [person] is of much better use to my communities than a split one" (57).[2] Yet, as I argue in Chapter 2, settler colonialism works to impede such integration through technologies of social engineering designed both to fragment Indigenous individuals and concomitantly to alienate those individuals from the lands, communities, and nations to which they belong. Settler colonialism seeks to constrain the humanity of Indigenous Peoples by attempting to induce denials of "intimate realities," thereby encouraging personal incoherence while threatening individuals' capacities to relate to each other and to other-than-human kin.[3] Settler colonialism endeavours to "destroy the fabric of Indigenous nationhoods by attempting to destroy our relationality by making it difficult to form sustainable, strong relationships with each other" (Simpson, "Not Murdered"). Stories of personal integrity and wholeness, like many of those analyzed in this book, provide maps for weaving together "intimate realities" with "meaningful way[s] to live in the world." They provide the connective tissue that draws the full, unfettered humanity of Indigenous individuals into families, communities, and nations in consensual, generative, and mutually nourishing ways. Indigenous masculinities, I argue in this book, are among the imaginative resources that can be gleaned from Indigenous literary art to facilitate these processes.

I tend to think of "masculinities" as tools for describing the qualities, actions, characteristics, and behaviours that accrue meaning within a given historical context and social milieu through their association with maleness, as maleness is normalized, idealized, and even demonized. Particularities of culture and history inevitably inform the makeup of the web, and movement between social contexts causes particular threads to gain prominence or to recede into the background as masculinities are conceived and expressed differently in kitchens, workplaces, classrooms, bars, and bedrooms. Yet what comes to be considered masculine within a given context bears a weight of accreted meanings that necessarily falls short of capturing the complex experiences of individual men (or others), even as those meanings continue to influence how people's identities are lived and understood.[4] Given the myriad ways in which heteropatriarchy has ravaged the lives of Indigenous people on Turtle Island—especially Indigenous women, girls, and queer, trans, and two-spirit people—it is unsurprising that within Indigenous Studies "masculinities" are often perceived as barriers to, rather than resources for, decolonization; at times, they are even understood to be weapons that tear at individual and communal bundles, sapping tools vital for healing and continuance.[5] But what if Indigenous masculinities themselves were conceived as medicines? What if Indigenous masculinities were recognized as sacred? In *Love Medicine and One Song: Sâkihtowin-maskihkiy êkwa pêyak-nikamowin*, Cree-Métis poet Gregory Scofield reminds us that medicines can harm as well as heal: "'Pêyahtihk,'[6] the old people would say. 'It is not to be taken lightly for the consequences are great and, if used improperly, often fatal'" (1). As social constructs in a volatile and oppressive reality informed by settler colonialism, masculinities can carry the weight of and perpetuate oppression, but they are not doomed to be always and only negative. To deny the beauty, vulnerability, and grace that can be expressed and experienced as masculinity is to concede to settler colonialism's myopic vision of the world; it is to eschew the creativity that is among our greatest gifts. This book weaves together stories of Indigenous life, love, eroticism, pain, and joy as teachings that articulate more complex, diverse, and human understandings of Indigenous masculinity than those inherited from settler colonialism, in the hope that the bundles of Indigenous boys, girls, diversely gendered youth, and others will not be impoverished of medicines in this world conditioned by settler heteropatriarchy. These are stories that explore and critique and create masculinities that might be of value or might be of harm, and they are stories that foster the knowledge to understand the difference. As Anishinaabe writer Kateri Akiwenzie-Damm argues, such storywork is necessary for cultivating conditions in which her sons will be "able to find a wider range of depictions of Indigenous men that will maybe inspire them . . . and teach them both in that Nanabozho way of what to do and what not to do. . . . They'll have more to draw on than I think Indigenous men have had in the past few generations" ("Affirming Protectorship" 181).

There remains, of course, a legitimate reason for anxiety in this enterprise. Simpson, for example, worries "that Indigenous masculinities reinforce the colonial gender binary, centering cis-gendered straight men (who are already centered in everything) instead of dismantling heteropatriarchy, and that the binary set up between feminisms and masculinities cages queer people out" (*As We* 137). For these reasons, Yellowknives Dene theorist Glen Coulthard argues that "critical indigenous masculinities should vacate not occupy space that indigenous feminist, queer and trans voices should occupy" (@denerevenge 27 Jan. 2016), and Simpson states unequivocally that "I am *not* suggesting that we center resurgence around masculinity, even critical masculinity" (*As We* 52; emphasis added). The utility of the present project thus depends upon its ability to illuminate artistic interventions that invigorate manifold, malleable, and generative conceptions of Indigenous masculinities *without* recentring "masculinity"—to borrow from Anishinaabe scholar Randy Jackson, the goal of this project is to facilitate fertile dialogue without "taking up . . . space in a way that crushes people out" (interview). We need to hold up stories that nourish and nurture, stories that generate space for other stories still, not stories that silence and segregate and deny the value of other perspectives: mutuality and generativity over hierarchy and coercion. If the cruel inertia of settler colonialism makes the reader skeptical of the enterprise, I understand, and I remain open to the possibility that the premise with which I began—that masculinities are redeemable as resources for decolonial work—is false. However, I genuinely believe it to be true and strive in the pages that follow to show you why by drawing on the brilliance of Indigenous literary artists.

## MASCULINITIES AS ETHICS, NOT IDENTITIES

Work on this project began over a decade prior to the crafting of this introduction. As a settler scholar of Indigenous literatures, I endeavour to be guided in my work by cues to criticism emergent from "the literature itself" (Blaeser 54), and in the mid-2000s I perceived a recurrent theme of surrogate brotherhood in recent novels by Indigenous authors from lands claimed by Canada. These novels depict the relationship between an introverted protagonist and a more demonstrably manly mentor figure with whom the protagonist performs acts of brotherhood.[7] In each of these stories, the protagonist must ultimately resist the siren pull of his surrogate brother's social capital and the captivating draw of that brother's propensity for violence in order to construct an endorsable identity. I speculated, at the time, that the similarities among the relationships depicted in these novels might betray anxiety about the limited models of healthy masculinity available to some Indigenous youth and the dangers within such contexts of turning to mainstream masculinities characterized by individualism and violence. To test this hypothesis, I sought out Indigenous masculinity theory, only to find that scant scholarly work in the area had yet been published: Ngāti Pūkenga theorist Brendan Hokowhitu's articles on Māori masculinity, popular culture, and sport offered the most significant and sustained interventions in the nascent field, and brief discussions of masculinity and men's issues could be found in the work of Indigenous feminist scholars such as Kim Anderson and Paula Gunn Allen and in the work of psychologists and anthropologists such as Eduardo Duran and Bonnie Duran. Almost nothing had been published on Indigenous masculinities and literature in the North American context beyond critiques of how depictions of Indigenous hypermasculinity proliferate in the fictional writing of settlers.[8] At the time, no book-length scholarly study of Indigenous masculinities in the North American context had yet been published.[9] Outpacing academics, as is often the case, Indigenous creative artists exposed gaps in the critical discourse, pointing toward and provoking urgently needed conversations.

As a settler, I had neither the knowledge nor the experience to begin developing the Indigenous masculinity theory toward which I believed Indigenous writers to be gesturing, but, in consultation with Indigenous colleagues and mentors,[10] I recognized that I could arrange opportunities for Indigenous thinkers from a wide array of genders and positionalities (not just cis-men) to reflect on masculinity in ways that might enable such theory to gestate. Between October 2010 and August 2013, I conducted twenty-three interviews with Indigenous artists, activists, academics, and Elders on the subject of Indigenous masculinities and gender, the majority of which were published in *Masculindians* in 2014, upon which I draw in my thinking for the present volume. *Masculindians* was part of a dramatic shift in the critical terrain during these years. Since the time that I began thinking critically about Indigenous masculinities, Kānaka Maoli scholar Ty P. Kāwika Tengan's seminal ethnography on the Hawaiian men's group the Hale Mua, *Native Men Remade: Gender and Nation in Contemporary Hawai'i* (2008), was published, followed by Diné scholar Lloyd L. Lee's *Diné Masculinities: Conceptualizations and Reflections* (2013)—these are the only two published monographs on Indigenous masculinities at the time of my writing. Hokowhitu's prolific work in the field has continued apace, supplemented by that of more junior scholars such as Robert Henry (Métis), Shane Keepness (Saulteaux), Erin Sutherland (Métis), and several others, as well as scholars of Indigenous gender and queer theory such as Lisa Tatonetti (settler) and Scott Morgensen (settler), who at times have turned their critical attention toward questions of masculinity. Scholarly gatherings on Indigenous masculinities have been held in Kingston, Ontario (2015), Edmonton, Alberta (2015), and Honolulu, Hawai'i (2016),[11] and the groundbreaking collection *Indigenous Men and Masculinities: Legacies, Identities, Regeneration*, edited by Cree-Métis gender theorist Kim Anderson and Cree scholar Robert Innes, was published in 2015. The critical context with which I am engaging in *Carrying the Burden of Peace* is therefore considerably different from what it had been when I began conceiving this work. Although I can speak only from my experiential reality as a white, able-bodied, cis-gendered, heterosexual, settler male—who is a father, husband, sibling, son, uncle, and university professor—I aspire in this volume to contribute nuance and creative energy to the burgeoning field of Indigenous masculinities studies by holding up the work of Indigenous literary artists, as well as sharing some of the critical considerations that have evolved for me throughout a decade of research and reflection, of questioning and listening. I offer this work to honour those who have engaged with me directly in the conversations that led to *Masculindians*, as well as those Indigenous scholars, artists, and activists from whom I have learned through their critical and creative work. The willingness of so many to share with me their experiences, wisdom, and expectations regarding masculinity and gender demonstrates not only their immense generosity and trust but also, I believe, sincere hope that those conversations would expand, gain traction, diversify, and develop. This book is a response, in part, to that hope and an expression of what I consider to be my responsibilities in relation to the gifts that I have received.[12] I acknowledge the limits of my knowledge and my awareness that any unintended adverse impacts of what I write here are likely disproportionately to affect Indigenous persons rather than me—particularly women, girls, queer, trans, and two-spirit people but also cis-hetero men and boys.[13] The responsibility for all that is shared here is my own, and I gratefully anticipate correction, elaboration, and critique from those for whom the issues engaged in this book are most vital. Although I understand that, in the words of Simpson, "there is virtually no room for white people in resurgence" (*As We* 228), I hope that the Indigenous creative and critical thought curated in this book can provide resources of value to that world-making imperative.

In a critical volume such as the present one, starting points matter, and I intend to begin this work in strength and beauty by discussing masculinities that persist outside the straightjacket of settler simulations and beyond the impoverished inheritance of what Morgensen calls "colonial masculinity." Ktunaxa poet Smokii Sumac's award-winning debut collection *You Are Enough: Love Poems for the End of the World* (2018) recognizes the utility of Indigenous masculinities while refusing to accept the dominant ways in which masculinities circulate in contemporary society. *You Are Enough*[14] in many ways is an honour song to the author's female-to-male (FTM) transition and, as such, untethers masculinity from the cis-male body while retaining masculinities as aspirational values.[15] Sumac's speaker asks, "without trusting men / how do i become / a man / worthy of trust?" (49). The poignant question reveals the conflicted contours of masculinity in Sumac's work: it betrays awareness of masculinities corrupted by violence—"our trained bodies know / dangerous men / the way they / won't listen let up" (49)—but remains committed to the possibility that masculinities can be understood and expressed differently. As Simpson directs, Sumac's speaker pursues a way of "being in the world" that aligns with his "most intimate realities," which means simultaneously honouring masculinities worth claiming and guarding against the replication of behaviours potentially legible as "masculine" that tear at the fabric of relationality and well-being. Significantly, the arbiter of worthy masculinities in Sumac's delineation here is trust, a relational imperative that overturns the hyperindividualism through which dominant masculinities tend to be understood. The kind of "man" whom Sumac's speaker desires to "become" is a question not of anatomy but of ethics: one who demonstrates relational accountability. The collection's ethos of becoming thus resonates with Scofield's description in *Masculindians* of consciously "working to become the type of man that I would like to have had in my life. So to become the type of father to my nieces and nephews, to be the type of lover to my partner, to be the type of friend to my friend.... That's what I've marked in my growing and evolving masculinity—to strive" ("Liberation" 216). Both Scofield and Sumac perceive masculinities in aspirational terms, not as teleological destinations or fixed identity formations; masculinities are creative tools, medicines among manifold others in one's bundle that can foster senses of integrity in the perpetual process of meaning making: "still always changing / still always transitioning," Sumac writes in *You Are Enough*, "just as we all are / always" (79).

Scofield and Sumac write into an imbroglio—a context in which Indigenous masculinities are at once overdetermined and underrepresented (at least in terms of their diversity and complexity). Each writer actively disavows self-centred and dominative masculinities while holding up other understandings, expressions, and performances of masculinity that augur alternative futures. The latter masculinities are delineated, for Scofield, via relational responsibilities (to kin, to lovers, to friends) and, for Sumac, by honouring consent as an ethical imperative. In Sumac's poem "haiku consent series or #makesexgreatthefirsttime," the speaker's commitment to consent overturns the insidious lessons of settler colonialism, creating conditions of "radical balance" in which "a revolution of sex" becomes possible (*You* 28). The poem begins with a battle cry—"forget the bad sex / i want to read the good" (27)—before interrogating how "bad sex" is actively fostered then normalized within heteropatriarchal society. The second section of the poem reads thus:

> my first time was good.
> when i say this to women
> they are often shocked

we are taught instead
it should hurt
that it's breaking
something inside you

not taught our pleasure
only shame
turn the lights off
normal is for him

did you get him off?
wait through long pounding hours
or just-a-minutes (this never happens)

taught to hold our breath
stare at how many ceilings
to-do list in mind

my first time was good
the consensual first time
the one that i count (28)

Depicting an experience prior to transition, Sumac's speaker reveals the radically divergent teachings about sex, sensuality, and power encountered by those whom dominant society genders male and those whom society genders female (repeating the word *taught* three times to stress the simulated nature of such lessons). Women are taught that sex is shameful and destructive—that it is "breaking / something inside you"—and, as such, are conditioned to disavow or unlearn their own "pleasure." Women are taught that their role in sex is to facilitate male pleasure—"did you get him off?"—which is why "normal is *for him*": the quotidian norms of heteropatriarchy coerce (some) men to imagine sex as something that one does *to* another and sexual gratification as something that one takes *from* another. As Justice critiques, "If the male body isn't giving harm, it's taking pleasure . . . either assaultive or extractive. One or the other, there's nothing else" ("Fighting" 145). Such myopic heteropatriarchal teachings, however, obfuscate desire's fluidity, as well as the capacity for sensual intimacy to be mutually generative (as I will discuss in Chapter 3); sensual pleasure, as Sumac's poetry celebrates, is anything but a finite resource.

Sumac's collection transcends these limited understandings of sex, gender, and sensuality by depicting erotic encounters among diversely gendered individuals and at various stages of the speaker's process of FTM transition[16] and by championing consent as a decolonial imperative. Consent, in Sumac's work, is a means of simultaneously honouring another's full humanity and cultivating the conditions necessary for genuine interpersonal intimacy; by transcending self-interest, consent enables the acknowledgement of another's *integrity* while making interpersonal *integration*—whether in terms of erotics or nation building—possible. Consent constitutes an ethic of care that is both vigilant and pliable: powerful yet gentle, responsive yet sovereign. In the fourth section of the poem, Sumac writes of a relationship in which the speaker's erotic attraction is not reciprocated. Rather than betraying a sense of rejection, the speaker offers that "you / are enough / / and you deserve above all / your autonomy" (31). Over the course of the collection, the titular phrase "you are enough" constitutes a developing cadence that maps the speaker's active cultivation of self-love in the face of settler colonial regimes of dis-integration and dehumanization. As such, its use here to honour another's autonomy via an ethos of consent implies an echoing back upon the self—consent, and the integrity that it nurtures, go both ways. Although addressed to the autonomous beloved, the reader recognizes the "you" in "you are enough" as simultaneously affirming the speaker's own self-worth, thereby enabling conditions of mutual well-being. Indeed, "you are enough,"[17] taken seriously, also means "I am enough." The dynamic interweaving of mutuality and autonomy creates the conditions of "radical balance" for which the poem ultimately calls, a revolution of gendered thought that shatters the shackles of heteropatriarchy.

Although the subtitle *End of the World* speaks to the apocalypse of colonial catastrophe, I am inclined to read it in aspirational terms: as an end to the world inherited from settler colonialism and the heteropatriarchal regimes of gender through which that world operates. Through consent, Sumac challenges his readers to "creat[e] the world / each ask / each yes at a time / co-write the story" (28). He not only dares to imagine a decolonial world but also gifts his Indigenous readers (and others) weapons with which to touch such a world into being[18]—one weapon is consent and another is the depiction of masculinities worth claiming. Wide-eyed and unflinching, Sumac's poetry is far from utopian, but neither is it apocalyptic; it is part of an inspired movement of young Indigenous artistic visionaries—including Billy-Ray Belcourt (Driftpile Cree), Tenille Campbell (Dene-Métis), Alicia Elliott (Tuscarora), Lindsay Nixon (Cree-Métis-Saulteaux), and Joshua Whitehead (Oji-Cree) writing in lands claimed by Canada—dedicated to singing into reality better ways of being in the world: "a revolution of sex / for every human" (28). In relation to the critical enterprise of *Carrying the Burden of Peace*, Sumac's poetry inspires me, challenges me, keeps me honest. It illuminates the vibrant possibilities of complex, diverse, non-dominative, and empowered masculinities tempered— or, better, *enlivened*—by consent. It shows that masculinities—those that we choose, not simply those that we inherit or confront—can be ethics rather than identities, medicines for the bundles of those who would choose to gather them. And, at the same time, it regis- ters possibilities beyond masculinity; the collection's celebration of "genderless space[s]" of consensual intimacy reminds readers that, if masculinities stagnate, calcify, and coerce, then we don't need them. And if masculinity does not suit us, as Sumac writes, then we can always "find a word that fits more" (19).

## WHAT IS AT STAKE IN A CRITICAL TURN TO INDIGENOUS MASCULINITIES STUDIES?

Even in light of creative interventions by Sumac and others, as well as the important critical developments catalogued above, the field of Indigenous masculinities studies remains at considerable risk of backsliding and reinscribing the very heteropatriarchal structures that it purports to critique. A few incidents in recent years coincid- ing with the increased institutionalization of the field indicate the ongoing potential for masculinities studies to engender unsafe conditions for Indigenous students, staff, faculty, and others—incidents about which a study such as the present one must be mindful and, in some cases, in which I myself am implicated. At the Indigenous masculinities gathering in Honolulu in 2016, representatives of the Hawaiian men's group 'Aha Kāne[19] were questioned by students about the place of queer and two-spirit people in the revitalization of traditional Hawaiian culture. The response of one of the group members implied a personal distaste for what he purported to be the unnecessary flamboyance of some queer Hawaiians,[20] thereby making queer and two-spirit participants in the gathering—as well as others—feel unwelcome and excluded. The fact that the organizers of the gathering, of which I was one, did not intervene at this point left students in the audience to call out the homophobic statement and to be the ones tasked with advocating for greater inclusivity.[21]

In April 2018, the University of Victoria in British Columbia suspended entry into its Indigenous Governance Program[22] after an independent third-party report found that the program left students "'traumatized'" because of "'discrimination'" and a culture of "'hypermasculinity' that provided little classroom space for diverse points of view" (Barrera). The report, compiled following interviews with thirty current and former students, staff, and faculty, observed a pervasive sense that the program had "'little tolerance for LGBTQ and two-spirited individuals'" (Barrera). Given the significance of the program as a hub for the theorization of decolonization and resurgence, the development of a climate of hypermasculinity intolerant of gender and sexual diversity presents cause for alarm and points to the difficulty of institutionalizing Indigenous masculinities studies without lending credence to the gender binary and to gender hierarchies—concerns articulated cogently by Simpson above. Furthermore, accusations of inappropriate and possibly predatory behaviour levelled on social media at the program's founder, Kanien'keha:ka scholar Taiaiake Alfred (considered by many to be an expert on Indigenous masculinities, although he has not written directly on the subject[23]), complicate matters further. Regarding his resignation from the University of Victoria in early 2019, Alfred cited "the ways I embodied toxic masculinity and how I did wrong and harmed people because of it" (qtd. in C. Wilson);

significantly, however, Alfred has not retreated from public life in the wake of his departure, and he has continued to give talks and perform consulting work in the field of Indigenous Studies.

In one further example, Saganaw Anishinaabe–Black scholar of Indigenous masculinities Kyle T. Mays authored an apology to "Indigenous womyn" for what he described as his own "toxic masculinity" in a 2017 blog post. Explicitly calling out "Indigenous cishetero" male academics for "harassing and sexually assaulting female students," Mays acknowledged that hypermasculinity in academia "festers and destroys an[y] possibility for change." "If we are serious about decolonization," he argued, "then we need to decolonize our behavior, ourselves, and imagine new ways of being Indigenous men."[24] The hypocrisy that Mays called out was brought into stark relief, however, when Cherokee scholar Adrienne Keene, on whose site Mays's work was originally posted, deleted the blog and eventually embedded it within a larger piece called "The Problematics of Disingenuous Public Apologies." Keene reported that she had been "approached by a woman . . . with the support of several other women who have witnessed and experienced problematic behavior" from Mays and that "recent behavior ha[d] not changed since the public apology," leading Keene to worry that "the continued presence of the post was allowing the behavior to continue." The attendant controversy illustrates how critical writing through the lens of Indigenous masculinities studies (purportedly in alliance with Indigenous feminisms and Indigenous women) risks sheltering further masculinist transgressions; it also illuminates the nuanced, rigorous, and collaborative ways in which Indigenous women and others refuse to permit the perpetuation of such hypocrisy. And it alerts us to dangerous discrepancies that can obtain between public-facing knowledge production and interpersonal behaviours behind closed doors, as well as the necessity, in Nixon's words, of "responsible community-led accountability measures" regarding "men" and "their toxic behaviors." I share these incidents not to imply that homophobia, misogyny, and/or hypermasculinity inevitably pervade Indigenous masculinities studies but to indicate the vigilance required to keep these corrosive inheritances at bay and to foster the inclusivity, generosity of spirit, and safety necessary for the field to contribute to "the dismantling of heteropatriarchy as the crucial nation-building exercise of our time" (Simpson, *As We* 92–93).

The stakes are undeniably high, as is illustrated by one more example, which registers the complicated interconnections among abstract ethical principles, embodied day-to-day struggles, and political realities that need to be navigated in this work. In 2014, Cree-Swedish poet and scholar Neal McLeod was witnessed striking his common-law partner in public and charged with domestic assault, ultimately taking "a plea deal, [going] on probation for a year and [being] eventually ousted by [Trent] [U]niversity after negotiating a settlement" (Tuffin). McLeod's criminal behaviour is salient given the public debate that it provoked, the author's previous claims to recovery from toxic masculinity, and his poetry's consistent attentiveness to themes of masculine violence. In *Songs to Kill a Wîhtikow* (2005), for instance, McLeod uses the mythical cannibal beast wîhtikow from Cree culture as a metaphor for the violent inheritances of settler colonialism with which contemporary Indigenous people must contend, and in *Gabriel's Beach* (2008) he discusses the "fire" of "Gabriel's Beach" as the strength, courage, and capacity for violence required for success in warfare, which risks proving to be disastrous in everyday life. On the basis of his critical and creative work, I was eager to conduct an interview with McLeod back in 2012. In that conversation, he acknowledges having "been a violent male in the past, both with males and with female partners," and having "signed up for a program to deal with these things" in his "mid-twenties." His claim that "we should talk about [gender-based violence] and think about how we got here" ("Tending" 209), which is presented in the interview seemingly teleologically in relation to eliminating violence against Indigenous women yet occurred prior to the assault leading to his conviction, is thus both prescient and insufficient: talking about it did not protect McLeod's former common-law partner. This contradiction also illuminates my possible implication in exacerbating conditions that I had set out to critique. Some of those to whom I have turned for expertise in Indigenous masculinities theory and whose work I have celebrated in publications such as *Masculindians* have proven to be violent and predatory—they have demonstrated the very behaviours that I had imagined my scholarship as working to eliminate.[25]

When *kisiskáciwan: Indigenous Voices from Where the River Flows Swiftly*, the first comprehensive collection of Indigenous literary art from Saskatchewan, was set for release in 2018, a group of Indigenous women writers from the province objected to the inclusion of work by McLeod, who, they argued, "to the best of our knowledge has not made amends to those he has harmed" (Lee et al.). The original signatories of the open letter—Erica Violet Lee (Cree), Nickita Longman (Saulteaux), Sylvia McAdam (Cree), Lindsay Knight (Cree), Night Kinistino (Cree), and Dawn Dumont (Cree)—asked the University of Regina Press (URP) and the editors of the collection "to honor the experiences of Indigenous women and abuse survivors by removing Neal McLeod from this anthology" and to "recognize the lifesaving necessity of supporting Indigenous women, girls, and Two-Spirit people who name abuse and abusers." In response, URP Director Bruce Walsh stated that, although the open letter's "concerns are ones with which I strongly agree and support," "I can't deliver what [its signatories] want. I must stand with our editor," because to do otherwise would be to "abandon [editor] Jesse Archibald-Barber's academic freedom" ("Publisher's Response").[26] Eventually, McLeod withdrew his work from the anthology, stating that "I do not want other writers to feel uncomfortable or feel as though they must choose between academic freedom and other values they hold dear. I do not want others to leave so I can stay" ("Neal McLeod").

The *kisiskáciwan* controversy sheds light on the fraught nature of balancing the need for identifiable actions to combat gender-based violence against Indigenous women, girls, and queer and two-spirit people and the importance of understanding the multiple factors and long history that inform intimate violence in Indigenous communities. The tension—as well as the urgency of finding ethical pathways beyond it[27]—is articulated effectively by Elliott: "I don't know how we can acknowledge the journeys and pain of Indigenous men like Neal McLeod . . . without silencing Indigenous women and two-spirit people. But I do know that ignoring it or excusing it is not going to help." At the time of the controversy, acclaimed Cree poet and fellow contributor to the collection Louise Bernice Halfe counselled the importance of retaining belief in the possibility of "redemption for those men who have worked hard to change their behaviors" ("Introspection"). Noting that "we can learn so much from the experiences and stories of these men and women who are in recovery,"[28] Halfe asked her Indigenous readers, "If there is no forgiveness, then what? What do we have? Is there no hope?" Her advocacy for "hope" resonates in complicated ways with open letter signatory Erica Violet Lee's suggestion that "Holding someone accountable for the harm they're causing to your community is not the same thing as throwing them away. It's the opposite. And it's done as an act of love for our community" (qtd. in Lederman). Although these authors disagreed publicly about McLeod's inclusion in *kisiskáciwan*, their aspirational commitments—Lee to "love for our community" and Halfe to the "humility, respect, and kindness [of] our community" ("Introspection")—remain animated by ethics of accountability. As Halfe states, Indigenous women "want men to accept their responsibility for violence and want accountability."

Not unlike Lee, Halfe demands that violent men work "hard" and genuinely "change their behaviors" as preconditions for "forgiveness." Not unlike Halfe, Lee resists notions of irredeemability—of "throwing [men] away"—but demands legible action to promote the safety of women, girls, and queer and two-spirit people. Nixon elaborates the complex moral, ethical, and practical considerations at play in these embroiled demands:

> Transformative justice in our communities would mean eventually allowing men who have hurt others back into community life. We must make sure the question does not become, What are we doing to ensure these men are welcomed back? It puts responsibility on those hurt to mediate abusive relations. We must focus on what these toxic men—who have hurt and might continue to hurt— are measurably doing within their relationships before we allow them back into community spaces. What do we require of them?

In the discussions of Halfe, Lee, and Nixon, forgiveness is neither a given nor an impossibility; it is a relational ethic that demands accountability and "work"; it is an objective that must be weighed in relation to community well-being and safety.[29] In contrast to such nuanced renderings, I worry that Walsh's recourse to "academic freedom" as a universal imperative in his response to the open letter risks belying the messiness of reality within the settler colonial present. The elevation of "academic freedom" to the realm of the irrefutable—rather than understanding it as a value to be weighed in relation to other values, especially when discussing the lived reality of persistent vulnerability to violence faced by Indigenous women—risks betraying, however unintentionally, a failure to listen.[30]

At the present impasse, Lee's elaboration of "wastelands theory" is helpful. Lee defines wastelands as "[s]paces that are considered not simply unworthy of defence, but deserving of devastation. . . . A wasteland is a place where, we are taught, there is nothing and no one salvageable. . . . Wastelands are spaces deemed unworthy of healing because of the scale and amount of devastation that has occurred there" ("In Defence"). Although the tactical exclusion of perpetrators such as McLeod—from collections or from communities—represents a performative disavowal, a form of banishment potentially marking such men as "unworthy of healing," Lee claims that "the heart of wastelands theory" is that "there is nothing and no one beyond healing. So we return again and again to the discards, gathering scraps for our bundles, and we tend to the devastation with destabilizing gentleness, carefulness, softness" ("In Defence"). The impasse is traversed through the achievement of balance between recognition, on the one hand, that "no one [is] beyond healing" and that many Indigenous men, in McLeod's own words, need to "find a way to heal, to make amends, to love, and to one day feel worthy of love" ("Neal McLeod") and recognition, on the other, that "concrete actions [are required] to build a future where gendered colonial violence is over" (Lee et al.). Each of these is necessary, I would argue, for all Indigenous women, children, queer, trans, and two-spirit people, and even cis-hetero men, to be safe and for communities to flourish; each is required to foster

Indigenous futures in which gender-based violence is unthinkable, in which "every Indigenous body" is "free to direct [its] energy and work towards a place of thriving" (Simpson, *As We*, 51; also see Lee et al.). Throughout this book, I strive for a cautious balance between insistence that neither individual Indigenous men nor concepts of Indigenous masculinity are irredeemable and awareness that toxic masculinity, hypermasculinity, and gender-based violence will stand forever in the way of Indigenous resurgence and decolonization.[31]

## THOSE WHO CARRY THE BURDEN OF PEACE

Building from the central premises (1) that settler colonialism has always been and continues to be a gendered enterprise and (2) that colonial interventions in Indigenous gender systems have adversely affected not only Indigenous women and queer, trans, and gender non-conforming folks but also—and at times differently—cis-Indigenous men, in Chapter 1 I endeavour to build a critical framework for discussing Indigenous masculinities that will not collapse back into a reinforcement of colonial heteropatriarchy. I turn to Indigenous literary art to uncover a vocabulary for speaking about Indigenous masculinities that does not rely upon what Driftpile Cree theorist Billy-Ray Belcourt calls "the putative givenness" of dominant ideas of masculinity imposed by settler colonialism ("Can"). I begin Chapter 1 by analyzing the gendered dimensions of settler colonialism in Canada as experienced by the Haudenosaunee (the confederacy of nations on whose lands the majority of this book has been written).[32] I then assess the capacity of Indigenous masculinities theory to engage productively with community concerns emergent from the first half of the chapter, paying particular attention to the creation story of Sky Woman and the story of Aionwahta and the Peacemaker as told by Kanien'keha:ka Elder Tom Porter. I conclude the chapter by championing a malleable form of Indigenous masculinity theory characterized by creativity and catalyzed by cross-pollination with Indigenous feminisms and Indigenous queer and two-spirit theory.

In Chapter 2, I examine the territorial dimensions of settler colonial technologies of social engineering in Canada. I argue that efforts to police gender in residential schools were motivated by the desire to efface embodied experiences of territorial persistence. Looking at testimony from the Indian Residential Schools Truth and Reconciliation Commission as well as autobiography, fiction, and poetry by residential school survivors, I consider how shame has been wielded historically in residential schools and elsewhere as a means of alienating Indigenous people from their bodies, their kinship systems, and their territories, with profound effects on understandings and experiences of gender. I conclude the chapter by classifying a trek of two thousand kilometres by a group of predominantly male Cree youth, known as the Residential School Walkers, as what Ty P. Kāwika Tengan calls "embodied discursive action" (*Native Men Remade*)—in this case action that self-consciously reintegrates gender complementarity while reconnecting the individual with the land in an expression of radical reterritorialization and sovereignty.

In response to the coerced alienations from the body examined in the preceding chapter, in Chapter 3 I ask what is at stake in sensual depictions of Indigenous male bodies. Although queer and two-spirit theory has been effective in destabilizing biological determinism and in recognizing the fluidity of gender concepts within many Indigenous worldviews, it has tended to retain a celebratory posture toward the feminine that has not been shared toward the masculine. For example, building from the work of Chrystos and Beth Brant, non-citizen Cherokee scholar Qwo-Li Driskill identifies "radical Two-Spirit *woman-centred* erotics as tools for healing from colonization" ("Stolen from Our Bodies" 59; emphasis added). In this chapter, I consider whether radical *man-centred* erotics—whether two-spirit, queer, straight, cis, trans, or otherwise—might participate in the decolonizing processes that Driskill champions.[33] I begin the chapter by examining a short story by Anishinaabe writer Leanne Betasamosake Simpson to illustrate the need to deconstruct what I refer to as the competitive ecology of gender that has been normalized through settler colonialism and to consider the generative power of intimacy as a decolonial ethic. I conclude the chapter with analysis of poetry by and interviews with Cree-Métis poet Gregory Scofield, whose work exemplifies a form of chosen vulnerability that serves to insulate expressions of masculine intimacy from lapsing into domination.

In Chapter 4, I build from the previous chapter's discussions of domination to consider the role of economics in policing forms of masculine identity through an analysis of Haisla-Heiltsuk writer Eden Robinson's fiction. I begin the chapter by employing theorizations of gift economy by Syilx intellectual Jeannette Armstrong and Sami scholar Rauna Kuokkanen in the study of two of Robinson's short stories in order to understand how the imposition of settler heteropatriarchy in North America—and particularly in the Pacific Northwest—has relied upon the naturalization of economic exchange through capitalism. I then turn to Robinson's *Blood Sports* (2006), a novel whose plot is impelled by notions of debt and indebtedness. Set in Vancouver's Downtown East Side, the novel is hyperconscious of economic conditions, with affluent, sociopathic drug dealer Jeremy exercising indebtedness to maintain control over his chronically impoverished cousin Tom. I am particularly interested in how the duo's antithetical core economic values—Jeremy's elitist domination through wealth and violence and Tom's selfless generosity—inform their radically divergent performances of masculinity. According to Kuokkanen, exchange naturalizes settler heteropatriarchy because it is "ego oriented" and "based on the values of self-interest, competition, domination, and individualism" (30); gift giving, conversely, can foster radically different gender imaginings because it is "other-oriented" and "based on the values of care, cooperation, and bonding" (30). I ultimately argue in this chapter that, although Tom concedes the legitimacy of the system of exchange over which Jeremy will always maintain control—suggesting at various points in the novel that "I *owe* him" (e.g., 50)—his stubborn refusal to abandon the logic of the gift allows Tom to animate alternative masculinities that exceed his cousin's hypermasculine violence and chart pathways toward more just and nourishing futures.

In Chapter 5, I analyze the multi-genre work of Tłįchǫ writer Richard Van Camp, whose oeuvre has proven to be consistently invested in questions of masculinity, intimacy, embodiment, and violence. Building from interviews conducted with Van Camp over the past decade, I elaborate the variety of models of masculinity developed in his short fiction, children's literature, and comics, recognizing the significance of themes of vulnerability, erotics, and brotherhood discussed elsewhere in the book. In particular, I pursue the often-unacknowledged affinities between humour and sensual intimacy in Van Camp's work before turning to his 1996 novel *The Lesser Blessed* as an investigation of the role of kinship in dealing with the contemporary struggles of Indigenous male-identified youth. I argue that the novel illustrates the danger of failing to honour kinship ties as ongoing and dynamic responsibilities. Hearkening back to the previous chapter, I analyze whether models of masculinity that privilege individual freedom over communal responsibility offer viable futures for the socially disenfranchised, such as several of Van Camp's protagonists. I then turn to Tłı̨chǫ practices of kinship to pursue how cultural models of pluralist, non-dominative masculinities can be mobilized in the ongoing reimagining of gendered identities for which the novel ultimately calls.

As a response to the call for visionary engagements with gender that I read in the works of the authors at the centre of this study, in the conclusion I revisit the central themes of the book to consider what flexible, non-dominative, vulnerable, sensual, embodied, and empowered masculinities look like through a series of reflections on Kanien'keha:ka-Heiltsuk filmmaker Zoe Leigh Hopkins's film *Mohawk Midnight Runners*. Rather than tying up the various argumentative threads of the book, the conclusion is intended to open up the conversation further by thinking about what Indigenous masculinities studies might look like in the years ahead. Returning to the place-based concerns of the introduction, I consider the Kanien'kéha word commonly translated as "warrior"—*rotiskenrakéh:te*—as a way of reflecting on the decolonial potential of Indigenous masculinities that exceed both colonial simulations and static notions of tradition. Although focalizing this book through a lens of warriorhood risks trading in stereotypes about the inevitability of collapse between masculinity and violence—particularly *Indigenous* masculinities and violence, as work by Brendan Hokowhitu, Brian Klopotek, and Gail Guthrie Valaskakis makes clear[34]—the constellation of ideas embedded in the Kanien'kéha term offers more fertile possibilities. As

Kanien'keha:ka activist and artist Ellen Gabriel explains, the word *rotiskenrakéh:te* is translated among the Kanien'keha:ka as "those who carry the burden of peace." According to Gabriel, "A real warrior uses peaceful means first; is one who honours, respects and practices peace in their daily lives but has the ability to protect the people and the land when a threat to their safety is imminent" ("Those").[35]

I chose *Carrying the Burden of Peace* as the title for this volume for a few reasons. First, the notion of warriorhood—both its problematics and its possibilities—came up frequently during my conversations on Indigenous masculinities with Indigenous artists, activists, academics, and Elders.[36] Second, "the English or French terms for warriors [bely] the movement of Indigenous peoples and our histories of resistance against colonial imperialism" (Gabriel, "Those"), and for this reason many Indigenous people argue that Indigenous languages should be mobilized to provide greater nuance and flexibility for roles and responsibilities. Third, the lands upon which I live and work are the lands of the Haudenosaunee people, and I consider it valuable both ethically and intellectually to learn from the knowledge traditions of the territories to which one is responsible as a settler colonist. Fourth, ideas embedded in the expression "carrying the burden of peace" are woven throughout every chapter in this volume, providing its skeletal structure and its argumentative compass. To *carry* something implies embodiment, territoriality, and movement, which are resurgent imperatives discussed in Chapter 2. A *burden* suggests responsibilities that extend beyond the individual, as discussed via erotic intimacy in Chapter 3, gift economies in Chapter 4, and kinship relations in Chapter 5. And, as Chapter 1 and the conclusion aim to articulate, *peace* within contemporary settler colonial realities is more than the absence of conflict; rather, it is a dynamic responsibility with creative, collaborative, and critical dimensions. "Carrying the burden of peace" suggests, to me, myriad possibilities for active, embodied, and accountable subjectivities that exceed the impoverished imaginings of colonial masculinities while drawing on systems of knowledge in which masculinities resonate markedly differently.

In "'Just Make Me Look Like Aquaman,'" Sumac addresses both the journey toward integrity and the disintegrating influence of

**Image 1:** Smokii Sumac, Vancouver, 2019. *Photograph by Tenille Campbell*

colonial trauma. Speaking of the latter, Sumac writes that *"those things stopped me from being able to know who I was. . . . They took me away from myself."* Later in the piece, interspersed with stunning photographs of the author's naked transitioning body taken by Dene-Métis artist and poet Tenille Campbell, Sumac shares that Campbell's photography "is medicine because she *sees* us." The vibrant interactions among Sumac's courageous claiming of bodily vulner-ability, Campbell's nurturing and affirming gaze, the expressive medium of photographic art, and the vibrant Vancouver seascape in which the photoshoot took place create conditions in which, as Sumac writes, "I am fully in the moment. I am fully myself. I take breath and continue to find space here in my body, present, and witnessed, just as I am." Looking at the resulting photographs, Sumac expressively honours Indigenous masculinities worthy of claiming: "And most importantly, for me, no matter what anyone else might say, I see a man. I see an uncle, a brother, a nephew, and I see, maybe for the first time, my mother's son."

"Carrying the burden of peace" is not necessarily about defeating an enemy or exhibiting personal strength and power but about "fight[ing] with love" in the service of "a future free of fighting" (Justice, "Fighting" 142). The writings that I analyze in this book suggest to me that individual integrity is crucial to self-worth, especially given the regimes of imposed shame with which Indigenous Peoples have had to contend for at least the past century. The opposite of shame is not pride but love: love for the self, love for human and other-than-human kin, love for the land, sky, and water. Warriorhood can be a gesture of that love. It can be a role to which one is called,[37] a cluster of responsibilities that one actively takes on, a constellation of behaviours, emotions, and ideas that provides purpose and fulfillment to the individual while serving the needs of the People. And masculinities might indeed be tools through which such responsibilities and behaviours become legible. As Simpson offers in "Caged," in *Islands of Decolonial Love*, "maybe the warrior, the one that carries the burden of peace[,] also carries the burden of love—of embracing connection in the face of utter disconnection. maybe there is no limit to love" (103).

# 1. INDIGENOUS MASCULINITIES AND STORY

> And I know I may be really good, but I can't teach my son to be
> a man because there's things that I don't know and never will
> know and choose not to know because it's not my responsibility.
>      The unfortunate thing is that most men in our community don't
> know those things either. . . . —JANICE HILL KANONHSYONNE
> ("Where Are the Men?" 17)

> How can you forget everything and be a man? —DANIEL DAVID
> MOSES (*Almighty Voice and His Wife* 21)

Of the Indigenous Peoples of Turtle Island, Mi'kmaq activist
Sakej Ward declares that "We are a warrior race." However,
according to Ward, the colonial process through which
European peoples have come to dominate much of North
America has obscured this truth, encouraging many Indigenous
Peoples to deny who they are and mistakenly "think of themselves
as colonized subjects of Canada." "We try to bring back roles and
responsibilities," Ward laments, "but we always fail to bring back
the traditional role that encompasses half of our people: the male
population" (qtd. in Alfred, *Wasáse* 67). Settler colonialism is a
project of acquisition—fundamentally and always about land. Colonization has displaced hundreds of thousands of Indigenous people
from sacred landscapes inhabited by their nations for millennia;
at the same time, colonial policies and practices have worked to
alienate many from tribal-specific roles and responsibilities. This
double removal—from physical landscapes and from senses of social

cohesion and purpose—can be understood as settler colonialism's deterritorializing imperative. In order to transform ecosystemic networks of meaning into exploitable resources, settler colonialism works to deanimate lands, waters, and skies by targeting for eradication the dynamic bonds of reciprocal relations (experienced as kinship) that obtain among Indigenous Peoples and their territories. The concept of territoriality provides a lexicon through which to register the land- and place-based dimensions of what I referred to in the introduction to this volume as integrity: the pursuit of "meaningful way[s] to live in the world" that are "consistent with [one's] most intimate realities" (Simpson, *As We* 120). Processes of integration, or *territorialization*, cultivate meaningful senses of self while animating reciprocal relations that splay outward to human and other-than-human kin and to constellations of animate places. In this sense, territoriality refers to connection, embeddedness, nesting—the integration of the self within a nexus of relations that extends beyond the self and beyond the human. "Deterritorialization," as I use the term here, refers to the active suffocation of such relations via settler colonialism's technologies of disorientation, disintegration, and ultimately dispossession. As Claire Colebrook explains, if territorialization refers to the "connective forces that allow any form of life to become what it *is*," then deterritorialization is the process through which a form of life is coerced to "become what it *is not*" (xxii). Deterritorialization is a process of coercive unmaking (disappearance) rather than remaking (assimilation).[1] In order to naturalize settler belonging through the commoditization of land as property, settler colonialism has sought both to erase Indigenous presence from the land and to transform Indigenous lives into *that which they are not*, interwoven processes that, as theorists such as Paula Gunn Allen, Lee Maracle, Qwo-Li Driskill, and Mishuana Goeman demonstrate, are always gendered. Settler colonial violence is enacted at the intersections of gender and race, with different (though interconnected) implications for those who identify as men, those who identify as women, and those who identify as both, neither, or otherwise. Cree-Métis gender theorist Kim Anderson has argued that, though "many Native women have been able to continue their traditional responsibilities of creation and nurturing, . . . many men's responsibilities have been greatly obscured by the colonial process," which has made it "more difficult for men than it is for women to define their responsibilities in the contemporary setting and reclaim their dignity and sense of purpose" (239)—conditions that inform Ward's demand to "bring back the traditional role" of Indigenous men and Timothy Sweet's argument that the "project of 'recovering the feminine'" in Indigenous communities must "be complemented by an endeavour to recover the masculine" (475).

*Carrying the Burden of Peace* is not a recovery project. Although I recognize tribal-specific teachings about masculinity to be resources of urgent value, like Ngāti Pūkenga scholar Brendan Hokowhitu,[2] I am skeptical of the romanticizing pull of the "traditional" and the fixity that the concept of "traditional masculinities" can imply. I also remain alert to the ways in which traditions can be affected by the centuries-long siege of Indigenous communities by heteropatriarchal Christian assimilation and thereby come to leave certain bodies and identities out. Nor does this book attempt to define Indigenous masculinities. As I argue elsewhere,[3] efforts to define Indigenous masculinities are doomed to failure by the diversity of Indigenous nations and communities from sea to sea to sea on the northern part of Turtle Island; by the inevitable evolution of understandings of gender within and among communities over time; by the contextual specificity of how gender is experienced and expressed by groups and individuals; and by the fact that "what comes to be considered masculine within a given context necessarily falls short of capturing the complex experiences of individual[s]" ("Into" 2). Furthermore, academic efforts to identify, theorize, and revitalize tribal-specific understandings of masculinity, in my view, are compromised if not conducted by scholars within the cultures under analysis, those whose "*living, primary, feeling citizenships*," to borrow language from Kanien'keha:ka scholar Audra Simpson, enable not only privileged access to knowledge but also the corrective vitality of reciprocal relationships that hold academics to account (175).[4]

In *Carrying the Burden of Peace*, I do not endeavour to authenticate Indigenous masculinities or to measure the distance between a mythic pre-contact past and contemporary expressions of identity. I am interested less in what it means to be an "Indigenous man" than in what allows some stories to nourish, validate, and (re)vitalize Indigenous senses of self—thereby fortifying individuals to serve their families, communities, and territories according to their gifts and passions—while others diminish identities and isolate, quarantine, and contain Indigenous freedom as expressed through gender. Which stories nurture individual *integrity*? Which serve to *dis-integrate*? Cherokee Nation scholar Daniel Heath Justice contends that there are stories that "give shape, substance, and purpose to our existence and help us understand how to uphold our responsibilities to one another and the rest of creation," and there are others that "are noxious, bad medicine" and "can't help but poison both the speaker and the listener" (*Why* 2). In this chapter, I engage with stories in a variety of registers to consider how the settler colonial imperative of Indigenous deterritorialization is bound to the diminution of Indigenous humanity and further to consider what this means for Indigenous masculinities. I analyze creation stories, political discourses, media representations, and films to think through how settler colonialism has conscripted gender in the enterprise of turning Indigenous people into that which they are not and how Indigenous individuals and communities—and particularly, for the purposes of this project, artists—have refused, asserted their collective humanity, and affirmed commitments to do gender differently.[5] Masculinity is a story. "Masculinities" are stories, just as "femininities" are stories, and how they are told, where, when, and by whom influence their meanings and how some of them come to illuminate others while placing still others in shadows, thereby obfuscating alternative horizons of possibility. As settler gender theorist Scott Morgensen argues, "other stories existed before this category, 'sexuality,' appeared or became dominant; and they can be retold, or new ones can be invented that leave the boundary-policing power of sexuality behind" (56). In short, the stories that we hold up matter. Justice argues, for example, that "the story of Indigenous deficiency"—which has been rehearsed in North American popular culture ad infinitum to dehumanize Indigenous men (as well as others)—"displaces . . . other stories, the stories of complexity, hope, and possibility. If the simplistic deficiency accounts are all we see, all we hear, and all that's expected of us, it's hard to find room for the more nourishing stories of significance" (*Why* 4). Here I set out to interrogate and understand stories that simulate, diminish, and quarantine Indigenous masculinities in order to open up space for discussions of Indigenous "stories of significance" in the chapters that follow.

I begin this endeavour by sitting with the language of "roles and responsibilities," not to reify problematic notions of biological determinacy or re-entrench the gender binary, but to consider whether roles and responsibilities offer the potential for non-prescriptive means of social integration that are generative for both individuals and communities. In my conversations with Indigenous artists, activists, academics, and Elders on the subject of Indigenous masculinities, the phrase "roles and responsibilities" came up again and again—at times because of specific questions that I was asking but just as often organically—and it can be found peppered throughout the burgeoning scholarship in Indigenous masculinities studies. However, anxieties persist about the potentially prescriptive nature of roles and responsibilities when understood in strictly gendered terms that might require one to deny aspects of one's full humanity in order to be recognized, validated, and integrated into the group.[6] As such, to be mutually generative for individuals and communities, roles and responsibilities are perhaps best understood as sites of creative negotiation between the needs of networks and the gifts and talents of individuals within them. Justice provides an instructive example from his youth involving hunting with his father: "I'd lean up against a tree with a novel and read, and he was good with that. You know, I had my rifle; I'd know if there was an elk coming, and being part of the hunt was my responsibility. So we adapted; we adapted some of these masculinist pursuits for my nerdy fantasies" ("Fighting" 135). Justice was not forced to conform to particular expectations of masculine identity, yet he recognized and acted upon his own responsibilities to the group's objectives in ways that enhanced both self-worth and group success: "[S]o it's a balance: you honour people's integrity, but you're also honouring what's bringing you together" (139). Here, as elsewhere, integrity speaks to the unique traits and desires that allow one to be fully oneself while also hearkening to the sense of shared purpose that fosters integration into a larger community.

Another concern involves the risk of treating roles and responsibilities as themselves identities rather than vehicles through which identities can be developed and expressed. When discussing roles and responsibilities during our interview in *Masculindians*, Stó:lō writer and theorist Lee Maracle clarified that "it's not a role. We *are* that.... I'm not a role. I'm a Wolf Clan, backward and forward visionary. That is my relationship to the whole. . . . That's what's going to take us from yesterday to tomorrow—this vision. And I keep it. It's my bundle" ("This" 39). Here Maracle distinguishes between *who we are*—in her own case, a "backward and forward visionary"—and the behaviours through which such identities become legible. To call one's identity a role is to diminish the richness and complexity of one's full humanity and to divert attention from the gifts in one's bundle toward a utilitarian assessment of duties taken on. "[I]t's not a role. We *are* that" reminds us of the limits of the language of roles and responsibilities, particularly when such language can become ossified in highly gendered ways that coerce conformity. In his seminal article "Native Ethics and Rules of Behaviour," Kanien'keha:ka psychiatrist Clare Brant identifies the ethic of non-interference as "one of the most widely accepted principles of behaviour among Native people," arguing that "a high degree of respect for every human being's independence" ultimately discourages "coercion of any kind, be it physical, verbal, or psychological" (535). Within a worldview that values the ethic of non-interference, roles and responsibilities cannot be identities; they are duties, commitments, behaviours, and interactions that constitute a dynamic interface between the gifts of individuals—their "bundles"—and the needs of the larger group, be it the family, the community, or the nation. In this way, the autonomy of the individual acts as a catalyst rather than an impediment to one's integration into the community. Using Brant's work, settler legal expert Rupert Ross elaborates that those who develop in a context of ethical non-interference tend to become "'layered' onto [the] extended family," thereby becoming "integral, as opposed to autonomous, parts of it" (22). The danger in contexts in which the ethic of non-interference has been assaulted by settler colonial policies of dispossession and imposed individualism is that roles and responsibilities might cease to function as resources for the organic affirmation of identities and instead become arbiters of one's ability to conform to preformulated expectations. In such contexts, the responsibility for "carrying the burden of peace," for example, might become ossified into a static, Westernized notion of "warrior"—saddled with hypermasculine baggage and misaligned with aspirations toward Indigenous futures.

To mitigate the potential for gendered coercion in roles and responsibilities discourse, Anishinaabe scholar Randy Jackson champions two-spirit theory, arguing that

> people bring their skills and their gifts to contribute to the well-being of that whole. In the context of two-spirit, it doesn't really matter what gender you are when you look at the world that way. And that's how I've untangled myself from the crushing roles and responsibilities of what it means to be a man, by understanding that that's not really about gender; it's about how do I as a person contribute to the well-being of my community. (interview)

Like Justice, Brant, and Maracle above, Jackson argues for the world-building possibilities of the interface between communal needs and individual gifts; however, he highlights the risks of layering gender onto this relationship. In this sense, his understanding of gender aligns with that of non-citizen Cherokee theorist Qwo-Li Driskill, who argues in *Asegi Stories: Cherokee Queer and Two-Spirit Memory* that "'Gender' is a logic, and a structural system of oppression, whose sole purpose is to categorize people in order to deploy systemic power and control. . . . Gender is a weapon to force us into clear Eurocentric categories, keep us confined in there, ensure we monitor each other's behavior, and then, while we are distracted, take our lands" (167). Although I agree that, as a system of categorization, gender is structurally predisposed to delimit,[7] I worry that the presumption that gender is everywhere and always oppressive might itself be delimiting and thereby obfuscate other more liberatory possibilities. Constrictive understandings of gender have certainly been deployed by settler colonial structures of power to quarantine Indigenous Peoples and "take [their] lands," but I wonder if gender might be thought of and enacted beyond such myopic paradigms. In much the same way that I argue throughout this book that masculinity should not be cast aside as irredeemable, I consider in this chapter whether gender systems might be identified, recovered, or imagined that are not "structural system[s] of oppression" but constellations of meaning through which Indigenous individuals (can) integrate into families and communities along diverse pathways that might be legible as non-coercive territorialization—as means of *becoming who they are, of fostering their own integrity while integrating into the whole.* I pursue this line of inquiry in accordance with the conviction that, although settler colonialism is an inherently gendered enterprise, settler colonial gender systems are not the only understandings of gender available to us. In other words, settler colonialism does not have a monopoly on gender, and the stories about gender that we choose to hold up and breathe life into matter.

I root this chapter's discussions in the knowledge traditions, critical theory, and creative art of the Haudenosaunee Confederacy for four main reasons. First, the lands upon which I live and work in Kingston, Ontario, are the territory of the Haudenosaunee People, as well as the Anishinaabe People, and many of the teachers and friends from whom I have had the privilege of learning during nearly two decades in this place as a settler colonist are Haudenosaunee.[8] Second, the generative balance of power along gender lines within Haudenosaunee communities, at various levels of governance and social relations, points in the direction of gender systems that do not solely "deploy systemic power and control," even as Haudenosaunee gender systems tend to be reliant on a gender binary. As Kanien'keha:ka activist and artist Ellen Gabriel declared at a national event of the Indian Residential Schools Truth and Reconciliation Commission in Montreal, "There's men's roles and there's women's roles, in a Haudenosaunee worldview, and there's no need to read more into it than that" ("Plenary Address"). I consider below whether such recourse to the language of "roles," especially while tethered to a binary construction of gender, might nonetheless prove to be liberatory provided that the ethic of non-interference remains culturally operative. Third, the image of the Mohawk warrior has come to symbolize Indigenous hypermasculinity in popular Canadian consciousness—"a symbol," in Audra Simpson's words, "not of the Kaianere'kó:wa or gendered forms of power and alternative forms of political authority and legitimacy, but of a contemporary, militant, and lawless savagery" (151). Fourth, as Kanien'keha:ka literary scholar Rick Monture argues, the Haudenosaunee have been remarkably "resistant to assimilationist policies over the past two centuries," at least partially, in his view, because of "the sustained power of the stories that are at the foundation of Haudenosaunee philosophical thought" (17).

I begin by discussing the depiction by Kanien'keha:ka Elder Tom Porter Sakokweniónkwas of the Haudenosaunee creation story to introduce ideas about gender that might exceed the structural containment of settler colonial gender systems. Then I illustrate how specific colonial interventions—from the *Indian Act* to residential schooling to capitalist consumerism—have been enacted to alter how roles and responsibilities function within Haudenosaunee communities. I then consider how popular cultural images of Indigenous men that rely on hypermasculine stereotyping risk exacerbating the alienation that settler colonialism has sought to engender between Indigenous individuals and their diverse and multiple communities. I conclude by returning to Porter's narratives from *And Grandma Said . . . Iroquois Teachings as Passed Down through the Oral Tradition* (2008) to analyze the story of Aionwahta as a rumination on condolence that guides listeners toward forms of healthy, non-dominative, and empowered masculinities, which might serve the cause of Indigenous continuance; if settler colonialism is structurally devoted to Indigenous deterritorialization, I argue, then the Aionwahta tale offers a vision of reterritorialization with specific implications for Indigenous masculinities.[9]

## CREATION STORIES AND GENDER COMPLEMENTARITY

The comparison of creation stories is nothing new in Indigenous literary studies. Cree playwright Tomson Highway, for example, interrogates the ideological implications of foundational spiritual myths and their relationships to language in *Comparing Mythologies* (2003), and non-citizen Cherokee writer Thomas King compares Judeo-Christian and Indigenous creation stories to initiate his critical reflections on Indigenous-settler relations in the lecture series *The Truth about Stories: A Native Narrative* (2003). Nor are such comparisons without risk; I am conscious that comparing Indigenous and European creation stories can again centre settler colonialism, when more instructive comparisons might well be made among diverse Indigenous creation stories or between Indigenous creation stories and those of diasporic and refugee populations. The following discussion, however, is intended to illuminate the symbiotic relationship among creation stories, place-based knowledge, and what I will refer to as ecologies of gender.[10] How we understand the world to have come into being influences profoundly our understandings of ourselves within it, with further implications for our understandings of gender. Because settler colonial policies of assimilation and deterritorialization have involved not simply the imposition of Euro-Western regimes of gender into Indigenous communities but also sustained attacks on the worldviews in which Indigenous ecologies of gender are embedded, I consider it productive to think about the Haudenosaunee creation story of Sky Woman together with the Christian creation story os Genesis. In doing so, I contend that, though the creation story of Genesis might be structurally predisposed to the germination of models of gender that function as "system[s] of oppression," the story of Sky Woman might provide tools for understanding gender as an ecosystem of meaning in which foundational respect for individual integrity works to insulate against coercive containment, even as gender continues to function as a vehicle for social organization.[11]

In his oral sharing of the Haudenosaunee creation story, Porter depicts Atsi'tsiaká:ion (Sky Woman) falling through a widening hole beneath a great tree in the Sky World, "tumbling, head over heels," through "the atmosphere" toward our world, which, at that time, contained "no land—no mountains, no valleys. The complete planet was surrounded by water. There was no kinda land anywhere." As she was falling, Atsi'tsiaká:ion was spotted by "a flock of blue herons" that "gathered that she wasn't from their world—the world of water. And," having neither fins nor webbed feet, "if she was going there, she would not survive." Taking pity on her, "they tried to intervene," saying, "Let's all fly together. We'll hook our wings together and make a soft feathery place so she can gently fall on our bodies." However, the additional burden of her weight soon led them to become "totally exhausted," so they convened a "council of birds" in which they determined to reach out to the water creatures below, thinking that "maybe together they can find a way . . . to help this lady." "So all the animals of the water world had a meeting." Although they were "completely befuddled," "the big turtle" offered humbly, "I don't really have an answer, either. But I might have a temporary answer. How about if when they get down here, you tell them to put that woman right in the middle of my back. I'll stay afloat on top of the big water, and I'll hold her up. And then we can try to keep thinking about what we might do to help her." The council agreed (47–50).

When she was placed upon Turtle's back, Sky Woman revealed the "seeds in her hand," which she had torn loose from Karonhià:ke, the Sky World, when attempting to steady her fall; they were to be her food source, "but there was no dirt [in which] to plant them." Remembering stories from their Elders about dirt "below [the] big water somewhere," the water animals determined to dive into the depths of the sea to retrieve it. First the beaver attempted and failed. "[T]hen the otter tried it. And then different ones tried it. They all took turns, but they *all* died. Finally a little tiny one, the smallest one—they call him anò:kien in my language, and in English that's *muskrat*—he came forward" and said, "Well, I'm not a good swimmer. I don't have a big tail like the beaver to propel me down in the water. All I am is just little old muskrat. And if they didn't make it, probably I'm not gonna make it either. But at least I'm *gonna try.*" After being below the surface of the water for the longest time of all, muskrat finally emerged appearing lifeless. "As they revived him, his eyes opened up, and he started to blink. And when they opened his little tiny black hand, there were some little granules of the dirt there, from the big water." Atsi'tsiak:ion took the dirt from muskrat's hand and some from his mouth,

> [a]nd she put it right there in the middle of the turtle's back. And then she started a kind of sideways shuffle walk in a circle where that dirt was in the middle. And as she started to move she started chanting the language of Karonhià:ke, for that's where she was from. . . . And as she went around there, the miracle of birth began. And the granules of dirt began to multiply and grow. Instead of a little speckle, it had become a pile. And as she continued to sing or to chant that song, it began to multiply even more. And not only that, but the turtle began to grow bigger in accordance with the growth of that dirt. . . . That was the miracle of birth. (50–53)

The Haudenosaunee creation story foregrounds the coming together of unlike things. In contrast to the creation story of Genesis—in which the universe is formed through a series of divisions when a single creative force, in the figure of a male God, separates light from darkness, Heaven from Earth, and land from water—Turtle Island is created through the collaboration of several figures that come together creatively to deal with the crisis of Sky Woman's introduction into the water world. As opposed to division, the Haudenosaunee creation story stresses convergence, as symbolized by the blue herons hooking their wings "together" to make a "soft feathery" bed to support Sky Woman. Here several creatures work collectively to solve the problem of Sky Woman's inability to survive in a landless environment. The herons unite to catch her before holding a council of birds and then reaching out "to the water creatures below" for consultation; the great turtle offers up a carapace for the land on which Sky Woman will live but requires muskrat to collect the necessary morsel of earth from the sea floor; muskrat retrieves the granules of dirt but relies upon the other swimmers and Sky Woman herself to animate those granules into a continent. The act of creation in this story is fundamentally collaborative, requiring several parties, each of which bears the capacity to engender positive change. Whereas the creation story of Genesis restricts the formation of the universe to a specific temporal period (from "the beginning" to "the seventh day") and attributes the creative act to a single cosmic force (the God figure), the Haudenosaunee narrative understands creation to both precede and exceed the story of Sky Woman (as suggested by the existence of both the Water World and the Sky World prior to her arrival and by the ongoing acts of creation suggested by the birth of her children after this chapter of Porter's version of the creation story closes) and to emerge from a plethora of sources (from the great turtle to muskrat to the council to Atsi'tsiak:ion herself).

The balance of creative power throughout the Haudenosaunee creation story signals an important difference from the story in Genesis. The primary active force throughout Genesis remains the God figure—again envisioned in the masculine—while the rest of creation either is acted upon or achieves surrogate agency through the overarching authority of the God figure; man's power over the beasts because of his being forged in the God figure's image (Gen. 1.27, KJV) is an example of the latter. The Haudenosaunee creation story has no such power structure. Although the herons have the authority to call together the council of water creatures, they cannot make decisions on behalf of the council or produce Turtle Island without the assistance of other beings. In fact, consensus-based decision making among first the birds and then the council of flyers and swimmers suggests not a vision of top-down governmental authority but an adaptive coalitional politics capable of coalescing to confront new challenges before dispersing into multiple sovereignties. Monture identifies as "one of the most significant features" of the creation story the "theme of change, adaptation, and development" through which "the Haudenosaunee are instructed to view life and society as in a state of constant movement and transition" (5). The Haudenosaunee creation story gestures toward the importance of balance within structures of power, whereas the story in Genesis gestures toward the importance of hierarchical authority, each of which has ideological implications for relationships within human societies and between humans and the natural world. Genesis weaves hierarchy into the creative process through the disparate valuing of the halves into which the universe is divided. For example, as Heaven is divided from Earth, the former is conceived theologically to be the superior of the two. Similarly, as day is divided from night, the former is afforded greater value, as evidenced by the description of the "great lights" by which the two are governed: "the *greater* light to rule the day, and the *lesser* light to rule the night" (Gen. 1.16, KJV). The term "rule" appears to be no accident either.

The role of hierarchy is illustrated even more powerfully in Genesis by humankind's prescribed relationship to the natural world: "[A]nd God said unto [man and woman], Be fruitful, and multiply, and replenish the earth, and subdue it: and have dominion over the fish of the sea, and over the fowl of the air, and over every living thing that moveth upon the earth" (Gen. 1.28, KJV). The duty of humankind, in this configuration, is forcibly to bring the natural world under human control, as suggested by the term "subdue," which requires a radically different valuation of the other-than-human than is implied by Sky Woman's reverence for the fecund and expanding natural world upon the turtle's back. Furthermore, the relationship between human and animal worlds in the Haudenosaunee creation story is predicated on mutuality and convergence, anathema to the "dominion" enjoyed by humankind in Genesis. Whereas the term "dominion" asserts human rule over "fish," "fowl," and "every [non-human] living thing . . . upon the earth," animal and human worlds in the Haudenosaunee creation story are fundamentally integrated. In fact, the survival of the human world depends on the active decision making of empowered flyers and swimmers. In this manner, whereas Genesis seems to suggest that humankind must conquer and control the natural world of plants and animals, the story of Sky Woman seems to suggest the importance of kinship relations among humans, plants, and animals with no element of creation ruling over any other.

The comparison that I am drawing here between the hierarchical division privileged in the Genesis creation story and the egalitarian unification privileged in the Haudenosaunee creation story forms some of the ideological backdrop to the discussions of gender with which I am concerned in this chapter and the book as a whole. If we extend the principle of hierarchical division to gender relations in Genesis, then men are placed in authority over women because the female is depicted as being derived from the male—"[a]nd she shall be called Woman, because she was taken out of Man" (Gen. 2.22, KJV)—and because men are presented as sharing affinity with the masculine God figure: "So God created man in his own image, in the image of God created he him" (Gen. 1.26, KJV). The power dynamic in the Haudenosaunee creation story is different since the first human is decidedly female and the creative power that in Genesis is isolated in the God figure is shared for Porter among a plethora of diversely gendered characters—some are given male or female pronouns, and others (e.g., the turtle) are not gendered at all. Sky Woman, as the first human, is also an active agent in the creation of Turtle Island along with the turtle, the muskrat, and the other council members, which come together in ceremony and with the aid of "the language of Karonhià:ke" to enable the dirt to expand in extraordinary fashion. Porter glosses this fecundity as "the miracle of birth," which appears to associate the emergence of Turtle Island with feminine creative power. Yet it is important to recognize that, in the story as Porter tells it, feminine creative power is not exercised to the exclusion of masculine creative power and that the dynamic nature of collaborative creation throughout the Haudenosaunee creation story is not a zero sum game—there is not a finite amount of power in exchange between those gendered male and those gendered female; rather, power is *generated* through the coming together of diversely gendered beings in common purpose. In Chapter 3, I borrow language from settler scholar Mark Rifkin to discuss this kind of gender thinking as "dynamic mutuality," which transcends the competitive ecology of gender naturalized by settler colonialism.

Yet, as Ellen Gabriel, Janice Hill, and Barbara Alice Mann all note, the structuring of Haudenosaunee society has been informed historically by a division of labour between men and women. In her study entitled *Iroquoian Women: The Gantowisas* (2000), Mann describes the process of "gendering" as "the most crucial common-place of the Iroquoian universe" (64). Yet the existence of "two . . . genders," in her view, does not "inevitably impl[y] antagonism" in

Haudenosaunee worldview (63). Rather than relying on the hierarchical binaries so crucial to Genesis—Heaven/Earth, day/night, human/animal, male/female—Mann argues that the Haudenosaunee principle of "twinship" recognizes and even celebrates difference while mobilizing that difference productively within kinship networks based on balance and complementarity: "As a reflection of [the] twinship principle, the genders are seen as simultaneously independent, yet interdependent, each gender one half of the paired, human whole. A pure expression of Iroquoian thought, the relationship between men and women in Haudenosaunee culture developed from the bedrock of principles [of] . . . reciprocity, balance, cooperation, mutuality, and the joyful coming-together of two to create one self-perpetuating whole" (90). Gender difference is not denied in Haudenosaunee thought, according to Mann, but Haudenosaunee societies take great care to ensure freedom from domination for both men and women. She calls the relationship between the genders in such societies "[e]qual and complementary, interdependent yet individual," arguing that

> the genders fall into natural halves that parallel one another, socially, politically, economically, and religiously. Neither gender interferes with the other's allotted half of existence. Each half is left to operate as it sees fit, so long as the ultimate outcome of activity forms a beneficial whole.
>
> In short, women do women's things, while men do men's things, together yet apart in their complementary spaces of the female-field and the male-forest. Thus, women farm, and men hunt, but, in the final analysis, all the people are fed. (97–98)

Although bordering on utopian in its assessment of Haudenosaunee gender equity, Mann's depiction simultaneously betrays the ongoing potential for gender coercion through the territorial segregation of the sexes and the conceit that gender difference is "natural"—in other words, the conception of genders as "natural halves" implies the possibility of biological determinism, and the assignment of spaces of belonging and unbelonging along biological lines creates opportunities for gender hegemony. However, the danger of prescriptively imposed gender identities is mitigated here, at least somewhat, via the ethic of non-interference. In a society in which individual autonomy is a principle value, the refusal of either gender to interfere "with the other's . . . existence" can be imagined to condition a more diffuse refusal to interfere with the development and expression of individual gender identities as well—perhaps even those that deviate from the binary altogether.

The gender system theorized by Mann and symbiotically related to the Haudenosaunee creation story can be understood to inform the governance structures of the Haudenosaunee Confederacy that preceded and have survived settler colonialism. At the time of initial sustained contact with Europeans, the Haudenosaunee Confederacy consisted of five nations, including the elder sibling nations of the Kanien'keha:ka (the Keepers of the Eastern Door), the Seneca (the Keepers of the Western Door), and the Onondaga (the Keepers of the Council Fire) and the younger sibling nations of the Oneida and the Cayuga; the Tuscarora became part of the Confederacy after American expansion left them landless, bringing the political union of Haudenosaunee nations to six. The Confederacy binds the nations together through kinship systems of clan-based social organization, subject to a democratic constitution known as Kaienere'kó:wa or The Great Law of Peace (Porter 97–113, 334–63). The political structures of the Confederacy ensure not only that all nations and clans are represented at the Grand Council Fire but also that women and men are mutually engaged in political decision making. Non-Indigenous historian J.R. Miller writes that,

> Simply put, the Iroquois developed complex and sophis-
> ticated institutions of government because their social
> circumstances [as large populations concentrated in
> semi-permanent agrarian villages] required that they have
> mechanisms for regulating relations among large numbers of
> people normally resident in one location. . . . [T]he women
> of their communities had prominent political roles. For
> example, clan mothers were responsible for selecting a new
> chief, and deciding to make war or peace also fell within

their jurisdiction. Iroquoians were matrilineal and matrilocal peoples, meaning that they traced kinship through the
mother's family, and when a man married he relocated to
the longhouse of his bride's family. Much of the prominence
of Iroquois women's public role seems to have stemmed
from their contribution in agriculture. In short, farming
was women's work, with the result that women controlled
the food supply and thereby gained great influence. (57)

Although we should be cautious of some of the causal implications of this analysis (insofar as Miller views the Haudenosaunee
political structure and the role of women in Haudenosaunee society as primarily products of "social circumstances" rather than
the agentive development of a society through cross-pollination
among worldview, territory, and conditions), his introduction to
Haudenosaunee governance illuminates an emphasis on gender
balance. For instance, although the male Sachem or Chief speaks
on behalf of his clan at the nation's council and, along with the
Sachems of the other clans, on behalf of his nation at the Grand
Council Fire, he carries no coercive authority over the people and
can be removed from his position by the Clan Mother if he does
not voice the people's will, as established through prior consensus.
The authority of the male Sachem, therefore, is radically different
from the authority of a prime minister or president and especially
from that of a monarch.

The role of the Sachem involves significant responsibilities rather
than heightened power and influence. His only means of instigat-
ing action is through the persuasiveness of his rhetoric; he cannot
compel his clan to do anything and is subject to their collective will.
It is unsurprising, therefore, that, as Porter notes, it is "forbidden
to *seek* leadership" (338) in Haudenosaunee traditional governance[12]
because such a pursuit betrays a desire for power that is anathema to the freedom from coercion so central to Haudenosaunee
worlview. According to Porter, the Kanien'keha word for Sachem is
"Roiá:nehr and it means *he's good*. And the [word for Clan Mother]
is Iakoiá:nehr, *she's good*. And the law is called Kaianere'kó:wa, *the
great good*. That's the Constitution. So compared to that, the word

'Chief' sounds degrading" (340). The authority of the male leader, Roiá:nehr, in this system is always tempered by the authority of the female leader, Iakoiá:nehr. Mann describes the role of the Clan Mother through the word *Gantowisas*, meaning "political woman, faithkeeping woman, mediating woman; leader, counsellor, judge. *Gantowisas* indicates mother, grandmother, and even the Mother of Nations. . . . *Gantowisas*, then, means indispensable Woman" (16). As indicated by Miller, Porter, and Mann, Clan Mothers are central to Haudenosaunee governance as primary overseers of the authority of male Sachems, as the holders of women's councils, as key figures of consensus building within the clan or nation, and as the arbiters of war and peace. Yet even the authority of Clan Mothers is tempered by checks and balances. According to Porter, the Clan Mother only "initiates" the central processes of governance and the selection of leaders; she does not dictate decisions. "All she does," he explains, "is she's the voice of the people of that clan" (340).

The matrilineal nature of Haudenosaunee kinship, the complex gender ecology of Haudenosaunee governance, the imperatives of non-interference and consensus building in Haudenosaunee decision making,[13] and the cultural emphasis on balance signalled by the coming together of Sky Woman, the great turtle, and the swimmers and flyers in the Haudenosaunee creation story all have profound implications for what might be described as masculine roles and responsibilities. According to Kanien'keha:ka Clan Mother and educator Janice Hill, in her home community of Tyendinaga Mohawk Territory, "the transition to the twentieth century and the twenty-first century hasn't been as easy for men, I think, as it has for women." Hill explains:

Our community is like a circle and everything inside the community is the responsibility of the women (so the social aspect of being a community is the responsibility of the women) and everything outside of the circle (so politics and war and dealing with foreign nations and anything like that) is the responsibility of the men. Now . . . we don't have anybody to war with anymore, so that takes away that responsibility. And men don't hunt as much, you know—and there's not the possibility if they're urban or don't have access to hunting grounds or haven't been taught how to hunt and fish—so that takes away that responsibility. And in terms of being political leaders and dealing with outside governments, that one still exists but even that platform has changed so much. . . . So, our men don't get to negotiate on the same platform as traditionally our men did, which makes that whole political role null and void. So then what? That void has been created and they haven't been taught to change that role in a different way, more positively. ("Where" 18)

Hill's eloquent plea for the need to reimagine roles and responsibilities in contemporary Haudenosaunee communities, especially among those who identify as boys and men, registers the importance of senses of purpose to identity formation, self-worth, and community health. In this way, she affirms—along with other Haudenosaunee theorists such as Gabriel and Porter—that Haudenosaunee society *is* highly gendered and that Haudenosaunee thought privileges a gender binary between men and women, male and female. Yet, as the preceding discussion of gender in the creation story of Sky Woman suggests, within a framework of complementarity and balance, and conditioned by profound respect for the autonomy of individuals via the ethic of non-interference, such a system does not *need* to prescribe gender identities. It does not need, as Randy Jackson warns, "to crush people out." In fact, I suspect, gendered roles and responsibilities within such a society—invigorated, opened up, and reimagined in the manner that Hill champions—might yet function as resources for the development of diverse identities that exceed the gender binary.[14] However, the capacity of such roles and responsibilities to be liberating rather than oppressive—to be world building rather than constraining—depends on the vitality of myriad integrated aspects of Haudenosaunee life.

Gender, within Haudenosaunee society, is integrated organically with other features of being. If other vital elements of the worldview to which gender is symbiotically related come under assault—such as the ethic of non-interference—then the risk of a binary gender model becoming oppressive to women, queer, trans, and two-spirit people, and even cis-men, is exacerbated. I began this section with a comparison of creation stories to illustrate how alternative understandings of the world's beginnings—nurtured in different lands, in different languages, alongside different histories—inform radically different worldviews and radically different gender systems. However, it is crucial to recognize that settler colonial assaults on Indigenous systems of gender have not been the inevitable by-product of that difference—a logical reaction to confronting something "foreign" by seeking to remake it in the image of the self. Settler colonial manipulations of Indigenous gender systems have been far more insidious, designed not to assimilate but to deterritorialize, not to make Indigenous people white but to make them who they are not and cease to persist *as Peoples*. This has involved a multi-pronged approach to the "management" of Indigenous Peoples through which various elements of Indigenous worldviews have come under attack, and it is to these assaults that I now turn.

## MANUFACTURING MASCULINITIES: PATRIARCHY AS POLITICAL POLICY

With the extension of settler colonial control throughout the eighteenth and nineteenth centuries, several factors conspired to undermine gender systems characterized by complementarity, twinship, and balance among the Haudenosaunee, including the diplomatic upheaval caused by colonial warfare, the loss of traditional territories in upstate New York, the decimation of animal populations because of settler encroachment, and the aggressive missionary work of several Christian denominations. In this section, I analyze the impacts of two specific colonial interventions—the *Indian Act* (1876) and the residential school system (1879–1996)—on Haudenosaunee ecologies of gender since those interventions work to displace, obfuscate, or render impracticable aspects of the masculine roles and responsibilities introduced above. Here I focus more on settler colonial intentionality and the tactical nature of technologies of deterritorialization than on discernible effects, with the recognition that Indigenous resilience has ensured that genocidal objectives have not meant the inevitable suffocation of culture and identity. I endeavour to track how the gender systems of the Haudenosaunee have been assaulted, fully cognizant that Haudenosaunee gender knowledge and expression have endured. As Monture illustrates in relation to his own community, "Obviously, the Six Nations at Grand River have been able to maintain a substantial portion of their traditional culture despite mounting pressures to assimilate into mainstream Canadian society" (17). And as Stó:lō theorist Lee Maracle affirms, "We might be doing different things 'cause we're running around in this hamster cage or we might be doing the same thing our ancestors always did because we've reached wholeness by some miracle. . . . We cannot *not* be ourselves" ("This" 35).

The *Indian Act* of 1876 brought together and formalized all previous legislation by the British Crown and the newly inaugurated government of the Dominion of Canada pertaining to Indigenous Peoples. This vast document, which has been added to and amended considerably over the past century and a half, has two primary functions: first, to categorize and define Indigenous identity; second, to legislate a political system for controlling Indigenous nations in a manner that ensures their subordination to the Canadian state. Each function has considerable implications for Indigenous gender relations. Certainly until 1985 and in many ways after that year,[15] these goals of the *Act* constituted a two-pronged attack on gender balance in Indigenous communities by seeking to silence the political voices of Indigenous women and imposing patriarchal systems of identification on often matrilineal and matrilocal nations such as those of the Haudenosaunee Confederacy. Aimed at the heart of Indigenous nationhood—the definition of group membership and the organization of structures of governance—this legislation, in the words of Bonita Lawrence, has "indelibly ordered how Native people think of things 'Indian'" (3–4).

Among the most significant aspects of national sovereignty is a group's right to determine its own membership, and prior to the *Indian Act* most Indigenous nations did so according to kinship ties, community integration, and consensus; Kanien'keha:ka were deemed Kanien'keha:ka because of their kinship commitments to

others within the Kanien'keha:ka Nation and the broader Haudenosaunee Confederacy and because they were recognized as such
by their communities, a process that had little to do with racialized
conceptions of "Indian blood." With the *Indian Act*, the Canadian
government began to determine who would legally be recognized
as Indigenous through the category of the "Status Indian," based,
among other things, on blood quantum. In the *Act for the Gradual
Enfranchisement of Indians* of 1869, which would become a foundational pillar of the *Indian Act* seven years later, the denial of community membership to individuals based on blood quantum was
introduced in relation to economic entitlement. Section IV states
that, "In the division among members of any tribe, band, or body
of Indians, of any annuity money, interest money or rents, no
person of less than one fourth Indian blood . . . shall be deemed
entitled to share." This section, in effect, exiled those of less than
one-quarter perceived Indigenous ancestry from their Indigenous
nations economically, irrespective of kinship ties or community
will. Such legislated banishment became even more striking along
gender lines. Section VI reads thus:

> Provided always that any Indian woman marrying any other
> than an Indian, shall cease to be an Indian within the mean-
> ing of this Act, nor shall the children issue of such marriage
> be considered as Indians within the meaning of this Act;
> Provided also, that any Indian woman marrying an Indian
> of any other tribe, band or body to which she formerly
> belonged, and become a member of the tribe, band or body
> of which her husband is a member, and the children, issue
> of this marriage, shall belong to their father's tribe only.

Through this section, the *Act* directly attacks the matrilineal clan-
based social structure of the Haudenosaunee Confederacy (as well
as those of other Indigenous nations), seeking to destabilize the
checks and balances that nurture gender complementarity to menace Indigenous communities toward the adoption of gender systems
resembling settler heteropatriarchy. In Haudenosaunee kinship, as
explained by Porter, a man retains his clan-based identity when he

marries, bringing the knowledge traditions of his heritage with him as he moves into the longhouse of his wife's relations. In the system enforced by the *Indian Act*, a woman's cultural identity disappears in the eyes of the government upon her marriage outside the group; in the tradition of settler heteropatriarchy, her identity is reconceived as subordinate to and dependent on that of her husband. The *Indian Act* thus strikes a blow at the heart of Haudenosaunee ecologies of gender by displacing women from positions of power in the home, and recasting them as dependent first on fathers and then on husbands, as well as in the broader community by denying the significance of women's heritage formerly affirmed through the matrilineal tracing of ancestry.

Seeking to divest power from the system of consensus-based governance employed by the Haudenosaunee for centuries, the *Indian Act* further imposed a band council system of quasi-democratic governance under the umbrella of Indian Affairs that fundamentally disenfranchised the female half of the Haudenosaunee population.[16] Section X of the *Gradual Enfranchisement Act* declares that "The Governor may order that the Chiefs of any tribe, band, or body of Indians shall be elected by the *male* members of each Indian Settlement of the full age of twenty-one years at such time and place, and in such manner, as the Superintendent General of Indian Affairs may direct, and they shall in such case be elected for a period of three years, unless deposed by the Governor for dishonesty, intemperance, or immorality." Far from the interwoven web of checks and balances in which Clan Mothers and Sachems work collaboratively to discern and act upon the will of the people through extensive consultation, compromise, and consensus building, the system imposed via the *Gradual Enfranchisement Act* was fundamentally incapable of cultivating consensus insofar as it barred half the population from participating in the political process as voters or potential leaders. Denial of the vote, of course, does not preclude any and all influence on political decision making, but such manipulation of Indigenous systems of governance must nonetheless be construed as a direct attack on Indigenous women's power and authority and on their roles within their families and communities. Given the interdependence of men and women within Haudenosaunee society, such manipulation should also be understood as affecting men's roles and responsibilities in ways that illuminate what I will call the false promise of patriarchy for Indigenous men. Although the governance structure imposed by the Dominion of Canada appears to place a monopoly of political power in the hands of Indigenous men, such power remains circumscribed by the will of white male Canadian overseers who "may order" tribal elections and are empowered to depose elected Indigenous leaders based on subjective transgressions such as "dishonesty, intemperance, or immorality." Under the *Indian Act*, Indigenous men's political power was imagined no longer to blossom from a dynamic ecosystem of relations among genders but to flow downward from the superintendent general of Indian Affairs to the governor to Indigenous male leaders and then to an Indigenous male electorate in an elaborate form of surrogacy. The defining feature of Indigenous leadership in this configuration, from the perspective of settler colonialism, is that it is contingent; it is subject to the will of settler authority. Through such legislation, the Dominion of Canada sought to domesticate Indigenous nations beneath the sovereignty of the Crown[17] and, in terms of gender, to foment an impression of Indigenous patriarchal power while ensuring that such power remained conditional (and ultimately could be denied, as illustrated in the vague clause about deposing Chiefs). Furthermore, the arbitrariness of the application of such power—far from uniform and consistent but subject as much to the whims of local agents as to larger policy dictates—served further to destabilize and thereby deteriorate the functionality of Indigenous gender knowledges. The point is that settler colonialism insinuated patriarchal power into Indigenous communities as a means of shoring up settler colonial rule while functionally delimiting the reach and impact of patriarchal power for individual Indigenous men. Thus, the manipulation of Indigenous gender systems evidenced by the *Gradual Enfranchisement Act*, at least in terms of political process, was less about remaking Indigenous societies in the image of the colonizer—at the interstices of race and gender, Indigenous men's power was envisioned structurally as *always subordinate* to white male authority and thus far from a mirror—and more about attacking the functional gender dynamics that constituted the lifeblood of Indigenous nations; such wielding of patriarchy was not assimilative but deterritorializing, designed to undermine the "constellations of care" within Indigenous communities in order to render those communities less viable and less politically resistant.

The most pervasive colonial technology of deterritorialization in lands claimed by Canada was undeniably the residential school system, which functioned from 1879 to 1996, removing over 150,000 Indigenous children from their homes, families, and communities to be educated in a Eurocentric manner (Truth and Reconciliation Commission). As with the false promise of patriarchy, the stated objectives of residential schooling—in the oft-quoted words of Canada's inaugural prime minister, John A. Macdonald, from 1887, "'to do away with the tribal system and assimilate the Indian people in all respects with the inhabitants of the Dominion as speedily as they are fit for the change'" (qtd. in Ennamorato 72)—are misleading at best. Although the schools were run by religious denominations representing the faiths of the majority of settler Canadians, were conducted in Canada's two official languages, and included, in most cases, some of the Eurocentric curricula experienced by settler students throughout the country, the development of equivalently educated students in residential schools, compared with the mainstream school system, was actively precluded by a plethora of factors. The schools were chronically underfunded and understaffed; classes were taught in most cases by clergy who had not been trained as teachers, as would have been the case in mainstream schools; students tended to be instructed during only a fraction of the school day (the proportion of which varied by school, over time, and among age groups but in almost all cases failed to meet the level experienced by contemporary settler students); and, during the majority of the decades in which residential schools were functioning, Indigenous students were educated for vocations that were on their way to obsolescence in industrializing Canadian society (e.g., domestic cleaning work for Indigenous girls and agricultural labour for Indigenous boys).[18] As such, even if the schools had not been sites of horrific abuse and neglect, as well as havens for illness, the vast majority of students emerging from them would have been ill-prepared for successful integration into Canadian society because of the structural limitations of the schools themselves—limitations about which the Department of Indian Affairs was aware but had scant intention of addressing.

Furthermore, during the periods in which residential schools were multiplying across Turtle Island and then were at their height, contemporaneous Indian Affairs policies actively prevented the absorption of Indigenous people "into the body politic," as Minister of Indian Affairs Duncan Campbell Scott proclaimed in 1920 to be the department's "objective" (qtd. in Milloy 46): the "pass system," brought into law in 1885 and functioning for almost sixty years thereafter, quarantined Indigenous Peoples of the prairie provinces on their reserves, preventing free movement throughout non-Indigenous communities without the written consent of Indian Agents; the policy of "centralization," implemented in Nova Scotia in the 1940s, actively removed Mi'kmaq and Maliseet families and communities near settler towns and cities, sequestering them on large reserves at Shubenacadie and Eskasoni.[19] As such, it is hard to treat the Canadian government's recourse to the language of "assimilation"—as heinous as that language is—as anything but disingenuous. The goals of Indian Affairs were not equality and incorporation but subordination and disappearance. As Roland Chrisjohn and Sherri Young put it, residential schools were "not, therefore, instruments of social engineering, intended to inculcate an alternative form of life: they [were] instruments of genocide, meant to produce things unrecognizable *at all* as human beings" (73). Despite the propagandist language of social integration used by government officials, residential schools were designed to *disin*tegrate and *de*territorialize, targeting the coherence of Indigenous individuals and communities for fracture.

In Chapter 2, I argue that residential schooling pursued its deterritorializing imperative largely through three forms of coerced separation: the severing of the mind from the body through impositions of Cartesian dualism, the severing of individual Indigenous students from their kin (particularly through spatial segregation by gender and age within the institutions), and the severing of Indigenous bodies from sacred lands and waters through carceral confinement within the schools themselves. In 1879, Macdonald explained the "residential" nature of the schools in this way:

> When the school is on the reserve, the child lives with its parents, who are savages, and though he may learn to read and write, his habits and training mode of thought are Indian. He is simply a savage who can read and write. It has been strongly impressed upon myself, as head of the Department, that Indian children should be withdrawn as much as possible from the parental influence, and the only way to do that would be to put them in central training industrial schools where they will acquire the habits and modes of thought of white men. (qtd. in "Residential Schools" 2)

Here again Macdonald uses the language of social engineering and assimilation—to "*acquire* the habits and modes of thought of white men"—while holding up segregation along a generational vector as a utilitarian measure through the separation of children from their parents. However, through the language that he invokes, Macdonald betrays that Indian Affairs policy might not be just about denying access to parents but ultimately about denying access to the dynamic mutuality of community. The jumble of words—"habits and training mode of thought"—suggests the difficulty of describing the integrated systems of meaning through which peoplehood exists and which residential schools were designed to deny Indigenous youth.

Such segregation was perhaps at its most aggressive along gender lines. One tactic for dis-integrating Indigenous communities was to deny the validity of gender balance and coercively naturalize a hierarchical gender binary that would privilege males while relegating females to positions of subservience. As the testimonies before the Indian Residential Schools Truth and Reconciliation Commission make clear, the residential school system enforced this objective, often brutally, with catastrophic implications for Indigenous girls, as well as for two-spirit and non-binary youth, whose humanity was denied by these disciplinary structures of classification. The religious orders that ran the schools impressed upon students that the domination of women by men was divinely sanctioned and natural, that the physical body was filthy and degenerate, and that sexuality and desire were inherently sinful, all of which constituted direct attacks on Indigenous gender complementarity while compromising the interpersonal dynamics through which integrated identity is affirmed and roles and responsibilities are rendered legible. Inuvualuk writer Anthony Apakark Thrasher recalls that "We were told [at residential school] not to play with the girls, because that would . . . be a sin. I thought that was strange, because I had played with girls before I came to school. Now they were telling me I shouldn't touch them" (14). Métis author Maria Campbell writes in *Halfbreed* that "the system that fucked me up fucked our men even worse. The Missionaries had impressed upon us the feeling that women were a source of evil" (144).

As I argue in the following chapter, residential schooling's tactical assaults on Indigenous gender systems, though not always or entirely "successful," of course, have had profound effects on the functionality of gendered roles and responsibilities within many Indigenous communities. Whereas I argued earlier that, by placing significant value on the ethic of non-interference and the balance of power between genders, the Haudenosaunee worldview fosters checks and balances that guard against gender-based oppression even in contexts in which a gender binary is naturalized,[20] the *Indian Act* and residential schooling have strategically targeted elements of the ecosystem of Haudenosaunee meaning making in efforts to throw it out of balance, thereby heightening the likelihood that gendered roles and responsibilities might be interpreted in heteropatriarchal terms. Given such tactical obfuscation of aspects of Indigenous worldviews, Dene scholar Glen Coulthard emphasizes the need to acknowledge how "the Indian Act has itself come to discursively shape, regulate, and govern how many of us have come to think about Indigenous identity and community belonging. As a result," he argues, "we have to be cautious that our appeals to 'culture' and 'tradition' in our contemporary struggles for recognition do not replicate the racist and sexist misrecognitions of the Indian Act and in the process unwittingly reproduce the structure of dispossession we originally set out to challenge" (103).

My point in this section has been that, despite recourse to the rhetoric of assimilation, "the white man's burden," and the civilizing mission of white settler heteropatriarchy by politicians and civil servants such as Macdonald and Scott, the evidence of gendered interventions in Indigenous lives, families, and communities via the *Indian Act*, residential schooling, and other measures suggests the primary impetus of colonial policy to be dis-integration and elimination rather than social engineering and assimilative re-production. Such policy initiatives bespeak a campaign of deter-ritorialization: not to *remake* but to *unmake*, and ultimately to legitimize that unmaking. This campaign has been, and continues to be, conducted through intensive attacks on the bodies and voices of Indigenous women (in the political arena and elsewhere) and those of queer, two-spirit, and non-binary Indigenous people. It has relied simultaneously upon the delimitation of Indigenous men's power through structural contingency as well as targeted violence against Indigenous men's bodies via the regulatory entities of the North West Mounted Police and the Royal Canadian Mounted Police, the judicial system, and the carceral apparatus of the state. Although the state's denial of Indigenous women's power might be imagined to have added to the power of Indigenous men, the false promise of patriarchy and the implications of communal dis-integration suggest otherwise. As theorists such as Kim Anderson and Bonita Lawrence have argued consistently, the disruption of gender bal-ance within Indigenous communities is always *also* an attack on the integrity and well-being of Indigenous men. Such attacks have borne spiritual, political, and educational dimensions, as discussed thus far, and semiotic ones. As Lawrence argues, although "systems of classification . . . forcibly supplanted Indigenous ways of anchoring relationships among individuals, their communities, and the land," such ruptures have been "facilitated . . . by the images of Native people that exist within the colonizing culture. . . . [R]acist images," she continues, "assist in normalizing government regulation of Na-tive identity even as they are central to creating its categories" (24). Although such images shore up colonial political power, they are often created and circulate beyond a strictly political realm, thereby attesting to the perhaps subconscious desire of settler populations to be absolved of complicity in colonial violence and dispossession. In other words, such images—which tend to rely upon notions of Indigenous masculinity that are discrete from the dynamic mutuality evident in Haudenosaunee social systems described above—act upon settler longing for the legitimization and therefore naturalization of the colonial enterprise, often by imagining Indigenous bodies as deserving of the violence to which they are routinely subjected and then scapegoating Indigenous men as the imagined source of such violence as well as the proper targets of disciplinary responses by the state. It is to such images—or "simulations"—that I now turn.

## MEDIA MASCULINITIES AND REGIMES OF THE IMAGE

If, as settler geographer Neil Nunn argues, "settler colonialism is a territorial project that is centred on the accumulation and control of dispossessed land," then the sustainability of such "control" depends on the cultivation of "a sense of legitimacy over the acquired land" (1337). For this reason, settler colonialism is deeply invested in the production of narratives that naturalize Indigenous dispossession as necessary and even inevitable. For settler awareness of colonial violence to be transmogrified into an experience that bolsters settler identities and senses of belonging and entitlement—rather than anxiety, guilt, and awareness of complicity—settler colonialism requires the culpability for such violence to be projected onto its victims. Settler criminologist Shiri Pasternak frames the conundrum succinctly: "[H]ow [do] you kill an Indian with a clear conscience?" (318). This haunting question registers how Indigenous dispossession and elimination are not just goals of political leaders but also unspoken imperatives woven deeply into the fabric of settler experience since, consciously or not, settlers genuinely wish to view themselves/ourselves as good. As such, the deterritorialization of Indigenous Peoples is not just a policy issue but indeed an issue of popular North American consciousness with undeniable semiotic dimensions. In this section, I examine the regime of images through which "Indigenous masculinity" has been, in a sense, *invented* by settler society,[21] normalized through semiotic proliferation, and then mobilized to justify the extension of the very violence out of which it emerged. The images of Indigenous men with which I am concerned in these pages tend to be isolated and decontextualized: they are removed from communal ecosystems of meaning making, like those within Haudenosaunee communities, in which autonomy and non-interference are balanced with interdependence through gendered roles and responsibilities. As such, these simulations betray settler imaginaries rather than Indigenous realities, with implications for both settlers—who are their primary audience and whose interactions with Indigenous Peoples are often preceded (and thus conditioned) by such images—and Indigenous Peoples themselves.

In *I Am Woman: A Native Perspective on Sociology and Feminism*, Stó:lō writer Lee Maracle argues that "the result of being colonized is the internalization of the need to remain invisible. The colonizers erase you, not easily, but with shame and brutality. Eventually you want to stay that way" (8). According to Chickasaw legal scholar James (Sákéj) Youngblood Henderson, this forceful erasure engenders for contemporary Indigenous people a "realization of their invisibility [that] is similar to looking into a still lake and not seeing their images. They become alien in their own eyes, unable to recognize themselves in the reflections and shadows of the world. As their grandparents and parents were stripped of their wealth and dignity, this realization strips Aboriginal [people] of their heritage and identity. It gives them an awareness of their annihilation" ("Postcolonial" 59). The systematic decimation of Indigenous social structures and the suppression of gendered roles and responsibilities have indeed contributed to crises of identity for some Indigenous people—crises that, though fostered by erasure and absence, are exacerbated by images of Indigeneity in popular culture that actually *stand in* for Indigenous presence; Anishinaabe theorist Gerald Vizenor terms such semiotic replacement "manifest manners" and "simulations of dominance."[22] Popular North American culture is saturated with stereotypical images of Indigenous people created and controlled by settlers for the benefit of the non-Indigenous majority. As Audre Lorde puts it succinctly in the Black American context, "'it is axiomatic that if we do not define ourselves for ourselves, we will be defined by others—for their use and to our detriment'" (qtd. in Jackson II 133). Such external control over definitions and image production has led Kanien'keha:ka scholar Patricia Monture-Angus to suggest that "growing up 'Indian' in this country is very much about not having the power to define yourself or your own reality. It is being denied the right to say, 'I am!'—instead finding yourself saying, 'I am not!'" (3).

Choctaw scholar Brian Klopotek argues convincingly that, "For at least the last century, hypermasculinity has been one of the foremost attributes of the Indian world that whites have imagined. With squaws and princesses usually playing secondary roles, Indian tribes are populated predominantly by noble or ignoble savages, wise old chiefs, and cunning warriors. These imagined Indian nations comprise an impossibly masculine race" (251). In tandem with the settler colonial move to suppress the political power of Indigenous women comes the representational move to re-present Indigenous cultures as overtly and hyperbolically masculine in non-Indigenous art, literature, film, and media—a move designed to recast Indigenous nations as a bona fide threat in need of amelioration through civility. Mainstream representations of Indigenous men in each of these fields have tended to remain within the restrictive triangulation of stereotypes that includes the "noble savage," the "bloodthirsty warrior," and the "drunken absentee,"[23] each deeply invested in the trope of the "vanishing Indian" that would naturalize the demise of Indigenous nations while delegitimizing the experiences of Indigenous women.

Some years ago I offered the following diagram (see Figure 1) as an interpretive tool for understanding the political work of legitimation in the service of which such images are marshalled. I titled it "Masculindians" to foreground its constructedness and therefore its inability to represent the actual lived experiences of Indigenous individuals and nations.[24] The noble savage is positioned at the top of the diagram because it represents what non-Indigenous North American society has romanticized as the most admirable features of Indigenous cultures: rugged autonomy, physical bravery, and spiritual connection with nature—all elements of idealized masculinity that non-Indigenous North Americans have worried have been depleted in the dominant culture over the past 150 years or so because of postindustrial urbanization and other factors.

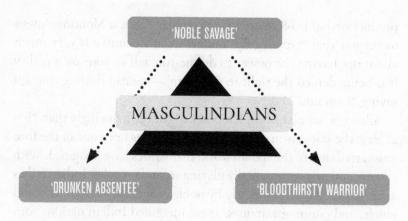

**Figure 1:** Masculindians: Simulated Stereotypes of Indigenous Masculinity

However, the noble savage is imagined as ill suited to survival in North American modernity, which pushes male Indigeneity within settler imaginaries toward one of the other points on the triangle, representing alternative pathways of degeneration. The bloodthirsty warrior is the embodiment of hypermasculine fury untempered by the spiritual dignity, restraint, and stoic endurance of the noble savage. In a continuum in which the noble savage represents the height of desirable "natural" masculinity uncontaminated by modernity, the bloodthirsty warrior moves dangerously beyond the ideal toward an extreme of masculine violence unmoored by reason or morality. The drunken absentee represents degeneration in the other direction. Unable to retain the dignity of the noble savage in the face of colonial oppression, the drunken absentee stereotype becomes immobilized and powerless, struggling not against a colonial enemy (like the bloodthirsty warrior) but against himself and his community through domestic violence, parental absenteeism, and protracted self-destruction through alcoholism or drug abuse. David Anthony Tyeeme Clark and Joane Nagel grapple with the political and ideological purposes of hypermasculine representations in literary westerns, arguing that such texts seek to recreate "hegemonic masculinity" among non-Indigenous North Americans through the depiction of "endless struggles with Indian supermen before they were, in the minds of the conquerors, overpowered, tamed, imprisoned, and thus emasculated, on reservations" (116).

The noble savage and the bloodthirsty warrior represent the *before* image in this scenario, whereas the drunken absentee represents the *after* image, with all of these depictions circulating to shore up the settler self.

As suggested above, the unrelentingly dignified, brave, and stoic noble savage signifies for mainstream audiences the pinnacle of Indigenous cultural development. The noble savage is generally a Chief or Medicine Man who commands the respect of his people. He is attuned to the natural world and deeply invested in the spiritual traditions of his people. In literary and filmic representations, the noble savage remains an advocate of his people's worldview despite the onslaught of European "civilization" while befriending (and often sacrificing himself for) a well-meaning European who has become an honorary member of the community. The noble savage is almost always portrayed as a tragic figure, as silent, solitary, and humourless. The latter features are demonstrated strikingly in the portraiture of British American painter George Catlin in his early- and mid-nineteenth-century artwork designed to document what he believed to be vanishing Indigenous cultures. Catlin focused much of his art on male leaders of Indigenous nations garbed in traditional regalia. Immensely popular in their time, Catlin's paintings presented a limited idea of Indigenous masculinity by often segregating male leaders from the contexts of their communities and rendering them in the style of European monarchs. Such paintings could thus be interpreted by non-Indigenous audiences as representing a form of coercive male authority akin to monarchy that bore scant resemblance to the lived realities of Indigenous nations such as those of the Haudenosaunee Confederacy. Catlin's portrait entitled *Not-to-way, a Chief* (1835–36) offers one such example (see Image 2). In the image, Not-to-way is painted in vivid colours standing alone upon a featureless landscape that fades into an abstract, cloud-filled sky. Gazing calmly, almost mournfully, off into a seemingly uncertain future, Not-to-way is depicted in relation to neither territory nor community, leading the viewer to question of whom and of what, in fact, he is "Chief." Catlin's *Letters and Notes on the Manners, Customs and Conditions of North American Indians* complicate matters further. Even though at the time of the painting Haudenosaunee nations

**Image 2:** George Catlin, *Nót-to-way, a Chief*, 1835–36, Oil on Canvas *Smithsonian American Art Museum, Gift of Mrs. Joseph Harrison, Jr., 1985.66.196.*

boasted populous communities with complex democratic structures of governance at various sites, including Akwesasne, Kanawake, Six Nations, and Tyendinaga, he painted few Haudenosaunee people, stating that "Of this tribe I have painted but one," and in this case choosing a "Chief" who, "though he was an Iroquois, which he was proud to acknowledge to [the painter,] . . . wished it to be generally thought, that he was a Chippeway" (see "Nót-to-way, a Chief"). Not only did Catlin frame his portraits to isolate subjects from the political and territorial vitalities of their communal lives, but also, in this case, he selected for artistic commemoration one living in exile from his tribal nation, intriguingly referring to him nonetheless as "a Chief." In such ways, Catlin's portraits served to simulate a model of Indigenous leadership with little relation to the reality of consensus-based systems of Indigenous governance, and they tended to obfuscate the interdependence among genders in Indigenous communities by focusing on isolated men.[25]

The noble savage in art, as in literature and film, is meant to be respected and admired but ultimately to be grieved because of his inevitable demise. The noble savage constitutes an anachronism because his attachment to a tribal worldview and lifestyle is portrayed as admirable but doomed in the face of European expansion. For example, in the films *Dances with Wolves* (1990), *Black Robe* (1991), and *The Last of the Mohicans* (1992),[26] audiences are encouraged to sympathize with the characters of Kicking Bird, Chomina, and Chingachgook, respectively. Each character displays several characteristics of the noble savage stereotype, yet ultimately (and inescapably) each fades away by the film's conclusion; he has no possibility of imagined persistence beyond the film's final credits. *Dances with Wolves* concludes with Kicking Bird, played by Oneida actor Graham Greene, retreating to the "winter hunting grounds" against the advancing American cavalry. Here winter carries with it the none-too-subtle symbolic charge that the Lakota Sioux culture for which Kicking Bird has become the film's figurehead is at the end of its existence, fading into the hills like the characters themselves. If the cultural demise is at all in question, the film ends with an epilogue declaring that thirteen years later "The great horse culture of the plains was gone and the American frontier was soon to pass into history."

In *Black Robe*, Montagnais leader Chomina, played by Kanien'keha:ka actor August Schellenberg, ultimately dies from wounds inflicted on him by his nation's Haudenosaunee enemies. Having refused baptism from the film's protagonist, Father Laforgue,

Chomina is depicted as returning to the dream world of his people as he dies, symbolically carrying their spiritual ways with him. The imagined demise of Chomina's spiritual system is reinforced in the film through Laforgue's eventual baptism of the entire tribe of Huron, whom he journeys to convert.

*The Last of the Mohicans*, adapted from the novel by James Fenimore Cooper, signals by its very title the extinction of an Indigenous culture. In the film, as in the novel, the final "Mohican" is the noble and brave Chingachgook, played by Lakota activist Russell Means. In the monologue with which the film concludes, Chingachgook not only declares himself the last of his people, a "race" that will die with him, but also frames this demise within the context of the inevitable demise of all Indigenous Peoples: "The frontier moves with the sun, pushes the Red Man of these wilderness forests in front of it until one day there will be nowhere left. Then our race will be no more or be not us. . . . The frontier place is for people like my white son and his woman and their children. And one day there will be no more frontier." Significantly, the Mohican Elder envisions a possible future for the film's European protagonists but not for his people or any other Indigenous nation. Chingachgook's words resonate with settler audiences because they encourage participation in a lament for tragic loss without the assignment of blame or culpability. It is the "frontier" that pushes Indigenous people from the "wilderness forests," not colonial policies, settler encroachment, or racialized violence; Indigenous dispossession and elimination are crimes without a perpetrator. And because this inevitable demise is voiced in stoic resignation by the noble savage, the settler viewer is invited to identify with that loss through mourning, placated by the observation that "once . . . [they] were here": performative grieving serves to instantiate settler futurity as *belonging* on stolen lands while Indigeneity is consigned to the past. The noble savage is inherently artifactual—always outside the flow of time, unchanging, fit only for museum display and never for endurance into settler modernity.[27] In fact, the "white son," played by Daniel Day Lewis, allows attributes of imagined Indigenous masculinity epitomized by Chingachgook to be inherited and preserved—perhaps even "perfected" by "white civility"—in the absence of actual Indigenous people. In this way, the film's dénouement participates in a discursive absorption of imagined Indigenous masculinity that has been in circulation at least since Ernest Thompson Seton began encouraging white settler boys to "play Indian" with the Woodcraft Indians and then the Boy Scouts of America, in efforts to cultivate rugged masculinity that would prepare them for white American manhood, at the dawn of the twentieth century.[28] In both the ethos of the Woodcraft Indians and the film, Indigenous people disappear or devolve, unable to cope with the advance of modernity, while the worthy attributes of vanishing (and imagined) Indigenous masculinity are absorbed into the mythology of settler belonging.

The remaining two points on the masculindians diagram illustrate potential responses to the inevitable demise imagined for the noble savage. The bloodthirsty warrior constitutes a hypermasculine reaction to settler colonial conquest, and the drunken absentee represents resignation to the demise of a people in which the Indigenous man becomes complicit in his own destruction through the narcosis of drugs and alcohol. In each of the three films mentioned above, the noble savage is placed opposite a bloodthirsty warrior figure. In *Black Robe*, the role of the latter stereotype is filled by a Haudenosaunee War Chief who, after delighting in the torture of Father Laforgue and his two male companions, cuts off Laforgue's finger and slices the throat of Chomina's young son with neither sympathy nor remorse. The role of the bloodthirsty warrior is played in each of the other two films by Cherokee actor Wes Studi. The nameless character played by Studi in *Dances with Wolves* is referred to in the film's credits as "the toughest Pawnee." The nemesis of Kicking Bird's Lakota band, he charges forward against overwhelming odds and meets his death defiantly, fist raised and shouting, his sacrificial rage here guaranteeing his eventual death. Studi's role as Magua in *The Last of the Mohicans* portrays even more blatantly the bloodthirsty warrior's irrational hypermasculine violence. A figure consumed by anger, Magua has dedicated his life to extracting revenge against his enemy, Colonel Munro. When asked by the French marquis, with whom he is allied, why he loathes the English colonel so intensely, he responds with the declaration that "Magua will eat his heart."

Speaking of himself in the third person, Magua is so fixated on vengeance that he cannot even put into words the reason for his anger; he collapses back on the violent act of revenge itself, thereby removing it from any meaningful context and obscuring its causal function. Magua is thus symbolic of a threatening hypermasculine violence that non-Indigenous North American society imagines within Indigenous cultures—a masculinity that cannot be channelled into productive actions through "civilized" logic; he is thus doomed to perpetuate violence until he too is killed.

The furious moment of defiant self-sacrifice imagined for the bloodthirsty warrior seems to be paired in mainstream North American consciousness with the protracted self-destruction of the drunken absentee, depicted as so wounded by unavoidable loss that he segregates himself from family and community and drinks himself to death. Rather than perishing in resistance like the former stereotype, the latter stereotype internalizes and is immobilized by the pain of his nation's cultural erasure; whereas the bloodthirsty warrior betrays a corrupted hypermasculinity untethered to rationality or restraint, the drunken absentee is emasculated, bereft of dignity, purpose, and virility. He thus performs the sapping of the strength of the noble savage and functions as evidence for the colonial hypothesis that the glorious elements of Indigenous cultural traditions have been contaminated and lost, and that Indigenous masculinities are anachronistic in the context of settler modernity, meaning that assimilation and Indigenous removal are not only justified but in fact necessary. These three stereotypical images—which I stress again are the products of settler North American imaginaries and desires rather than representations of Indigenous realities past or present—therefore serve a variety of purposes for settler colonial power. The stereotypes of masculindians serve to justify colonial expansion and act as evidence of the success of colonialism. The drunken absentee provides evidence of Indigenous degeneration that legitimizes settler colonial interventions in Indigenous communities and shores up the benign self-image of the colonizer as the cure, not the cause, of Indigenous suffering. The bloodthirsty warrior, although perhaps admirable in his fearlessness and compelling in his recourse to hypermasculine violence, provides a foil for colonial conquest; he is the perfect enemy who, in defeat, bolsters the masculinity of his settler conqueror.

According to literary critic Elizabeth Cromley, "The manhood of the Indian" in white literary representations historically has been "attached to their ruthless violence, so when readers imagined Indians as actors in these stories, they saw men, physically courageous and bold, yet unable to channel their masculinity into 'civilized' and productive acts" (269), which leads to what Michael Wilson identifies as the "central white criticism of Indian 'nature': Indians' alleged lack of masculine self-control" (132). Through literature, art, film, and media, settler audiences can imbibe the supposedly "virile" and "natural" Indigenous masculinity of bloodthirsty warriors but then perfect that masculinity through the "civilizing" force of interpretive restraint. In this delineation, the drunken absentee serves as evidence that the hypermasculine violence of the bloodthirsty warrior has been subdued and contained by colonial power and that the noble savage—so admired and romanticized in non-Indigenous literature, film, and art—has become an anachronism. Thus, although the decimation of Indigenous societies is portrayed as tragic within this constellation of stereotyped images—insofar as the loss of the noble savage is to be mourned—the settler self-image is exonerated of complicity because it is all presented as inevitable; it seems as if it could have happened no other way.

Although these stereotyped images are simulations created by settlers to serve colonial agendas, they bear genuine consequences for Indigenous men and Indigenous communities because they condition how Indigenous men are perceived and treated by settler society, and they offer cues to how Indigenous men are expected by some to behave, thereby delimiting the routes through which such men can seek power and social capital. In a contemporary context in which many Haudenosaunee and other Indigenous men have been systematically alienated from community-specific roles and responsibilities and continue to be disempowered by racism and economic and political disenfranchisement, the images of Indigenous hypermasculinity circulating in popular culture can become attractive to some Indigenous men because of the power that they betray—a form of surrogacy in a context of systemic oppression. Chippewa

**Image 3:** Face to Face (a photo that came to be Canadian media shorthand for the Kanehsatake land reclamation). *Shaney Komulainen, photo featuring Private Patrick Cloutier (left) and Anishinaabe Warrior Bradley Larocque (right), September 1, 1990.*

scholar Gail Guthrie Valaskakis suggests that this is how "images of . . . Indians" produced by and for mainstream North American culture come to be "appropriated by Indians themselves" (38). Focusing on the "monolithic representations of Indian militants" in the media during incidents of Indigenous resistance, Valaskakis argues that the trope of the "military masculine" (39)—which bears a direct lineage to the stereotype of the bloodthirsty warrior—becomes potentially attractive to "young warriors . . . [who] reappropriat[e] the media's monolithic, military representation of the bandana-masked, khaki-clad, gun-toting warrior and the western Plains warrior from which it has evolved" (60).

Images such as Shaney Komulainen's iconic photograph of Anishinaabe activist Bradley Larocque and Canadian military private Patrick Cloutier engaged in a standoff, taken at the Oka Land Reclamation of 1990 (see Image 3), participate in a regime of images that cultivates a simulated stereotype of violent, individualistic, and

ultimately vanishing Indigenous masculinity while naturalizing settler colonialism and state power. Komulainen's photograph resonates
with settler Canadians for a number of reasons, not least of which
is the ease with which it maps onto the semiotic field of masculindians. In the photograph, Cloutier's unmasked face encourages
identification with the settler viewer, and his apparent youthfulness
implies futurity threatened by a menace. In contrast, the masked
Larocque is obscure and ageless, turned away from the camera, and
his opacity serves to place the possibility vested in Cloutier at risk.
Unable to see Larocque's eyes, the settler viewer is unlikely to register
his full humanity, relegating Larocque to the semiotic category of
violent Indigenous hypermasculinity fostered through centuries of
colonial policies and cultural production. Significantly, his "military
masculinity" in the photograph is decontextualized; although the
strength of conviction embodied in his posture and his capacity to
wield violence, as evidenced by the visibility of his assault rifle, offer
tangible models of resistance to Indigenous viewers, the framing of
the photo as a person-to-person conflict individualizes and deterri-
torializes the events in ways that simplify and therefore misrepresent
them. The sacred pines for which the Kanien'keha:ka and their allies
struggled are signalled only by blurred foliage in the background,
and the intergenerational and multi-gendered network of kinship
involved in the administration of Kanien'keha:ka decision making
is entirely absent from this scene of two men engaged in conflict.
Larocque becomes interpretable in this image as an isolated wielder
of hypermasculine violence rather than one embedded within his
community, fulfilling his responsibility of protectorship—in Leanne Betasamosake Simpson's words, "[s]tanding up, speaking out
and protecting Indigenous lands, nations and bodies" ("Powerful
Legacy"). A Kanien'keha:ka activist and spokesperson during the
Oka conflict, Ellen Gabriel argues that Komulainen's photograph
"perpetuates a violent stereotype founded in history, a stereotype
that has not yet dissipated from the public conscience . . . [and] is
not reflective of our struggle. Our struggle includes men, women
and sadly . . . even children of our nations who for hundreds of years
. . . have been forced to fight heartless colonialists for their lustful
grab of our lands and resources" ("Those"). Disentangled from the

web of relations and the very land with and for which Larocque struggles, his image risks being absorbed into the iconography of the bloodthirsty savage rather than illustrative of responsibilities "to protect the people and the land when a threat to their safety is imminent" (Gabriel, "Those")—carrying the burden of peace.

Gabriel argues, in contrast, that, "if any image reflects the reality that *Onwehón:we* peoples have endured throughout our history with colonial forces, it is the racists burning their nightly effigies of a Mohawk 'Warrior' in Chateauguay during the Oka Crisis" ("Those"; see Image 4). That image powerfully represents the "reality" of settler colonial oppression precisely because it focuses on a fiction: the effigy. The effigy of a Kanien'keha:ka warrior, in the words of Anishinaabe theorist Gerald Vizenor, is "the absence of real natives— the contrivance of the other in the course of dominance" (vii), yet it has genuine consequences for Indigenous people. It is removed from the land, quarantined from networks of kinship and community, and held aloft as isolated, anonymous, and fundamentally *un*human; yet, as the plurality of the word *warriors* scrawled down the effigy's left leg implies, it is a caricature mobilized to incite and justify violence against Indigenous people broadly, in the service here of Québécois nationalism, as evidenced by the two fleur-de-lis flags. In this way, images of non-Indigenous Quebecers burning the Kanien'keha:ka effigy betray (1) the simulated nature of the "menace" of Indigenous masculinity, which, as a construct of settler society, is fundamentally incapable of representing Indigenous realities; (2) the audience by and for whom this semiotic construction has been produced and whom it is intended to serve, displayed by the white mob clustered around the burning figure, whipped into a frenzy of anti-Indigenous racism; and (3) how such symbolic violence is embroiled with and foments actual violence.

As Métis scholar Robert Henry notes, "Indigenous males are constructed in popular discourses and media as predictably . . . violent toward themselves and others" and, as such, "are more easily identified as criminals or participating in criminal behaviour" (192), which serves to corroborate settler intuition that Indigenous men are in need of pacification by the coercive power of the state. (In the image opposite, the word *Alcatraz* is visible above the effigy's

**Image 4:** Settler Citizens of Chateauguay Burn the Effigy of a Kanien'keha:ka "Warrior." *Peter Power*, Toronto Star, *1990*.

head.) As statistics from Corrections Canada and research studies by Robert Henry, Elizabeth Comack, Alison Piché, Susanne Reber and Robert Renaud, and others demonstrate unequivocally,[29] Indigenous men are targeted for state violence, removal to carceral spaces, and premature death at rates that far exceed national averages. "[I]n comparison to non-Indigenous Canadians," Robert Alexander Innes and Kim Anderson show, "Indigenous men have shorter life spans, . . . are more likely to be incarcerated, and are murdered at a higher rate" ("Introduction" 4). The level to which Indigenous men are imagined by the settler population to be "violent and dangerous" is "highlighted," for Innes and Anderson, "by the number of shooting deaths of unarmed Indigenous men by police officers, with relative impunity and with little outcry from the public" (10). To put it starkly, Indigenous men are targeted for premature death because they are constructed in the settler imaginary as less than human, as threatening to white Canadian prosperity, and therefore as responsible for the very violence to which they are subjected.[30] In Neil Nunn's words, Indigenous lives "fall outside the regulatory category of the Human, and as a result . . . are subject to elimination" (1342).

Although one could reach to scores of examples of Indigenous victims of such horrors—from Leo LaChance to Neil Stonechild to Melvin Bigsky to Joey Knapaysweet to Jon Styres and on and on and on—the murder of twenty-two-year-old Cree man Colten Boushie by fifty-six-year-old white farmer Gerald Stanley and his acquittal by an all-white jury on February 9, 2018, present an appallingly telling narrative not only because of the details of the killing but also because of how the killing has been treated by the police, the judicial system, and the broader Canadian public. The murder took place as Boushie and four friends, returning home from swimming, got a flat tire and drove onto Stanley's farm looking for help. Stanley testified in court that, as he approached the vehicle at close range, his weapon went off accidentally, striking the unarmed Boushie, asleep at the time according to the testimony of others, in the back of the head.[31] Treating the young Indigenous occupants of the vehicle not as victims in this case but as criminals themselves, the Royal Canadian Mounted Police raided their homes, including that of Boushie's mother at the very moment that she learned of her son's death.[32] In the courtroom, the all-white jury accepted Stanley's claim that "his semi-automatic handgun went off accidentally—an extremely rare 'hang-fire'" (Union of British Columbia Indian Chiefs). And, in the wake of this miscarriage of justice, many settler Canadians have been quick to join the chorus condemning the twenty-two-year-old murder victim and exalting the actions of his murderer. Cree-Saulteaux scholar Gina Starblanket and Cree scholar Dallas Hunt note, for example, how "outspoken farmers in the Saskatchewan farming community [have advocated] for violence" in the wake of this tragedy, viewing themselves, along with Stanley, "as heroic frontiersmen taming the wild and cultivating their little outposts of empire." Ben Kautz, a farmer and town councillor in Saskatchewan, wrote on the site of the Saskatchewan farmers' Facebook group that "In my mind his only mistake was leaving witnesses," and another member of the Facebook group wrote that "He should have shot all five of them, [and been] given a medal" (qtd. in Nunn 1339). These statements reveal the horrific extent of some settlers' devaluing of Indigenous lives; they also betray the deep investment of many settler Canadians in the simulated stereotypes of Indigenous criminality as a precondition of settler entitlement to land, property, and capital, and, as we see in the Stanley case, the visible endgame of such narratives is the actual deaths of Indigenous people and the calculated refusal to bring justice to settler perpetrators.

To reiterate, settler colonialism is a deterritorializing project; it seeks to constrain Indigenous movement (through removal from sacred landscapes and carceral confinement of various types) and to contain Indigenous identities (through the proliferation of dehumanizing stereotypes). As I argue throughout this book, settler colonialism struggles not to remake Indigenous Peoples in the image of the colonizer but to unmake and eliminate them in the service of settler appetites for land and property. As Nunn notes in relation to public responses to the Boushie murder, "across the media, countless people decried high property crime rates in their communities and sympathised with Stanley, suggesting that he was simply a victim of unfortunate circumstance" (1340). The great sleight of hand in all of this is that settler colonial society, which has coercively created social problems in many Indigenous communities, has displaced the burden of culpability largely onto Indigenous men, cast as perpetrators rather than victims—as corrupt band councillors who, instead of the *Indian Act*, are responsible for political dysfunction in their communities; as profiteers who, instead of settler resource exploitation and capitalism, are responsible for the misuse of their lands and the ravaging of the environment; as congenitally abusive tyrants who, rather than misogynist settler deviants, the systemic structure of settler heteropatriarchy, and coercive interventions in Indigenous ecologies of gender, are responsible for the gender-based violence to which disproportionate numbers of Indigenous women and girls are subjected. These are the very stories of Indigenous deficiency about which Daniel Heath Justice warns us in *Why Indigenous Literatures Matter*—stories that dehumanize and diminish and ultimately kill. We need stories that demonstrate Indigenous diversity and the full humanity of Indigenous Peoples, stories that eclipse the impoverished iconography of Indigenous hypermasculinity simulated by settler colonial society to serve its own legitimation and its insatiable appetites, stories that imagine and enact Indigenous futures through creativity and love. As Justice argues, we need stories that "affirm Indigenous presence—and our *present*" (xix), stories of embodied action that, to paraphrase Simpson, put bodies back on the land with intentionality and integrity.

## CONDOLENCE AND MASCULINE INTEGRITY

I began this chapter with calls from Sakej Ward to "bring back" the "traditional role" of Indigenous men and from Timothy Sweet to "recover the masculine" in "tribal societies." Although we must be skeptical of recovery projects that attempt to define, authenticate, and thereby "fix" Indigenous masculinities, the Haudenosaunee creation story of Atsi'tsiaká:ion (Sky Woman) presented above does offer some guidance on the invigoration of gendered roles and responsibilities that might exceed the "structural system of oppression" about which Qwo-Li Driskill warns in *Asegi Stories*. The telling of the story of Sky Woman by Tom Porter gifts listeners and readers with valuable insights into the contours of such

48

roles and responsibilities among the Haudenosaunee, including (1) the necessity of gender balance, complementarity, and twinship; (2) the notion of identity as fostered through integration into, rather than individuation from, the community; (3) the understanding of individual power as persisting within contexts of reciprocal responsibility; and (4) the recognition that the valuing of individual integrity evident in the ethic of non-interference—even in contexts in which roles and responsibilities are gendered—can insulate against the coerced imposition of gender identities onto community members. These values inform the matrilineal and matrilocal spatiality of Haudenosaunee society, and they undergird the care taken to ensure gender balance within the traditional governance structures of the Haudenosaunee Confederacy. However, as I have attempted to show, Indigenous systems of governance have come under relentless attack from the Canadian government through deterritorializing impositions such as the *Indian Act* and residential schooling, and the worldviews that those structures express and uphold have been similarly assaulted by representations of Indigenous hypermasculinity in mainstream art, literature, film, and media. Such spiritual, political, educational, and semiotic impositions on Indigenous gender systems have been undertaken tactically to devalue the voices of Indigenous women and queer, trans, and two-spirit people and to alienate Indigenous men from nation-specific roles and responsibilities in order to speed the dispossession of Indigenous lands and waters and to naturalize the sovereignty of the Canadian state. Although the heteropatriarchal dimensions of this process might be imagined to enhance the power of cis-hetero Indigenous men, such "empowerment" has always been circumscribed by the dehumanization of settler colonial rule; as settler colonialism *dis*integrates Indigenous communities in the service of elimination, it pressures Indigenous men, like Indigenous women and others, to become what they are not.

Yet the ideas and values placed under erasure by settler colonialism are not gone. The masculine roles and responsibilities that Janice Hill argues need to be reclaimed among the Haudenosaunee have not disappeared, even as they have been assaulted in the myriad ways described above; just as the traditional governance system of the Haudenosaunee Confederacy continues to function—at times in alliance and at others in conflict with the band council system imposed by the Canadian government—so too knowledge pertaining to gendered roles and responsibilities persists, and Haudenosaunee communities are, "all these years later, struggling to find our way back to those teachings" (20). I conclude this chapter with Tom Porter's telling of the tale of Aionwahta because it shares knowledge that might be considered part of that "struggle"—but not in a prescriptive way. Rather, Porter's evocative narrative guides Haudenosaunee listeners toward conditions of clarity and strength in which roles and responsibilities might be remembered, rekindled, and (re)created. The tale of Aionwahta offers political teachings that characterize just and equitable structures of governance at the same time that it offers critical teachings about gender relations and the dynamic interface between story and futurity. It provides a template for ceremonies of condolence by delineating the responsibility of those within the Haudenosaunee web of kinship to bring those who have been thrown out of balance by grief, trauma, and oppression back to their full humanity. In these ways, the Aionwahta story addresses alliance—commitment to the well-being of others with whom one is in relationships of reciprocal responsibility—and thereby fortifies Haudenosaunee communities grappling with centuries of gendered colonial violence through collective models for resurgence and reterritorialization.

Aionwahta was a man living in Onondaga at the time of the Peacemaker's journey to unite the clans and nations of the Haudenosaunee Confederacy under Kaianere'kó:wa, The Great Law of Peace. A man of witchcraft desired Aionwahta's wife, but she rejected his advances, so he produced medicine that made her grow sicker and sicker until she died. "'Because if I can't have her, nobody's gonna have her.' That's what he thought." This man then sought the affections of Aionwahta's seven daughters one by one, each of whom rejected his advances and each of whom he killed, leaving their father utterly broken and disconsolate. In despair, Aionwahta began to walk "aimlessly, in no particular direction. He just walked." He even walked into a small lake "covered from shore to shore with a blanket of geese and ducks," not caring if he should drown. When the birds flew up out of his way, however, they carried in their feathers so much of the water that they drained the lake—"that's how many were in there." As he walked upon the lake's muddy bottom, Aionwahta spied quahog shells, which he picked up and began to thread upon strings of sinew so that they "formed different variations of white and purple." And as he finished each of his strings, Aionwahta declared that

"With this string I made from this wampum that I found, if there is somebody in the world that is as sad and tearful, as full of grief as I am, with nothing to live for, . . . I would go see them. And I would take from the very beautiful blue sky a pure eagle feather. And I would wipe the dust of death from the sad one's ears, so that he could hear the children talk and sing and laugh again. So that he could hear his children and nephews when they speak to him. That's what I would do with this wampum if I knew somebody who was as sad as I am. I would console them by taking the death from their ears."

And then he picked some more up and he strung them. And he said, "If there was somebody as sad as I am, walking this earth, I would take, from the very beautiful clear blue sky, a soft little deer skin that's like white cotton. And I would wipe the tears from his eyes. I would use that cloth to wipe the tears, the pain of lonesomeness away from him. So he can see again the beauty of our Mother Earth and the beauty of his children and nephews and nieces. So he can see life again. That's what I would do, if there was somebody as sad as I am, to lose their whole family that they love."

Then as he continued to walk, he found some more of those same beads on the ground. And he strung them up. "With this wampum," he said, "if there was somebody in this world who was as sad as I am, with heaviness upon them, what I would do is I would take from the very beautiful blue sky, a medicine water and I would offer it to him. So when he drank it, it would dislodge the grief and the sadness, about the loved ones who died in his family. That way he could eat again and the food would taste good. And that way he could speak without a stutter to his loved ones, the ones that remain on earth. . . . And that's what I would do, if there was somebody who was in as much grief as I am." (Porter 293–96)

The tale of Aionwahta is a story of gender-based violence and a rumination on how communities thrown into chaos by the suppression of cultural ethics can be nurtured back to balance. The witchcraft man is villainous even before he commits the act of murder because he denies the free will of the women whom he covets; he fails to honour each woman's integrity, thereby violating the ethic of non-interference through acts of coercion, domination, and violence. Betraying modes of thought resonant with settler heteropatriarchy, he commoditizes the eight women as interchangeable possessions, ultimately deeming his own libidinal desires of greater worth than his victims' very lives—"Because if I can't have her, nobody's gonna have her." At the same time, by focusing primarily on Aionwahta and paying scant attention to the experiences of the women themselves, this version of the tale risks participating in the very economy of heteropatriarchy established by the witchcraft man's thinking and behaviour.[33] With two men as the story's only fully realized characters, this telling risks capitulating to a homosocial triangle in which the women become objects of exchange through which the conflict between agentive male subjects is enacted (see Sedgwick). When I teach this story in undergraduate classes, students seldom fail to point out their desire to know what happens to its villain; conditioned by the dominant mores of heteropatriarchal culture and prompted by the triangulated conflict in the story, they expect comeuppance. If the story were a Hollywood film, then the witchcraft man would surely be punished—likely at the climax via some spectacular act of violence by Aionwahta that placates the audience by, in a sense, "setting things right." However, Porter refuses to appease such desires, telling us nothing of vengeance toward this mass murderer of Indigenous women. In fact, Porter implies that what happens to the killer is somehow beside the point. Unlike Magua from *The Last of the Mohicans*, who, as a simulation of Indigenous hypermasculinity emergent from the settler colonial imaginary, seems to be capable only of thoughts of violence, Aionwahta is depicted in a manner that exceeds the structural constraints of heteropatriarchy. Whereas hypermasculine retributive justice sustains the masculine-centric thinking through which gender-based violence proliferates, Porter's tale offers something far more radical and ultimately, I argue, far more useful to decolonial futures.

Although isolated by the extremity of his grief, Aionwahta does not succumb to the lure of individualism (via despair or violence) but mobilizes his own suffering in the imagining of ceremonies capable of bringing the broader community back to balance at a time of profound hardship and disorder. Trading enmity for empathy, Aionwahta embeds his own struggle for healing in a purposeful commitment to the reawakening of others to the core values of his community. In other words, by taking upon himself the *responsibility* of enabling others to re-experience their full humanity, Aionwahta defines for himself a *role*, the exercise of which enables his own full humanity to be re-experienced as well. In the process of mapping out what he will do should he meet one "as sad and tearful, as full of grief as [himself]," Aionwahta assigns himself practical tasks that provide a sense of purpose while demonstrating his dedication to the well-being of others. Each of these tasks—"wip[ing] the dust of death" from the ears, "wip[ing] the tears" from the eyes, and "dislodg[ing] the grief" from the throat—is designed to allow aggrieved individuals to be more fully alert to, and expressive of, their true selves at the very moment when Aionwahta once again "live[s] deliberately and with meaning" (Simpson, *As We* 16). The relationship of the individual to the community in this configuration is mutually generative; Aionwahta finds *himself* through the act of enabling others to find *themselves*, and that solidarity is reciprocated when he eventually meets the Peacemaker and is condoled in precisely the manner that he has envisioned for others.

Porter's telling of the Aionwahta tale can therefore be interpreted, in my view, as a nuanced teaching about roles and responsibilities: it offers a practical expression of what roles and responsibilities might look like in a community context, and it theorizes the limitations of such roles and responsibilities within the Haudenosaunee worldview.

Through the depiction of Aionwahta as one alienated from his true self by grief and then reoriented through communal purpose, we see how adopting a community-embedded role can create conditions of possibility for the development and expression of an endorsable identity. At the same time, through the precise actions that Aionwahta undertakes, the tale offers a philosophical rumination on cultural ethics that need to remain operative to ensure that such roles and responsibilities become neither prescriptive nor oppressive. Simpson reminds us that "Heteropatriarchy isn't just about exclusion of certain Indigenous bodies, it is about the destruction of the intimate relationships that make up our nations, and the fundamental systems of ethics based on values of individual sovereignty and self-determination" (As We 123). The act of condolence involves the nurturing of such "intimate relationships," and the ceremony that Aionwahta envisions is fundamentally committed to "individual sovereignty and self-determination." He seeks not to impose particular perspectives upon those whom he condoles but to open them up to perspectives ever more their own. Their eyes are opened so that they can see the world more clearly. Their ears are cleansed so that the words of others are less likely to be misinterpreted and so that kinship relations can be affirmed and celebrated. And their throats are unclogged, not so that they can parrot the vision of Aionwahta, but so that they can reclaim their own voices. Aionwahta seeks neither to coerce nor to persuade; rather, he uses words and actions to engender conditions in which the voices of others might be raised in sovereign ways. Given the significance of non-interference to Haudenosaunee "systems of ethics," the roles and responsibilities championed in this story cannot be imposed or prescriptive (even if they are gendered), if they are to foster regeneration and resurgence. Roles and responsibilities within such a value system are open-ended, active engagements aligned with gifts and talents that create horizons of possibility for the building of individual and communal strength. This, in my view, is (re)territorialization.

Porter's telling of the Aionwahta tale augurs the potential for imagining masculine roles and responsibilities in non-prescriptive, non-dominative ways that might nourish Indigenous futures. According to the model of condolence shared in the story, this is not about dictating gender identities but about enabling Indigenous people to negotiate "meaningful way[s] to live in the world that [are] consistent with [their] intimate realities" (Simpson, *As We* 120). My argument in this book is that this process can be understood in gendered ways—provided that such understandings are non-coercive—but that it does not have to be. As theorists such as Janice Hill argue, a particular hunger for such roles and responsibilities persists among many who identify as Indigenous boys and men because of the specifically gendered ways in which settler colonialism has complicated "the transition to the twentieth century and the twenty-first century" for them (20). As such, turning to the language of "men" and "masculinities" can be useful, provided that such language is opened up to transcend the myopic hierarchies of settler heteronormativity. Hill is candid in her assertions that Haudenosaunee boys deserve "ceremonies" and "rites of passage" during their journeys of maturation and "to be passed over to the men" at specific stages "to learn man things" (21). Within Haudenosaunee ethics, however, such guidance ought not involve specific expectations about gender identities but should cultivate thoughtful reflection on the alignment of one's gifts with the needs of the people. Hill illustrates this powerfully through the example of her youngest son: "I believe he has the capacity to be a leader. He can be empathetic. He can be compassionate. I've been told by many people that he's good medicine. . . . But he needs to learn how to use that in a good way and what his responsibility is going to be with that medicine he carries" (20).

The Aionwahta story encourages us to understand gender roles and responsibilities in ways that exceed settler heteropatriarchy while honouring individual talents and gifts; the story demonstrates how nurturing individual integrity can actually foster one's integration into communities made richer by one's presence. The story does not necessarily give us answers but teaches us to ask the right questions with humility and a commitment to listen. It does not map out a final destination but teaches us how to travel softly and with purpose. It does not describe and analyze its vision but teaches us how to truly see. These are lessons not only of ideology and gender but also of literary studies—the modality of critical analysis through which the case studies that follow in this book will be conducted. As Aionwahta strings together the quahog shells of various sizes and hues, he mobilizes a symbolic system of non-alphabetic writing that can be translated into meaning by knowledgeable readers. The strings of wampum that he places in his pouch act as an archive of his experience, detailing his desperation in the wake of loss. This creative act, however, does more than document the past; it transforms past experiences into ceremonies capable of inspiring change in the present and the future. Aionwahta's visionary distillations thus act in much the same way as do Indigenous literatures according to Daniel Heath Justice's cogent characterization: "They remind us that we're the inheritors of heavy, painful legacies, but also of hope and possibility, of a responsibility to make the world better for those yet to come. . . . [T]hey help us make sense of our continuity and strengthen our struggle to put the world, at long last, back in balance" (*Why* 210–11).

# THE
# LAND
# AND THE
# BODY

# 2. SHAME AND DETERRITORIALIZATION

White supremacy, rape culture, and the real and symbolic attack on gender, sexual identity and agency are very powerful tools of colonialism, settler colonialism and capitalism primarily because they work very efficiently to remove Indigenous peoples from our territories and to prevent reclamation of those territories through mobilization. . . . They work to prevent mobilization because communities coping with epidemics of gender violence don't have the physical or emotional capital to organize. They destroy the base of our nations and our political systems because they destroy our relationships to the land and to each other by fostering epidemic levels of anxiety, hopelessness, apathy, distrust and suicide. They work to destroy the fabric of Indigenous nationhoods by attempting to destroy our relationality by making it difficult to form sustainable, strong relationships with each other. —LEANNE BETASAMOSAKE SIMPSON ("Not Murdered, Not Missing")

Sexual shame was a weapon used against us. Sexual shame was never ours. . . . [W]hatever shame we have around sexuality is one of those dubious gifts of colonialism that was intended to destroy us as individuals, as peoples, and destroy our links to one another, to the land, and to ourselves. —DANIEL HEATH JUSTICE (McKegney et al., "Strong Men Stories" 263) n October 2011, during a survivors' sharing circle at the Atlantic National Event of the Indian Residential Schools Truth and Reconciliation Commission (IRS TRC), a Cree woman recalled in eloquent and shattering testimony her forced separation from the younger brother for whom she had cared prior to residential school incarceration. Seeing her brother alone and despondent on the boys' side of the playground, the survivor recounted waving to him in the hope of raising his spirits, if only for a moment. A nun in the courtyard, however, spied this forbidden gesture of empathy and kinship and immediately hauled the young boy away. To punish him for having acknowledged his sister's love, the nun dressed the boy in girls' clothes and paraded him in front of the other boys, whom she encouraged to mock and deride his caricatured effeminacy.[1] In her testimony, the survivor recalled the hatred in his eyes as her brother was thus shamed—hatred not for his punisher but for her, his sister, whose affection had been deemed transgressive by the surveillance system of residential school acculturation.

What became clear to me as I witnessed the woman's testimony was that this punishment performed intricate political work designed to instruct boys to despise both girls and "girly" boys and to disavow bonds of kinship. The punishment's dramatization of gender opposition, its construction of the feminine as shameful, and its performative severing of intergender sibling relationships informed the type of masculine subjects whom those involved in administering residential school policies were invested in creating. Furthermore, it became clear that these punitive pedagogies of gender cannot be disentangled from the years of rape that the survivor went on to describe enduring from a priest at the same institution. Nor can the gender dynamics of these impositions be extricated from her expressed vexation that she still refers to the baby whom she later birthed in the residential school at age twelve as "him," even though the child was torn from her before she could discern his/her biological sex. These acts of psychological, emotional, spiritual, and physical trauma constitute embroiled elements of the same genocidal program, one that has sought not only to denigrate and torment Indigenous women but also to manufacture hatred toward Indigenous women in shamed and disempowered Indigenous men.[2]

In this chapter, I focus on the coerced alienation of Indigenous men from their own bodies by colonial technologies such as residential schooling. I argue that the gender segregation and the derogation of the feminine and the bodily that occurred systematically within residential schools in Canada were not merely by-products of Euro-Christian patriarchy; they were not just collateral damage from aggressive evangelization by decidedly patriarchal religious orders. Rather, this nexus of coercive alienations lay at the very core of the Canadian nation-building project by which the residential school system was motivated. The systemic manufacturing of Indigenous disavowals of the body served—and serves—the goal of colonial dispossession by troubling lived experiences of ecosystemic territoriality and effacing kinship relations that constitute lived forms of governance. For the purposes of this argument, ecosystemic territoriality refers to an abiding relationship of reciprocal knowing with(in) a specific constellation of geographic places; such relationships are enacted and affirmed through embodied practices and rendered meaningful through the embedding of personal experiences and stories within narratives of intergenerational inhabitation—they allow a being to *become what it is*.[3] Following Mark Rifkin, I understand the attack on "native social formations . . . conducted in the name of 'civilization'" as an "organized effort" to make Eurocentric notions of gender "compulsory as a key part of breaking up indigenous landholdings, 'detribalizing' native peoples, [and] translating native territoriality and governance into the terms of . . . liberalism and legal geography" (*When* 5–6). This process of translation serves to delegitimize Indigenous modes of territorial persistence and thereby to enable Indigenous deterritorialization—in the sense both of forcing Indigenous Peoples to "become what [they are] not" (Colebrook xxii)[4] and of removing Indigenous Peoples from particular land bases in order to make way for environmental exploitation, resource extraction, and non-Indigenous settlement. These are coerced *dis*integrations designed to dispossess and to disappear. I contend that each of these objectives was at play in residential school policy and practice in Canada—in a manner aligned with other coercive interventions in Indigenous lifeways throughout Turtle Island, from manipulations of Indigenous governance systems to Indian boarding school legislation to gendered interventions in familial lineage structures. In this chapter, I thus rehearse the preliminary steps of a crucial inquiry in the post-TRC era: if the coordinated assaults on Indigenous bodies and on Indigenous ecologies of gender are not just two among several interchangeable tools of colonial dispossession but in fact are integral to settler colonialism, then can embodied actions that self-consciously reintegrate gender complementarity be mobilized to pursue not simply "healing" but also the radical reterritorialization and sovereignty that will make meaningful decolonization possible?

I proceed in this chapter by theorizing the technologies at play in residential school obfuscation of what Rifkin calls "indigenous forms of sex, gender, kinship, . . . and eroticism" (*When* 5) through an analysis of selected literary depictions by residential school survivors that focus on gender segregation and the shaming of the body.[5] I then assess the political fallout of such impositions through a reading of Cree poet Louise Bernice Halfe's "Nitotem." I argue that Halfe's poem depicts the *dis*integration of a young Cree man's sense of embodied personhood through shame, a process in which his body becomes instrumentalized as a weapon capable of assaulting both women and the very principles of kinship that hold his community together. I conclude the chapter by considering the potential for what Kanaka Maoli scholar Ty P. Kāwika Tengan calls "embodied discursive action" (*Native Men* 17) by Indigenous men to reaffirm bonds of kinship and enact cross-gender solidarities that might encourage Indigenous reterritorialization. A model of such action is offered by the Residential School Walkers, a group of predominantly young Cree men who walked 2,200 kilometres from Cochrane, Ontario, to the Atlantic IRS TRC event in Halifax in support of residential school survivors. I examine a variety of Indigenous contexts—including Gwich'in, Mi'kmaq, Inuvialuit, Māori, and Maoli—to demonstrate the widespread and systematic nature of settler colonial technologies of disembodiment; yet, having begun with the testimony of a Cree residential school survivor, I hinge the chapter on the analysis of a poem by a Cree writer before culminating it in a discussion of the extraliterary, embodied actions of Cree men who, I argue, model what has been referred to as the "ideals of the *okihcitâwak* ('worthy men') from *kayâs* (long) ago" (McLeod, *Gabriel's Beach* 10).[6]

Before I continue, I wish to explain that I chose to begin with a paraphrase of this survivor's testimony aware of the fraught ethics of witnessing. I was one of perhaps twenty witnesses encircling the intimate survivors' sharing circle in Halifax when this testimony was delivered directly across from where I was sitting. I took no notes at the time, but when I returned to my hotel room later that evening I recorded recollections of the day: documentation, field notes, emotional debriefing. The testimony in question affected me a great deal—as it appeared visibly to affect others in the room— and I have thought about it many times since that day. It has also profoundly influenced my thinking about Indigenous masculinities as I have worked on this project. As such, I believe that it is necessary to acknowledge and honour that influence by engaging further with the words that this survivor chose to share that day. Although survivors are made aware that their statements will be audio and video recorded and that all testimonies gathered in Sharing Circles with the Survivor Committee are therefore "public," such sessions are not available for streaming on the IRS TRC website like the testimonies offered before the Commissioners' Sharing Panels. For this reason, I could not return to and transcribe the testimony in the survivor's own words. I approached the IRS TRC media liaison to ask whether a transcript of the testimony might be available and whether the IRS TRC has protocols through which researchers (or others) might contact specific survivors to seek permission to discuss their public testimonies in ways that those survivors would deem respectful. I was informed that there were no such protocols in place and that the testimony I sought was available in neither transcribed nor audiovisual format; if I wished to discuss this testimony, I therefore needed to use my own words to express my memory of the survivor's statement, thereby risking misrepresenting her experiences or, worse, manipulating her testimony to forward my own critical arguments in this book. As has been argued in relation to multiple international TRCs, the position of the academic onlooker can be characterized by voyeurism and consumption devoid of accountability—tensions amplified by my status as a settler. I am aware, therefore, that the safest position ethically is to avoid discussing this testimony altogether.

However, I have been reminded in my discussions with Indigenous colleagues and friends that silence is not an apolitical stance and that ethical witnessing of trauma involves working toward the ideological and political changes that will create conditions in which decolonization becomes possible. At the close of the IRS TRC Regional Event in Victoria in April 2012, Justice Murray Sinclair encouraged all of those present—Indigenous and non-Indigenous— to take their experiences of the event home to their families and communities and to share those memories in the service of change ("Closing Remarks"). Because I believe that the survivor testimony in question performs important work in the service of understanding colonial impositions on Indigenous ecologies of gender that will forward possibilities for decolonization, I include the paraphrase even as I know that doing so is ethically troublesome. As an unnamed survivor declares, "My story is a gift. If I give you a gift and you accept that gift, then you don't go and throw that gift in the waste basket. You do something with it" (Assembly of First Nations 161). This chapter is part of my effort to "do something" with this gift.

## BREAKING BONDS OF KINSHIP

"It could be *anytime* in the 1920s or 1930s," writes Gwich'in author Robert Arthur Alexie (9), announcing the representative nature of a young boy's arrival at residential school with his little sister in the 2002 novel *Porcupines and China Dolls*. The siblings are "herded into a building and separated: boys on one side, girls on the other. The young girl tries to go with her brother, but she's grabbed by a woman in a long black robe and pushed into another room. The last thing he hears is her cries followed by a slap, then silence" (10). "Sometime during his first month," Alexie continues, the young boy will "watch his sister speak the language and she will be hit, slapped or tweaked. He'll remember that moment for the rest of his life and will never forgive himself for not going to her rescue. It will haunt him" (12). The boy's feelings of powerlessness, guilt, and vicarious pain provide context for the dysfunctional gender dynamics in the novel's contemporary social terrain; they also resonate all too frequently with the testimonies of residential school survivors. Of the close to one hundred testimonies that I have witnessed either in person or on the IRS TRC's podcasts,[7] the vast majority reference the pain of separation from siblings, also mentioned in testimonies found in several collections, including *Resistance and Renewal* (1988), edited by Celia Haig-Brown; *Breaking the Silence* (1994), edited by the Assembly of First Nations; and *Finding My Talk* (2004), edited by Agnes Grant. Shubenacadie Indian Residential School survivor Isabelle Knockwood argues that traditionally, among the Mi'kmaq, "Older brothers and sisters were absolutely required to look after their younger siblings. When they went to the Residential School, being unable to protect their younger brothers and sisters became a source of life-long pain" (60). At the IRS TRC event in Halifax, Keptin of the Mi'kmaq Grand Council Antle Denny elaborated: "We all come from a nation where family is the most important thing. As an older brother you're taught to look after your younger brother and your sisters, and in these schools we could not even do that. When you look at the stories that I have heard, it makes me . . . quiver."

In *The Circle Game: Shadows and Substance in the Indian Residential School Experience in Canada*, Roland Chrisjohn and Sherri Young invoke Erving Goffman's term "permanent mortification" to theorize the lasting impact of the incapacity to protect loved ones from residential school violence. Chrisjohn and Young demonstrate how the pain of witnessing "a physical assault upon someone to whom [one] has ties" can engender enduring shame or "the *permanent mortification* of having (and being known to have) taken no action" (93). The terminology is apt insofar as the word *mortification* is defined as both "humiliation" and "the action" of "bringing under control . . . one's appetites and passions" through "bodily pain or discomfort" ("Mortification"); it also evokes a sense of benumbing. Public displays of violence and humiliation were used in residential schools not only to produce a docile and obedient student population but also, more insidiously, to discourage empathy and weaken reciprocal relations of kinship. The experience by which the young boy is "haunted" in Alexie's novel indeed begins as empathy—the vicarious torment of hearing his sister suffer. Yet shame becomes the cost of that empathy and ultimately works to condition its suppression. The initial pain at another's agony becomes contaminated by guilt and is thereby repositioned within the onlooker. Thus, the burden of the perceived experience endures a forced migration from the primary victim to the onlooking loved one actively discouraged from future empathetic impulses by the trauma of the experience. The pain becomes, in a way, an archive of perceived personal inadequacy that isolates and alienates, standing between—as opposed to uniting in their suffering—the siblings so tormented. Although the act of suffering together has the potential to strengthen interpersonal connections—as Anishinaabe writer Basil Johnston's celebration of the community forged among the boys at St. Peter Claver's Indian Residential School in *Indian School Days* attests—the institutional will was clearly to use such technologies to alienate the individual as completely as possible from social and familial ties and to recreate her or him as a discrete, autonomous (albeit racially inferior and undereducated) individual within the Canadian settler state.

Within the rigidly patriarchal ideological space of the residential school, the corrosion of kinship bonds through permanent mortification undoubtedly bears gender implications. Inuvialuk writer Anthony Apakark Thrasher's autobiographical discussion of residential school social engineering instructively documents how boys were taught to disrespect women and to view their own bodies as sinful:

> We were told not to play with the girls because it was a sin. I found this strange because I had played with girls before I came to school. At home I used to watch after my sisters Mona and Agnes. I even learned how to mix baby Agnes's milk. I loved them. But now I wasn't supposed to touch them and thinking about girls was supposed to be dirty. . . .
>
> One day Sister Tebear from the girls' side of the school accused George, Charlie, Adam and me of sinning with the girls in the basement. We were all out at the playground at the time. But Sister Tebear pointed me out with the three other boys and we were brought in before Sister Gilbert

and Father L'Holgouach. We were strapped to a bed and whipped with a three-foot watch chain made of silver. Sister did the whipping and Father okayed it. My back was bleeding, but something else burned more. Shame. It was branded in my mind. After this the silver chain never left me. Even to this day you can see the scar on my back. (23)

Thrasher depicts a series of assaults on his youthful understandings of gender, embodiment, and propriety. His role as a responsible brother is recast as sinful, and he is "protected" from the feminine by segregation. When he is actually able to engage in embodied acts of youthful play that are gender inclusive, such actions are disciplined in a manner that insists on the inherent sinfulness of the flesh and reinforces hierarchical binaries of male over female and spirit over body. These teachings, in effect, are etched onto Thrasher's skin in scar tissue. The body is marked by punishment as a physical reminder of the supposed filthiness of desire, a conception that denies the existence of sensuality that is not always already sexual. The shame that Thrasher evokes here is layered: he is shamed for the supposed sin of sexual desire, which Sister Gilbert seeks to beat out of his body, and for his weakness (both physically and in relation to the biopolitics of Aklavik Roman Catholic Residential School) as a young male unable to fend off the wrath of a female overseer. And as Sister Coté demonstrates dramatically, the boys are taught to perceive women as inconsequential, inferior, and grotesque: "She lined us boys up against the wall and showed us what she thought of girls—'Winnie, Wilma, Rosie, Mary, Jean, Margie, Lucy, Annabelle . . . this is what I think of them!' And she spat on the floor and stamped her foot on it. 'That's what I think of them!'" (23).[8]

Survivor accounts from the IRS TRC and elsewhere indicate that Sister Coté's pedagogy of gender is far from uncommon. Knockwood, for instance, recalls the nuns at Shubenacadie providing

their own version of sex education, which was that all bodily functions were dirty—dirty actions, dirty noises, dirty thoughts, dirty mouth, dirty, dirty, dirty girls. [Sister] took one girl who had just started her first period into the cloakroom and asked her if she did dirty actions. The little girl said, "I don't know what dirty actions are Sister. Do you mean playing in the mud?" [Sister] took the girl's hand and placed it between her legs and began moving it up and down and told her, "Now, you are doing dirty actions. Make sure you tell the priest when you go to confession." (52)

What makes Thrasher's depiction of the nuns' denigration of the feminine particularly troubling is its contextualization within a narrative that ultimately betrays some of the anti-female views thrust on Thrasher as a boy. For example, later in his memoir, he glosses a sexual encounter involving six Inuit men and two female prostitutes with the comment that "These nice-looking women had less morality than the most primitive people you could ever find" (74–75). "Entirely absent from Thrasher's recollection," as I argue elsewhere, "is any self-reflexivity about the 'morality' of the men implicated in this sexual act" (*Magic Weapons* 97). Rather, Thrasher falls back on chauvinistic teachings, like those of Sister Coté, that paint women as the source of all transgression. Whereas elsewhere he "laments the colonial conditions that have rendered Indigenous subsistence so difficult that many must rely on [criminalized] activity (like prostitution) to survive," here he supplies no such context and simply subjects the women "to the vexing and highly gendered moral codes he encountered in residential school, . . . even employing a specious evaluation of the women according to notions of primitivism (similar to those wielded in residential school denigration of Indigenous culture and history)" (97). My point is that, through the residential school's refusal to affirm familial bonds between siblings, its segregation of male students from female students, and its indoctrination of Indigenous youth with heteropatriarchal Christian dogma,[9] the Canadian government sought to alienate Indigenous men, such as Thrasher, from Indigenous nation-specific understandings of gender. In this way, the Canadian government worked to efface "traditions of residency and social formations that can be described as *kinship* [that] give shape to particular modes of governance and land tenure" (Rifkin, *When* 8). The violent inculcation of shame was a principal tool in this process of social engineering, and the conscription of some Indigenous men into settler colonial regimes of misogyny and the related violence against women and others have been two of its most damaging and protracted effects.[10]

## THE MANUFACTURE OF GENDERED VIOLENCE

Louise Bernice Halfe's inaugural poetry collection, *Bear Bones and Feathers* (1994), explores the legacies of colonial interventions in Cree ecologies of gender. A former student of Blue Quills Indian Residential School in St. Paul, Alberta, Halfe includes several poems that explicitly or implicitly locate residential schooling among these interventions, paying close attention throughout the collection to how the stigmatization of Indigenous bodies is implicated in the (re)production of intimate violence. The poem "Valentine Dialogue," for example, depicts a conversation between two women in which one struggles to fend off impulses toward self-blame after disclosing that she has contracted a sexually transmitted infection:

> Mudder says I'll never lift it down.
> Fadder says I'm nothing but a cheap dramp.
>
> Shame, shame
> Da pain in my heart hurts, hurts.
>
> My brown tits
> day shame me
> My brown spoon
> fails me. (ll. 18–25)

Halfe has worked for decades with other Indigenous women in Saskatoon to rebeautify the concept of the "'brown spoon,'"[11] a term used historically to denigrate Indigenous women's sexuality. With other members of the "Brown Spoon Club," Halfe has sought to honour "not only the power of spoon but the community of spoon where people are nurtured from it, where we give feast to the people, they lick it, they nurture themselves with it, and they give birth from it" ("Calm Sensuality" 50). The Brown Spoon Club has fought to recognize and celebrate Indigenous women as desiring embodied subjects rather than passive objects of male desire. "Valentine Dialogue" dramatizes the difficulty of this pursuit: even as the speaker describes men with a "Snake in dair mouth / snake in dair pants," she responds to the assertion that "Fadder . . . / always say mudder a slut" with the concession "Guess I must be one too" (ll. 15–16, 51–53). Although the poem depicts a relationship of reciprocal support between the two women speakers, it nonetheless betrays the consistent dehumanization with which they must contend, which conditions their beliefs about who they "must be" and, as Halfe demonstrates throughout the collection, informs their vulnerability to violence.

The poem "Stones," on the other hand, tracks anxiety and even panic among men about their feelings of physical inadequacy. Such feelings are externalized in the poem through games such as billiards and golf, through which men act out displeasure with the limitations of their sex organs by unleashing torrents of emotion on symbolic testicles. "Men day / hang dere balls / all over da place," the poem begins. "[W]hat I didn't no," the speaker continues,

> is day
> whack dem
> fundle dem
> squeeze dem
> dalk to dem
> whisper to dem
> scream at dem
> beg dem
> pray to dem
> g ah sh
> even
> swear at dem. (ll. 1–16)

This somewhat satirical portrait of Indigenous masculinity carries an ominous edge as the inability of men to "be satisfied"—even though "wit all dat whacking / day should of come / a long dime ago"—is shown to compel them toward sexual conquest:

dere still
jiggling dem
between dere legs
drying to find
different hole
to put dem in. (ll. 51, 48–50, 53–58)

The corrosion of self-image dramatized in "Stones," like that in "Valentine Dialogue," operates through the denigration of Indigenous bodies to compromise sensual intimacy and collaterally to endanger Indigenous individuals and communities. Several of Halfe's poems are populated by women characters whose corroded senses of self-worth beneath the weight of settler colonial oppression inform their vulnerability to the violence that often erupts out of men characters' feelings of hopelessness and inadequacy.

Halfe examines this dynamic closely in the poem "Nitotem," which offers a chilling portrait of a young boy abused at residential school who returns to his home reserve and rapes multiple women. The poem begins with Halfe's speaker observing the intensification of the boy's isolation through residential school violence. Sister Superior "squeezed and slapped" his ears until they "swelled, scabbed and scaled" and the boy could no longer "hear the sister shouting / and clapping her orders at him / or the rest of the little boys" (ll. 2, 4, 5–7). The assault on his ears—emphasized by the alliterative connection among the action, its perpetrator, and its effect—impedes both his sensory experience of the world and his social connection with the other boys. Deafened to his environment, the boy becomes imprisoned within his own body and unable to participate fully in the homosocial community of children, a separation stressed formally by the line break between "him" and "the rest of the little boys." His exile is then consummated at the poem's close when the boy-turned-young-man walks with "shoulder slightly stooped," never looking "directly at anyone. / When spoken to he mumble[s] into his chest. / His black hair cover[s] his eyes" (ll. 30–33).

The third and fourth stanzas provide the turn in the poem that locates a causal relationship between the shaming of the body, the derogation of the feminine, and sexual abuse in residential school,

on the one hand, and the eruption of misogynistic violence in Indigenous communities, on the other:

> He suffered in silence
> in the dark. A hand muffled his mouth
> while the other snaked his wiener. He had no
> other name, knew no other word. Soon it was no
> longer just the hand but the push, just a gentle
> push at first, pushing, pushing. Inside the
> blanket he sweated and felt the wings
> of pleasure, inside his chest the breath burst
> pain, pleasure, shame. Shame.
>
> ♦♦♦
>
> On the reserve he had already raped two
> women, the numbers didn't matter.
> Sister Superior was being punished. It was
> Father who said it was woman's fault
> and that he would go to hell. (ll. 16–29)

In one sense, the three symbols separating these stanzas represent
a temporal shift that emphasizes the intergenerational legacies of
residential school abuse as the sexual violence endured by the young
boy spills out into the community. Yet I argue that there is more to
it. The three symbols that Halfe uses to formally fracture the poem
hint at the three amputations that I am arguing were enacted at
residential schools to subdue empathy in the service of Indigenous
deterritorialization: first, the severing of mind from body (and the
derogation of the bodily); second, the severing of male from female
(and the derogation of the feminine);[12] and third, the severing of
the individual from communal and territorial roles and responsibilities (and the concomitant derogation of kinship and the land).

The separation of mind and body in "Nitotem" becomes legible
through psychoanalytic and trauma theories that view the suppression of bodily experience as a dissociative response to trauma.[13]
Unlike the suppression of bodily sensation as a means of escaping

cognitive recognition of acute violation, however, the fissure engendered between subjectivity and embodied experience in Halfe's
poem is not momentary but chronic. Driftpile Cree scholar and poet
Billy-Ray Belcourt "recruit[s] misery" to describe such experiences of
bodily containment and psychological assault "because [misery] does
not rest on the eventful" but "blends into ordinary time." Belcourt
argues, "Misery wears you down, effecting both a corporeal fragil-
ity and an intellectual fatigue that double as sociality's background
noise" ("Meditations" 3). The opening and closing lines of "Nitotem"
map the suppression of the boy's sensory experience, via assaults
by Sister Superior that compromise his hearing, while the weight
of shame draws his face to his chest, delimiting his capacity to see.
At the same time, his embodied subjectivity is further threatened
as private moments are transformed into public spectacles: "Here
everyone looked / and laughed at your private parts. / Soon they
too were no longer private" (ll. 13–15). With his "private parts . . . no
longer private," the boy is coaxed to perceive his body as distinct
from his personhood. Elsewhere, Belcourt identifies as "the sensation
of Indigeneity" a "sense of unbodiedness, of having been made to
be unbodied." "The fundamental violence of colonialism," Belcourt
argues, "is perhaps the inculcated sense . . . that your body is not
yours to keep, that it is never solely yours to maintain sovereign
control over" ("To Be Unbodied").

The stanzas from "Nitotem" quoted above depict the transfer-
ence of an experience of sensory "unbodiment" into the realm of
the sensual. The boy's conflicted experiences of "pain" and "pleasure"
provoke confusion within the dogmatic ideological space of the
residential school. Halfe's frantic language of "pushing, pushing"
and "sweat[ing]," which leads to "the wings of / pleasure," propels the
stanza into the experiential chaos of the "breath burst[ing] / pain,
pleasure, shame. Shame." The second "Shame" here comes down like
a verdict, carving the poem in two, both formally and temporally.
The last of three sets of alliterative pairs, this final term—repeated—
stands alone, its own sentence (in both grammatical and judicial
senses). "Shame" manifests as a tool of erasure cutting the boy off
from the pleasures of the body, enacting a symbolic amputation—or
one might even say a symbolic beheading or castration—that denies

integrated, embodied experience through the violent imposition of a form of Cartesian dualism. The mind is forced through trauma to treat the body as that which is other than self, creating conditions in which, as the poem's next stanza depicts, the body can become a weapon.

## DISEMBODIMENT AND HYPERMASCULINITY

The coerced disembodiment of Indigenous men is further complicated by the semiotic treatment of Indigenous males in popular culture primarily as bodies, as discussed in the previous chapter. As Brendan Hokowhitu argues in the context of Māori masculinities, the synecdochic stand-in of Indigenous male body for Indigenous male-embodied agentive subject demonstrates "the link between enlightenment rationalism and colonization, where the enlightened reason of European man, in a Cartesian sense, was allegorically opposed to the physicality of the unenlightened, the savage. The process of colonization did not mean [that Indigenous men] were to reach the echelons of enlightened reason, however: rather what was imperative to the colony was the domestication of their physicality, the suppression of their passions, the nobilization of their inherent violence" ("Māori Rugby" 2322).

Settler colonialism has borne many of the same tenets in North America, collapsing Indigenous men with physicality while technologies of social engineering such as residential schools have sought to limit embodied experience and replace it with fear of and revulsion for the body. Hence the absolute panic revealed in maniacal punishments of bedwetting, erections, and vomiting documented in the historical literature on residential schooling.[14] Because "hypermasculinity has been one of the foremost attributes of the Indian world that whites have imagined" (Klopotek 251), and the "manhood of the Indian" in popular cultural representations has remained tethered to "ruthless violence" (Cromley 269), Daniel Heath Justice demonstrates that Indigenous male bodies have come to be viewed as "capable of and a source only of violence and harm. When that's the only model you have, what a desolation, right? When your body, the only way your maleness is or should be rendered is

74

through violence, through harm, through corrupted power. Oh, it's just tragic" ("Fighting" 144). Justice calls such "models of hypermasculine maleness . . . a catastrophic failure of imagination, as well as a huge ethical breach" (145).

I argue that the ideological fallout of settler colonial imaginings of Indigenous masculinity undergirds a paradox within supposedly assimilative social engineering in Canada: on the one hand, the inherent physicality and violence of those racialized and gendered as Indigenous males have been continually reinscribed through the media, literature, film, and art (as argued in Chapter 1); on the other, violence and shame have been wielded systematically through residential schooling, the *Indian Act*, and the legal system to discourage sensual, embodied experience. I contend that some of the legacies of trauma coming to light in the testimonies of residential school survivors during the IRS TRC can be understood, at least partially, as a consequence of treating those racialized and gendered as Indigenous males *only* as bodies (without "the advanced intellectual and moral capacity to master their masculine passions" [Bederman 85]), then systematically manufacturing disavowals of the body through shame. Among the effects of such pernicious pedagogies is the recasting of Indigenous male bodies as distinct from subjectivity and selfhood, as tools to be used and discarded. And this coerced *dis*integration—this state of "unbodiment" at the collision point among Cartesian dualism, imposed racial inferiority, and corporeal disgust—works to sustain violence through the instrumentalization of bodies thus alienated.

Indeed, the fracturing of mind and body, as depicted in "Nitotem," is not strictly a consequence of individual experiences of abuse (though these experiences are undoubtedly at play), nor is it merely a product of Christian reverence for the soul over the body. Rather, it is a key weapon within the dispossessive arsenal of settler colonial policy, designed to deterritorialize Indigenous nations and corrode Indigenous sovereignties by compromising embodied connections to place and to kin. In residential school pedagogies of gender, shame was activated through the derogation of the body, coercing children's humiliation with their physical selves in order to produce docile subjects. At the same time, this shaming of the body constituted a primary tactic for removing physical beings from ecosystemic relations with their environments. As the sensory capacity of the body was assaulted—as evident by the "scabbed" and "scal[ing]" ears of the title character in "Nitotem"—the potential for ongoing experiential connection to place was suppressed. Thus, it was not just the physical removal of the child from ancestral territories and communal connections that forwarded the Canadian colonial agenda but also the targeted attacks on the child's frameworks for interacting with the other-than-human. Just as the body became instrumentalized as a tool of the alienated agentive subject (body ≠ self), so too the land became coercively alienated as an exploitable resource. Rather than upholding an ethos of reciprocity in which "the tribal web of kinship rights and responsibilities . . . link[s] the People, the land, and the cosmos together in an ongoing and dynamic system of mutually affecting relationships" (Justice, "'Go Away'" 151), residential school technologies of social engineering were mobilized to isolate the individual student as discrete, disembodied, and deterritorialized. If one is a disembodied soul, then one can be anywhere; however, if one is an embodied individual indigenous to a specific territory and tribal nation, then one inhabits a series of relationships to place along with the roles and responsibilities of ecosystemic persistence. To be clear, I contend that the bodies of Indigenous youth have been deliberately targeted for violence and humiliation within residential schools (and beyond) for the purpose of suppressing embodied experiences of land and of kinship. And the denial of these embodied experiences was calculated to extinguish Indigenous modes of social formation, nationhood, and territoriality. To dispossess Indigenous youth of their capacity for integrated, embodied experience has been to dispossess Indigenous nations of land and sovereignty. Leanne Betasamosake Simpson encourages Indigenous people to understand such interventions as *expansive dispossession*—"as a gendered removal of our bodies and minds from our nation and place-based grounded normativities" (*As We* 43–44)—and to recognize, therefore, the "responsibility" to generate "Indigenous freedom" by "creating generations that are in love with, attached to, and committed to their land" (25).

Both fictional and (auto)biographical depictions of residential school testify to the debilitating effects of alienation from lands and land-based practices. Métis writer Maria Campbell's character Jacob is described as "jus plain pitiful" after his release from residential school because "[h]e can['t] talk his own language" and "he don know how to live in da bush" ("Jacob" ll. 108–10). Thrasher explains in his memoir that "Every time I'd go home from school I saw older boys who . . . couldn't survive. . . . [I]n winter teenaged boys who should be able to trap and hunt had to rely on their parents. . . . Some also forgot how to speak Inuvialuktun" (84). In *Indian School Days*, Johnston portrays the year of his release from residential school as being characterized by the struggle for survival, recounting several abortive attempts to generate means of subsistence, from hunting raccoons to selling chopped wood to skinning squirrels. In each case, his lack of territorial knowledge and his disconnection from the community ensure failure until he ultimately determines that it would simply "be better to go back to school" (178). In this way, his narrative tracks the perverse effectiveness of residential school technologies of deterritorialization.[15] It is perhaps with similar struggles in mind that Campbell's speaker exclaims, "No matter how many stories we tell / we'll never be able to tell / what dem schools dey done to dah peoples / an dere relations" ("Jacob" ll. 103–06).

The title of Halfe's poem "Nitotem" is translated in *Bear Bones and Feathers* as "my relative, could be anyone" (128). What is interesting about this translation is that terminology pertaining to Cree-specific systems of kinship that extend beyond biological lineage—or *wâhkôtowin*—actually devolves through the conditions depicted in the poem into a marker of anonymity. Scholar of Indigenous education Linda Goulet notes that the word *nitotem* carries with it connotations of intimacy; it suggests "those to whom I am open." Whereas the identifier "my relative" (or "my intimate relation") should affirm interpersonal connections and clarify the individual's roles and responsibilities within the kinship structure, here the term fails completely to identify the poem's title character: he "could be anyone." The systematic assault on Indigenous ecologies of gender and Indigenous kinship structures enacted through the separation of boys and girls, the shaming of the body, and the

corrosion of empathy creates conditions in which the cyclical violence depicted in Halfe's poem proliferates. The number of women
raped "didn't matter" because the unbodied, alienated, and wounded
title character has been actively prevented from recognizing their
humanity—he fails to recognize them as kin. Having been robbed
of the capacity for integrated spiritual, physical, emotional, and
mental experiences, he no longer perceives himself as a participa-
tory element of the world that he inhabits; his empathy is destroyed.
In this way, the violent suppression of embodied experience, along
with the manufacture of gender animosity, can fracture and *disin-
tegrate* not only the individual victim of residential school violence
but also the community, the nation, and the expansive web of kinship relations—largely through shame. In Simpson's words, these
processes "work to destroy the fabric of Indigenous nationhoods
by attempting to destroy our relationality by making it difficult to
form sustainable, strong relationships with each other" (*As We* 93).
These are the legacies of over a century of residential schooling in
Canada that imperil aspirations toward meaningful "reconciliation"
between Indigenous and settler populations on Turtle Island and
cast a dark shadow over the discussions of Indigenous masculinity
in which this book is invested.

## EMBODIED DISCURSIVE ACTION AND RADICAL RETERRITORIALIZATION

In his presentation at the Fall Convocation of the University of
Winnipeg in 2011, Chair of the IRS TRC Justice Murray Sinclair
indicated that, for survivors of residential schooling, "the greatest
damage from the schools is not the damaged relationship with
non-Aboriginal people or Canadian society, or the government or
the churches, but the damage done . . . to the relationships within
their families." Sinclair argued, therefore, that "Reconciliation *within*
the families of survivors is the cornerstone for all other discussions
about reconciliation" ("Presentation").

In the final section of this chapter, I turn to the 2,200-kilometre
trek undertaken by a group of predominantly young Cree men
from Cochrane, Ontario, to Halifax in support of residential school

survivors in order, first, to consider the possibility for mindful, embodied actions to intervene in the "*expansive dispossession*" described in the chapter's preceding sections and, second, to consider the role of such actions as groundwork upon which reconciliation within families and perhaps even Indigenous resurgence can be pursued. I take this direction to guard against presumptions about the perverse "success" of the settler colonial regimes of social engineering that I have been analyzing, which risk obfuscating ongoing Indigenous agency. Indigenous literary art is the central focus of this volume because of its ability to map the affective experiences of both settler colonial violence and Indigenous persistence without ever conceding creative agency or denying the "much larger memory that stretches all the way back" (Driskill, *Asegi* 138). Literary expression cannot be written off simply as evidence of victimry, as I argue in my book *Magic Weapons: Aboriginal Writers Remaking Community after Residential School*, but illuminates the ongoing expressive agency of writers. The Residential School Walkers embody similar forms of creative agency in the extraliterary world through their actions and their words through what Ty P. Kāwika Tengan calls "embodied discursive action." I ultimately contend that the Residential School Walkers perform three mutually formative reterritorializing acts that serve the vision that Sinclair described. The first involves honouring the body as integral to and indivisible from the agentive self. The second involves affirming responsibilities to and roles within the family—with "family" construed in accordance with Cree principles of *wâhkôtowin* that extend beyond the limits of nuclear family biology. And the third involves (re)connecting with the land as an active principle of kinship and Indigenous resurgence.

Patrick Etherington Jr., then a twenty-eight-year-old man from the Moose Cree First Nation, explained to reporters during the walk that, when the generation preceding his "went to residential school, they became hard; they didn't know how to love, and they passed this on to us" (qtd. in "Walkers"). He added, on a personal note, "My dad and me, for a while there, the love was always there but sometimes he's never showed it" (qtd. in Narine, "Creating Awareness"). In an online testimonial posted on YouTube, Etherington elaborated:

When they went to residential school, the survivors had to become tough almost. And they had to become like robots . . . in order to survive. . . . And then when they left the residential schools . . . a lot of them didn't deal with it. . . . So by them not dealing with it, they actually passed it down on to us, the younger generation.

And I see it in our communities all the time. . . . We're still like robots almost. We don't know how to feel. We don't know how to express ourselves. I see that all the time on my reserve. It's starting to show its ugly face now too, in my home community of Moose Factory, through suicides. . . .

So that is the main reason I'm walking: the issue of suicide. We have to try and break this cycle. We got to learn to feel again. Got to learn how to love. Because those survivors were deprived of it. They were deprived of love when they were at those schools. (qtd. in CSSSPNQL 2:54–5:31)

By identifying the marathon walk as a strategy for addressing the emotional and sensory legacies of residential school experiences, Etherington Jr. affirmed the capacity of embodied actions to self-consciously reintegrate minds and bodies and to foster emotional literacy—with "learn[ing] to feel again" maintaining both sensory and affective valences.

In his welcoming address at the IRS TRC national event in Montreal in April 2013, Kanien'keha:ka Elder John Cree used the metaphor of a journey to express the need for emotional and physical (re)integration. He stated that the longest distance that a man will ever travel is the distance needed to bring together his head and his heart. Cree's words resonate with the Residential School Walkers' journey, both literal and symbolic, involving the physical movement of wilful bodies over territory while affirming struggles within agentive subjects toward integrated personhood that honours embodied persistence and feeling.

Their movement on the land can therefore be usefully understood as what Tengan calls an "embodied discursive practice" in which "men come to perform and know themselves and their bodies in a new way" (*Native Men* 151). For Tengan, "bodily experience, action, and movement [play] a fundamental role in the creation of new subjectivities of culture and gender" (87). The young men of the Residential School Walkers used the "bodily experience" of consensual (as opposed to forced) "movement" over territory to better "know themselves and their bodies"; in this way, they contested the fiction of Cartesian dualism and resisted the colonial pressures of both coerced unbodiment and forced relocation. By walking and speaking publicly, these individuals strove to enact, embody, and model non-dominative yet empowered subjectivities as Cree men, subjectivities that honour the capacity to "feel" and to "love" while exhibiting physical strength, stamina, and masculine solidarity.

By sharing the walk with his father, Patrick Etherington Sr., and his father's wife, Frances Whiskeychan, Etherington Jr. engaged in locatable actions designed to reclaim the intimacy and familial connection that residential school policy was designed to suppress. However, the vision of family that the walkers travelled to "reconcile" exceeds the biologically determinate (and patriarchal) conceptions of family imposed on Indigenous nations by the *Indian Act*.[16] At the Atlantic IRS TRC national event, the Etheringtons and Whiskeychan spoke of Robert Hunter, James Kioke, and Samuel Koosees Jr.—the other young men from their community who participated in the journey—using familial pronouns as sons and brothers, thereby evoking Cree ethics of kinship. Etherington Jr. traced the intergenerational contours of such ethics, proclaiming that "I'm doing it for the survivors—but more for the youth. There is a big problem with suicide in my community. The youth are lost." Reaching out to the generations preceding and following his own, he articulated a community-oriented sense of commitment, of responsibility. He added in Halifax that "I walked for my buddies who did it and for those that have attempted it" (qtd. in Sison). Constructing their embodied actions in a narrative of communal purpose, the Residential School Walkers exercised responsibilities embedded in Cree ethics of kinship to enable Cree (and Indigenous) continuance. In this way, this group of young Cree men, whose interpersonal connections were nourished along stretches of open road between Cochrane and Halifax, served the needs of their community in ways that resonated with the Cree role of *okihcitâwak*. According to Okihcitâwak Street

Patrol founder Colin Naytowhow, the *okihcitâwak* "were considered the warriors of the camp, monitoring the women and children, making sure the elders were taken care of, made sure the camp was kept safe." "That's the teaching we want to bring back," Naytowhow continues. "To let people know we are here to help" (qtd. in Smoke). Such connections to Indigenous warriorhood were certainly not lost on the walkers themselves, photographed throughout their journey in T-shirts displaying the word *Warrior* in bold letters, depicting images of nineteenth-century Indigenous warriors, or bearing the Kanien'keha:ka warrior flag.

The community of worthy young men strengthened on the journey appears to embody principles of kinship and thereby to serve Indigenous modes of territoriality in which such kinship is embedded. To affirm Cree kinship is to affirm Cree relations that extend to the other-than-human and therefore to the land. That is why the particular form taken by the Residential School Walkers' public action is so significant. The 2,200-kilometre journey is not merely symbolic. It is a testament to embodied relations with territory; it is an assertion of ongoing Indigenous presence, an expression of resilience, and an affirmation of belonging. In short, this journey constitutes an act of radical reterritorialization that honours and reclaims the land through embodied discursive actions that simultaneously honour and reclaim Indigenous bodies—it is an act of *re*integration that affirms individual and community integrity. And, of course, both land and body are essential elements of personhood from which residential schooling was designed to alienate Indigenous youth.

Ironically, the opportunities created at IRS TRC events for the walkers to discuss the experiences of their journey were often characterized by a peculiar stillness that masked the physicality of their feat. For example, in Halifax, an ad hoc session was organized to honour the walkers at the close of the survivors' sharing circle in which the testimony that begins this chapter was offered. In a windowless testimonial space, each of the walkers was encouraged to translate his or her experiences of the monumental trek into words. Although the testimonies proved to be eloquent and powerful, the disjuncture between the physicality and motion of their content and the stillness of their form was somewhat unsettling.[17]

As a useful supplement to these testimonies, Samuel Koosees Jr. has since posted on the internet a video featuring photographs from the journey that emphasizes the dynamic connections among the walkers, the beautiful territories through which they travelled, and the emotions engendered through their embodied discursive actions.[18] Of particular interest here are photographs in which the men lampoon the touristic monuments of colonially imposed provincial borders. In one case, the four men are shown in subsequent images leaping toward and then hanging from the "Welcome to New Brunswick" sign (5:07–5:16). In another, tricks of perspective are employed to portray Etherington Jr. crouched and apparently holding the miniature bodies of Samuel Koosees Jr. and James Kioke in either hand in front of the "Welcome to Nova Scotia" sign (6:17–6:28). Each of these photos is preceded immediately by images that evoke masculine strength. In the first case, the four young men are shown in consecutive photos walking together in solidarity and purpose, with the leading walker holding a ceremonial staff. Note in Image 6 that visible in the reflection of the leading walker's glasses (symbolizing vision) are, on his left, the ceremonial staff and, on his right, the camera; walking collectively forward, the men are simultaneously reflecting on what has come before. Juxtaposing images that evoke spectres of Indigenous warriorhood with images that humorously exploit perspectival shifts to trouble the solidity of settler colonial borders (Images 7–9), the video engages in a creative remapping that honours the strength, humour, and agency of the Residential School Walkers along their reterritorializing trek.

At the Atlantic IRS TRC event, Etherington Jr. described long stretches of silence as the group travelled the edge of the highway. As they walked and walked, he noted, his companions' heads were bowed to the earth. Only on reflection did he realize that he too had his head down, much like the figure in Halfe's poem "Nitotem" who "walk[s], shoulders slightly stooped / and never look[s] directly at anyone" (*Bear Bones* ll. 30–31). "What are we doing?" Etherington Jr. recalled asking himself before commanding his gaze upward to

**Image 5:** Residential School Walker with Ceremonial Staff. *Source: Frances Rose Whiskeychan and Patrick Etherington Sr.*

**Image 6:** Three Residential School Walkers: (left to right) Patrick Etherington Jr., Robert Hunter, and Samuel Koosees Jr. *Source: Frances Rose Whiskeychan and Patrick Etherington Sr.*

**Image 7:** Residential School Walkers at the New Brunswick Border. *Source: Frances Rose Whiskeychan and Patrick Etherington Sr.*

**Image 8:** Target Practice. *Source: Frances Rose Whiskeychan and Patrick Etherington Sr.*

**Image 9:** Perspectival Play at the Nova Scotia Border. *Source: Frances Rose Whiskeychan and Patrick Etherington Sr.*

survey the world around him. "And it was beautiful," he concluded on the panel. His words, it seems to me, offer a visual image that resonates with survivors' testimonies that document the debilitating imposition of shame as well as the struggle to regain senses of self-worth. Walking in solidarity with his kin and raising his eyes to honour the landscape, Etherington Jr. rehearsed an embodied cultural pride that settler colonial policies attempted to deny him. The action itself was a physical expression of selfhood and cultural integrity, and its public avowal at the IRS TRC event heightened its resistant force while extending its pedagogical reach. The model of non-dominative Cree masculinity enacted and articulated by Etherington Jr. and his companions offers both "survivors" and "youth" a prototype for the reformation of what Tengan calls "masculinities defined through violence" (*Native Men* 151), in a manner that refuses to disavow masculine strength, physicality, and agency. To borrow the words of Daniel Heath Justice, "That's a warrior's act, as well, to know what's needed to be done and to do it boldly and without need of response. To fight against shame through love" ("Fighting" 145).

Etherington Jr. saved his final comments in the sharing circle at the Halifax event for residential school survivors—those targeted most directly by the colonial technologies of *dis*integration, *disem*-bodiment, and *de*territorialization. "This is what I've done for you," he said. "This is what I've *chosen* to do for you." With the insertion of the word *chosen*, he affirmed ongoing individual agency even as he declared himself accountable to others in an expression of kinship responsibilities. This choice, this willed performance of embodied discursive action, attests to the ultimate failure of residential school social engineering. Like the words of the anonymous survivor whose testimony began this chapter, Etherington Jr.'s words and actions are a gift to be honoured. Etherington Jr. refuses the identity of inevitable victim: he will not self-define as a second-generation product of residential school violence, of the denigration of the body, and of the obfuscation of gender complementarity; rather, he instantiates himself as one voice among many that would call the elements of peoplehood back into balance.

# 3. JOURNEYING BACK TO THE BODY

his mouth brushing mine
is a flat stone
skipping the lake's surface
and oh his tongue
a spawning fish jumps
over and over the waterfall
is maskwa pawing
all his winter hunger
so I yield up roots and berries
and lie back
my whole abundant self

—GREGORY SCOFIELD, from "Ôchim ♦ His Kiss"
(*Love Medicine and One Song* 10)

It is not without fear
and memories awash in blood
that I allow you to slip between
my borders
rest in the warm valleys
of my sovereign body

—QWO-LI DRISKILL, from "Map of the Americas"
(*Walking with Ghosts* 11)

n an interview in *Masculindians*, Cree-Métis poet Gregory Scofield observed that "people have oftentimes taken the spirit out of sex and sexuality. And if they haven't entirely taken the spirit out of sex and sexuality, they've long since stopped looking to the ceremonies that accompany those things" ("Liberation" 220). Given the tactical assault on Indigenous bodies and desires executed through colonial technologies such as residential schooling, anxieties about sex as ceremony are unsurprising. Indigenous bodies have been racialized and gendered sexually aberrant for centuries within settler North American imaginations, at the same time that such bodies have been targeted for shame, humiliation, and violence by colonial regimes of discipline, as discussed in Chapter 2. As Oneida gender sovereignty activist Jessica Danforth asks, "What better way to colonize a people than to make them ashamed of their bodies?" (122). Because of the shame and sexual violence to which Indigenous individuals are routinely subjected in settler colonial contexts, sex and sexuality remain dangerous and potentially volatile subjects.[1] Yet, as Cherokee Nation scholar Daniel Heath Justice argues, "To ignore sex and embodied pleasure in the cause of Indigenous liberation is to ignore one of our greatest resources. It is to deny us one of our most precious gifts" ("Fear" 106).

During a roundtable discussion on Indigenous masculinities in February 2013, I quoted Scofield's comments about sex as ceremony and asked Scofield how spirituality might be braided together with physical intimacy, sensuality, and sexuality to serve the aims of Indigenous empowerment and gender complementarity. "The pathway back," he argued, "is for men to know their own bodies, to know the vulnerability that lives within their bodies, and to honour that vulnerability" (McKegney et al., "Strong Men Stories" 261). In this chapter, I focus on vulnerability and male embodiment to explore potential pathways toward decolonial ecologies of gender.[2] I conceive of vulnerability here in two senses. The first sense pertains to the risks associated with physical intimacy in the shadow of colonial technologies of dispossession characterized by body-shaming practices designed to induce Indigenous deterritorialization—risks laid bare in the previous chapter and the epigraph above from Qwo-Li Driskill's aptly titled "Map of the Americas."[3] So what is at stake in opening up one's body to intimacy and sensual pleasure in a context shadowed by racialized and gendered shaming and by settler colonial sexual violence? The second sense involves the dangers associated with focalizing analysis through the lens of Indigenous masculinity and identifying "the male body" as the locus of investigation, each of which risks trading in biological essentialisms and gender binaries anathema to many Indigenous gender systems. So what is at stake in naming and affirming "masculinity" and "maleness" in a context conditioned by ongoing settler colonialism and heteropatriarchy? I ultimately ask in this chapter and this project: Can cis-gendered Indigenous male bodies be celebrated as sacred in ways that do not risk furthering the dispossession of Indigenous women, girls, two-spirit, and trans people?[4]

In what follows, I argue

1. that, despite the aforementioned risks, Indigenous masculinities remain valuable to decolonial enterprises, provided that such masculinities are liberated from the impoverished inheritance of settler colonial regimes of gender and that their theorization remains alert to the generative wisdom of Indigenous feminist and Indigenous queer and two-spirit thought; and

2. that the bodies of *all* Indigenous people can serve the cause of Indigenous resurgence, even of those who self-identify as male and/or masculine, provided that such embodied identities do not foreclose on the expressive self-identification of others and that, in the words of Anishinaabe scholar Randy Jackson, they do not "tak[e] up more space in a way that crushes people out."

To pursue these arguments, I turn first to the creative art, scholarship, and activism of Michi Saagiig Nishnaabeg writer Leanne Betasamosake Simpson, which betrays heightened awareness of the dangers that attend Indigenous women, girls, and queer and two-spirit people because of the catastrophic impact of "colonial masculinities"[5] yet courageously continues to champion (con)sensual intimacy and "decolonial love" as embodied resurgent acts through which Indigenous futures are nurtured.[6] In other words, Simpson's response to the violent impositions of settler colonial gender systems is a "generative refusal" (*As We* 9)[7] to acquiesce to her own (and her characters') attempted disembodiment and deterritorialization and the affirmation of Indigenous bodies in relationship with each other and the land—including bodies identified as male. Simpson claims space for embodied intimacy in ways that exceed settler colonial regimes of gender and thereby awaken possibilities for Indigenous masculinities emergent from Indigenous worldviews and experiences. I then turn to the erotic poetry of Cree-Métis writer Gregory Scofield, which awakens readers to the importance of naming and affirming male bodies (especially Indigenous male bodies), thereby illuminating embodied theories of Indigenous masculinity. I argue that Scofield conscripts sensual avowals of embodied persistence in the assertion of territorial rights and responsibilities, and he does so through a creative vernacular that celebrates erotic agency while refusing to participate in the pathologization of Indigenous men.

In these ways, I argue in this chapter that consensual vulnerability, as a modality of masculine expression[8] illuminated by Simpson's and Scofield's work, can act as a medicine that resists the determinism, dogma, and hegemony of settler regimes of gender while avowing the embodied persistence of all Indigenous people. Such vulnerability, I argue, both relies on and enacts an ecological model of gender, characterized by "dynamic mutuality" (Rifkin, "Erotics" 177)[9] liberated from the tenor of anxious scarcity within the competitive ecology of gender inherited from settler colonialism. Such liberation enables the imagining, embodying, and enacting of diverse, non-dominative modalities of being that might be legible as Indigenous *masculinities*—not as colonial masculinities performed by Indigenous people but as expressions of gendered being emergent from Indigenous thought and action. My point is that the cost of accepting "masculinity" as beholden only to the corrosive cluster of qualities with which it has been associated by virtue of settler colonial history—of viewing "masculinity" as so saturated by destructive meanings (and so complicit in genocide) as to be irredeemable—is significant, and it risks divesting Indigenous communities of valuable weaponry that might be employed in the struggle for decolonial futures. Indigenous literary art not only illuminates the terrain of struggle but indeed affirms and envisions the weapons themselves.

## LEANNE BETASAMOSAKE SIMPSON AND THE
## RESILIENT UTILITY OF MASCULINITY

In his contribution to *Indigenous Men and Masculinities: Legacies, Identities, Regeneration*, Ngāti Pūkenga scholar Brendan Hokowhitu argues that "Indigenous masculinities . . . can and should be treated as a largely untapped rubric for examining the propagation of power in the colonial context" ("Taxonomies" 83). This rubric has remained "largely untapped" because of anxieties about the utility of "masculinity" as a category, given the centrality of heteropatriarchy and male supremacy in the colonization of the Americas, and because of resulting skepticism about the liberatory potential of modes of inquiry that would claim "masculinity" as their object of study. These concerns are expressed cogently in two tweets by Dene political theorist Glen Coulthard, who stated on December 3, 2015, that "I was more convinced when 'masculinity' was a problem not a solution in our indigenous studies analyses" and argued on January 27, 2016, that "critical indigenous masculinities should vacate not occupy space that indigenous feminist, queer and trans voices should occupy." Coulthard is not alone in perceiving masculinity as a "problem." Kim Anderson, Jonathan Swift, and Robert Innes note that many participants in their study of Indigenous masculinities "struggled with the concept of 'masculinity,' equating it typically with hegemonic, patriarchal, or hypermasculine identities that they were . . . trying to escape" (287); as such, the authors note that several Indigenous participants identified "'masculinity' as a behavior to recover from" (289).

In "Can the Other of Native Studies Speak?" Driftpile Cree scholar Billy-Ray Belcourt provides a critique of Indigenous masculinities studies that usefully illuminates the tenor of such concerns. Although his work champions "Indigenous Feminism" as "a world-building project" that asks "us to think about how to think about living differently," Belcourt remains critical of the "cruel nostalgia" and "putative givenness of qualifiers like 'masculine.'"[10] The phrase "putative givenness" is significant since it registers how accreted "common sense" notions of the "masculine" can displace, override, and police alternative gendered imaginings and thereby sustain colonial power structures rather than work toward their eradication. Recognizing the adverse implications of the reification of violent and dominative masculinities, Belcourt seeks—in a manner that echoes the work of Morgensen—"to build a critique that cuts to [colonial masculinity's] roots and envisions its end" (Morgensen 55). Because "masculinity" is ultimately considered irredeemable, decolonization, in Belcourt's argument, requires its transcendence rather than its reinvestment with new meaning and subsequent mobilization within decolonial struggles.[11] Although registering misgivings similar to those of Belcourt, Daniel Heath Justice questions whether colonialism's coercive delimitation of masculinities to solely the terrain of violence might constitute "a catastrophic failure of imagination, as well as a huge ethical breach." "When . . . the only way your maleness is or should be rendered is through violence, through harm, through corrupted power," he notes, "[o]h, it's just tragic." Thus, though registering along with Belcourt that such putative masculinities serve the embroiled causes of settler colonial violence and Indigenous dispossession, Justice posits that "literature ought to give us alternatives" ("Fighting" 144–45).[12]

In light of Justice's call for alternatives, I argue in this chapter that, though colonialism has adversely affected understandings of gender throughout Turtle Island, settler heteropatriarchy does not *own* Indigenous masculinities. In fact, the latter continue to be envisioned, enacted, embodied, and experienced in ways that exceed the binary logic of gender models inherited from colonial power and in ways that affirm, support, and are guided by Indigenous feminist and queer and two-spirit voices. So the problem is not solely with "masculinity" but also with the coercive delimitation of what gender and power can mean in contexts shadowed by settler colonialism; thus, I worry that the active turning away from Indigenous masculinities as a potentially decolonizing rubric—though entirely rational—risks reaffirming negative stereotypes of masculinity as its de facto meaning while deauthorizing and obfuscating behaviours that might yet be legible as "masculine" but exceed the impoverished iconography of what Morgensen identifies as "colonial masculinity." After all, settler colonialism is insidiously effective insofar as it limits the tools available to envision and enact its demise. Undergirding my position here, of course, is what Hokowhitu calls "the now conventional theoretical position within gender studies that gender is constructed" ("Taxonomies" 81). I tend to think of "masculinity" as a conceptual tool for describing qualities, actions, characteristics, and behaviours that accrue meaning within a given historical context and social milieu through their association with maleness. Although informed by relations of power, such associations are neither inevitable nor fixed. Thus, masculinity is neither biologically determinate nor stable over time. If we recognize masculinity as unfixed and malleable, then our enthusiasm to critique—and eradicate—those elements of masculinity that have been damaging to Indigenous nations and the land should be matched by our enthusiasm to identify, generate, and reclaim alternative understandings of masculinity that will nourish Indigenous Peoples, protect the land, and render ever more viable a decolonial future.[13]

I read Simpson's *Islands of Decolonial Love* as a sustained rumination on the consequences of settler colonial interventions in Indigenous gender systems and the difficult necessity of breathing new life into alternative understandings of gender.[14] In the three-page story "indinawemaaganidog/all of my relatives," Simpson makes three mutually implicated moves that I consider of value to Indigenous masculinities studies when operationalized together: the story *critiques* models of masculinity inherited through settler colonialism; it *reclaims* alternative gendered understandings from Indigenous worldviews; and it *imagines* and *enacts* new ways of expressing and inhabiting Indigenous masculinities characterized by consensual vulnerability and the refusal of anthropocentrism. Although attentiveness to creativity has been overshadowed at times in Indigenous masculinities studies by the urgent tasks of critiquing settler heteropatriarchy and reclaiming Indigenous knowledges about gender, Simpson's work demonstrates that creative artistry is imperative to the pursuit of decolonial futures.

Simpson's story begins thus: "i am standing on the wharf in cap saint louis just wondering, when a guy i've never met shows up." The introduction of the male stranger immediately signals the narrator's awareness of the spectre of violence against Indigenous women by which the story will be haunted. Admittedly a "guarded" person who "makes it a policy not to talk to people unless absolutely necessary," the narrator confesses being "suspicious" when the unknown fisherman named etienne offers to take her out on the Atlantic free of charge. "nothing in life is free," she rehearses in her head. "there is no such thing as a free lunch" (*Islands* 11). Through the use of interior monologue, Simpson exposes how the interactions between the story's two central characters are mediated by the gender dynamics of settler colonialism. It is therefore no surprise that, when "he offers his hand so [she] can step down onto the deck of the boat," the narrator "refuse[s] . . . because we need to get a few things straight right from the beginning and this is one of them." Yet, despite efforts to destabilize what appears to be an instantiation of a chivalric code in which the literal *captain* of the boat's purported generosity in transporting said *damsel* might well come with expectations of libidinal repayment, her mind remains alert to her vulnerability to violence. As they "drive away from shore," she thinks about "dexter and all the scenarios."[15] With characteristic dark humour, Simpson registers the real dangers that persist for her narrator in a world conditioned by colonial masculinities[16]: "we drive past a kayaker and kumbaya plays in my head and i stand up and wave like a happy person so he'll remember me when the cops question him later" (12).

However, despite the narrative's hyperconsciousness of the potential for victimization, Simpson takes care to acknowledge the persistence of the narrator's agency. After arriving at a colony of seals, the narrator notes that "they stampede into the sea reminding me of dogs and sheep and buffalo and etienne asks me if i want to go farther," and on "impulse" "i say yes" (12). Although the narrator's response is reactionary and impulsive, the boat's course is determined through a form of negotiation that indicates the potential for flexibility in how gender dynamics will be expressed in the story. Thus, the very conditions that exacerbate the narrator's vulnerability—the two are alone together on the ocean—actually create the opportunity for imaginative difference and potentially even change. Opening the door to alternative imaginings via Indigenous masculinities, Simpson's narrator *decides* that etienne "is mi'kmaq because he could be and even though that probably means nothing it makes [her] feel less nervous" (12). In this manner, the delimited and totalizing colonial masculinities that have conditioned the narrator's entirely rational anxieties throughout the story are exposed as incomplete, as not retaining a stranglehold on the spectrum of actions available to etienne, which then enables the narrator to begin to register her host's humanity more fully.

etienne expresses such difference in two key gestures of masculine vulnerability. First, he explains to the narrator "how the feds kicked his family out of the park and paid them three hundred and fifty bucks for their land in 1968 and they bulldozed the house" (12), alluding to the mass eviction of more than twelve hundred predominantly Acadian and Mi'kmaq residents in the creation of Kou-chibou-guac National Park in New Brunswick and thereby acknowledging his own victimization by the Canadian government. Rather than allowing the legitimate anger emergent from this historical injustice to stand between them, etienne shares this information to affirm his own subjectivity and thereby to foster the possibility of genuine connection with the narrator. Second, when a northern gannet then swims over to the boat, "etienne hands [it] a fish and says 'the bird is my family, all of this, the fish, the seals, the water—this is my family'" (13). Simpson's narrator describes this philosophical admission and accompanying embodied gesture as etienne's "reveal." The term indicates here a dual openness: both his openness to alternative conceptions of family, territoriality, and gender that signal his defiance of the constraints of colonial masculinities and his willingness to expose himself fully—and vulnerably—to his audience. In this way, etienne reveals his commitment to a worldview that transcends the anthropocentrism of settler heteropatriarchy (and potentially its attendant gender hierarchies—see Chapter 1) while affirming his masculine subjectivity by nesting his identity within a web of kinship relations articulated in ecological terms.[17] These gestures of openness—of agentive or *chosen* vulnerability—are productive insofar as they enable a form of mutual recognition between the characters that is uncontaminated by the gendered logics of settler colonialism: "our eyes meet," Simpson's narrator says, "because now he has my attention." The passage continues thus:

> i walk over and hug him and he is the kind of person that can give and receive a real hug and i'm not one of those people because my alarm system goes off when people touch me and i freeze up and shut down. this time that doesn't happen. i decide to kiss him and it's perfect and easy and we make out void of awkwardness but with a clearly defined beginning and a clearly defined ending. then he drives back to shore while i gut the fish in the back of the boat using his terrifyingly sharp knife, feeding the guts to the gulls and the gannets. he drops me off on the dock. we thank each other. we say goodbye and i pay attention to each step, instead of looking back. (13)

Simpson's depiction of the kiss as a *decision* highlights the narrator's agency in the encounter; however, the structural qualities of the sentence refine that agency as non-hegemonic and consensual—it is exercised in a manner that respects rather than suppresses etienne's own enduring agency. The use of polysyndeton—"*and* it's perfect *and* easy *and* we make out void of awkwardness"—compels the reader forward with the energy of erotic engagement while registering a movement beyond the self and into the mutual domain of the "we." The redemptive nature of such mutuality is then reaffirmed through the alliterative connection between the "gulls" and "gannets" and the "guts" by which they are nourished. Thus, the motion of the passage is both centripetal and centrifugal—it depicts the coming together of bodies in a way that awakens awareness of the connections that extend beyond the self and beyond the human. The fact that the paragraph is bookended by references to the narrative "I" further suggests that, although it tracks the coming together of two people through consensual vulnerability and erotic intimacy, such merging neither eclipses nor obscures the identities of the central characters; it nurtures and affirms them.

So what then does all of this have to do with Indigenous masculinities? The term "masculinity" does not appear once in the tale, which seems to be interested only tangentially in etienne's maleness, is focalized through a female narrator, and is written by an Anishinaabekwe author.[18] Yet the story seems to me to interrogate brilliantly both the role of colonial masculinities in conditioning the threat of violence toward Indigenous women in contemporary Canadian society and the ways in which the normalization of such masculinities works to inhibit the kinds of interpersonal connection that might push back against colonial degradation through decolonizing solidarities (or, as Simpson foregrounds in the title to her collection, through *Decolonial Love*). The opportunity for genuine connection between the story's two central characters emerges only as etienne expresses his subjectivity in ways that transcend the tropes of colonial masculinity by which the narrator feels threatened. Only then can she truly "see" him. He humbles himself by sharing his own victimization by governmental land seizure; he enacts his capacity to nurture by feeding the gannet; and he articulates a non-anthropocentric conception of "family" that extends beyond the human, thereby illuminating an understanding of kinship (and therefore gender) not constrained by the nuclear family models naturalized by settler heteropatriarchy. Through these gestures of consensual vulnerability, etienne is able to "reveal" his identity in a way that dispels the presumptions about colonial masculinities by which the narrator's perceptions of him have been clouded, which thereby enables sincere interpersonal connection—connection engaged in in an embodied manner. Erotic intimacy as a ceremony of mutual nourishment.

While speaking at Queen's University in Kingston, Ontario, in March 2015, Simpson declared the need to envisage and enact what she called "sovereign sites of intimacy" in the service of decolonial struggles ("Islands"). It strikes me that Simpson offers a paradigmatic example of one such "sovereign site" in the erotic encounter between etienne and her narrator. The site is indeed sovereign not because the central characters have achieved fundamental and lasting liberation from the influence of the settler colonial nation-state—the presence of the "terrifyingly sharp knife" at the story's close reminds us that the gender dynamics of settler colonialism persist beyond the story's final page. Rather, the site becomes sovereign in the present moment through the characters' embodied self-expressions, which transcend colonial constraints. Erotic intimacy is here made possible, I argue, by mutual vulnerability in which *masculinity* is operative. As illustrated by her willingness to open herself to the initial embrace, despite not being "the kind of person that can give and receive a real hug," followed by her decision to instigate the kiss, it is clear that not only etienne but also the narrator proves to be vulnerable. My focus on *masculine* vulnerability is not meant to obscure the agentive vulnerability of the narrator but to suggest that etienne's *performance* of vulnerability as a man is essential to the establishment of the conditions of relative safety needed for the narrator's consensual vulnerability to become possible. As Anishinaabe scholar Randy Jackson illustrates in relation to his own community-based critical practice, "it's . . . about unhinging yourself from the things that are causing the problem and trying to be more human about it, more human about how you be with people. And if we can be vulnerable in that kind of situation, it gives other people permission to be vulnerable too and open up and create that safe space" (interview). Because etienne carries into their relationship masculine privilege, which has informed the violent heteropatriarchal context by which the story is shadowed, his gesture of vulnerability generates liberatory possibilities that, when carefully tethered to respect for the narrator's decision-making autonomy, can be ultimately realized through consensual erotic intimacy.[19] And this intimacy is fundamentally creative. It builds something; it creates the sovereignty that it seeks. The space claimed together in the boat, therefore, is not just a critical one in which the corrosive characteristics of colonial masculinities are identified, interrogated, and purged; etienne and the narrator imagine and express something new, something indebted to Indigenous ecologies of gender, something collaborative, something sovereign.

## EMBODIMENT, ECOLOGY, AND DYNAMIC MUTUALITY

Among Simpson's strengths as an artist is her ability to register the ongoing impacts of settler colonialism on her characters without depicting their actions as predetermined by those influences; she does not concede to victimry but honours the full humanity of her characters by illuminating their resilient agency. In a blog post entitled "Upheaval," Cree activist and scholar Erica Violet Lee dares to yearn for sovereign Indigenous futures like those illuminated in Simpson's work while similarly refusing to let colonialism off the hook: "I want a moment to mourn the nutrients spilled, to accept this trauma as our kin, and then I want to move on. I want to live in a world where being a native woman is not synonymous with heartache and things past, but with happiness & things to come." "I cannot be disappearing," she writes, "if I insist upon a celebration in the midst of upheaval." As evidenced by her narrator's efforts to "pay attention to each step, instead of looking back," Simpson, like Lee, focuses actively on "things to come," thereby demonstrating a commitment to creating the "world" in which she "want[s] to live." Erotic intimacy in Simpson's story constitutes a modality of "celebration" that fortifies the narrator for the journey ahead—a journey in which she is likely to face further denials of her humanity yet will have the strength, the reader is convinced, defiantly to endure.

The nourishing moment of consensual vulnerability in "indinawemaaganidog/all of my relatives" is all the more important because, in the context of settler colonialism, it is exceptional. As the narrator of another short story from *Islands of Decolonial Love*, "buffalo on," explains, "we're all hunting around for acceptance, intimacy, connection and love, but we don't know what those particular med'cines even look like so we're just hunting anyway with vague ideas from dreams and hope and intention, at the same time dragging around blockades full of reminders that being vulnerable has never ended well for any of us, not even one single time" (85). Here memories of trauma discourage interpersonal connection even as the desire for such intimacy persists. Another way to say this is that the pervasive violence of settler colonialism creates conditions of non-consensual vulnerability for many Indigenous people—particularly girls, women, and queer and two-spirit persons. As Jessica Danforth argues, such vulnerability "does not happen by accident and is not a pre-existing social location. Instead young women are *made* vulnerable by any number of historical, social, political and economic factors that create vulnerable situations and circumstances for them" (paraphrased from a keynote address by Oliver et al. 907). Métis poet Joanne Arnott elaborates such conditions and their consequences for Indigenous intimacies:

> It's very delicate territory because I don't think we've seen an end yet to the reality that young Aboriginal women walking down the street are seen as someone it's safe to attack. That is just so. It permeates. I haven't visited a region in Canada where that is not so. . . . So, I don't know how any of us develop and maintain these good loving sensual, sexual relationships with men of our choosing without that being a factor—without the interference of having unwanted sex, without having extreme disrespect and extreme danger of a life-and-death scenario, having those things inflicted upon us. . . . So setting aside the question of who is to blame for any individual woman's victimization, we could just sit back and say, "Holy fuck! that happens a lot, all across Canada, in every community." And it happens systemically. And it happens that the repercussions are still not very much. (202)

The internalization of these dehumanizing lessons, according to Kateri Akiwenzie-Damm, informs "an underlying acceptance of violence against Indigenous women in the mainstream," and "the real outcome is that it's not safe for Indigenous women" ("Affirming Protectorship" 181).

In the brief passage above from "buffalo on," Simpson's narrator registers these realities while subtly refusing to capitulate to domination. The passage, though painfully forthright, remains aspirational because the narrator and members of her immediate community continue the hunt for "acceptance, intimacy, connection and love," even in the face of what Driskill might call "memories awash in blood" ("Map" 11). Traumatic memories, which condition rational fear of vulnerability and potentially the unwillingness to open oneself to sensual intimacy, are described as "blockades full of reminders." Although "blockades" might be interpreted strictly as barriers to intimacy that stand between the self and others, I read Simpson's evocative word choice through the lens of her commitment to Indigenous resurgence and therefore as conjuring up expressions of Indigenous sovereignty that disrupt the smooth functioning of settler colonialism. Simpson repurposes the concept of the blockade such that deep understandings of how the gendered violence of settler colonialism discourages interpersonal intimacy become part of the Indigenous reader's activist arsenal in the service of "dismantling . . . heteropatriarchy as the crucial nation-building exercise of our time" (*As We* 92); the inspired knowledge shared in her stories *becomes* the blockade that might prevent the reproduction of colonial masculinities and the naturalization of violence against Indigenous girls, women, and queer and two-spirit people. The hunt for the "particular med'cines" of "acceptance, intimacy, connection and love" continues indeed because the "vague ideas from dreams and hope and intention" are given shape by stories such as those found in *Islands of Decolonial Love*. In Arnott's words, "What I vision, no matter how outlandish or different from where I'm at right now, it's something that I can realize and what I have to honour is the distance. . . . I have to build up earthwork underneath the dream until that dream is resting on the earth, and that's the reality we've come to" (196).

In an article for *Red Rising Magazine* entitled "Land, Language and Decolonial Love," Erica Violet Lee affirms the resurgent potential of erotic intimacy in this way:

> As Indigenous people in colonial worlds, our vulnerability
> is non-consensually consumed and it is rarely ours to own.
> Daring to claim love and desire for Indigenous bodies in
> the face of ongoing colonialism is a liberatory act of vulner-
> ability. Allowing love to flow beyond the edges of our skin
> (in the form of touch), our lips (in the form of language),
> and our eyes (in the form of tears) is necessary and radical
> in a world where we're taught to believe those borders are
> impassable. So when we love each other, it is potent enough
> to heal the trauma and chase away the violence. So when
> we love it is wider than the prairies. So when we love, the
> bellies of our ancestors are filled with laughter and good

food. When we love each other, pipelines shut down and borders open and logging machines jam.

Here, as elsewhere, Lee dares to celebrate Indigenous eroticism and, like Simpson and Scofield, encourages us to think about how gender knowledge emerges from and is in constant orientation to the land and its animate inhabitants across the spectrum of the human and other-than-human. Given that colonial interventions in Indigenous gender systems have always been motivated by the desire to gain access to and exploit the land (see Chapters 1 and 2), affirmations of the embeddedness of gender knowledges within specific landscapes carry power. Although the gender system imported to support colonial conquest relies on the deanimation of land, the naturalization of adversarial relations between humans and other-than-humans, and a corresponding belief in the inevitability of opposition between men and women, Indigenous gender knowledges, as theorized by critics such as Paula Gunn Allen, Kim Anderson, Beth Brant, Qwo-Li Driskill, Brian Joseph Gilley, Mishuana Goeman, Sarah Hunt, Daniel Heath Justice, Lee Maracle, Leanne Simpson, Lisa Tatonetti, and Eve Tuck (and others), most often foreground relationality and complementarity. The difference is between a closed binary system, on the one hand, in which power is in competitive exchange between men and women and between people and the environment within an imagined habitat of scarcity, and open pluralist systems in which relations among differently gendered individuals and groups can actually *generate* power, on the other. The former is the ecology of gender that naturalizes the settler colonial system by displacing the burden of oppressive colonial history onto intimate interpersonal relationships involving Indigenous individuals (which thereby become the terrain in which gender equality is meant to be pursued), whereas the latter is a decolonizing ecology of gender in which networks of relationships can be marshalled to confront injustice in a manner that builds from but extends beyond the interpersonal. One is a structure of containment, whereas the other is a catalyst to expansive creativity. For clarity, I refer to the former as a competitive ecology of gender and the latter as an ecology of gender characterized by dynamic mutuality. Dynamic mutuality resonates with Simpson's theorization of "Kina Gchi Nishnaabeg-ogamig" as "an ecology of intimacy":

> It is an ecology of relationships in the absence of coercion, hierarchy, or authoritarian power.
>
> Kina Gchi Nishnaabeg-ogamig is connectivity based on the sanctity of the land, the love we have for our families, our language, our way of life. It is relationships based on deep reciprocity, respect, noninterference, self-determination, and freedom. (*As We* 8)

Community ecologists divide competitive ecological relations into three categories. The first is "interference competition," in which one group seeks directly to impede the growth of a competing group. The second is "exploitative competition," in which one group consumes resources that are therefore no longer available to the competing group. The third—and perhaps most significant to the concerns of this chapter—is "apparent competition," in which two groups share a common predator that constrains their growth, thereby making it appear as though they are competing with each other. In a settler colonial context, this is useful for understanding lateral violence as emergent from individuals' inabilities to confront the institutional and systemic sources of their oppression that can lead to the displacement of internalized rage onto others. As Bonita Lawrence argues, Indigenous women "face phenomenal levels of violence in [their] communities, but that is a function, in fact, of histories of male powerlessness in the face of colonialist violence" (qtd. in Anderson 276). I bring competitive ecology into the conversation here to illuminate the myopic nature of ideological structures that would conceive of gender competition as *inevitable* and *natural* and thereby reinforce colonial imperatives separating men from women and Indigenous Peoples from their lands. The naturalization of such models reinforces colonial heteropatriarchy, even as it identifies pathways for women and gender-non-conforming individuals to seek power (by seizing it from cis-gendered, heterosexual men). Yet, by imagining heteropatriarchy as the ongoing and inevitable context in which decolonization is pursued, I argue through my interpretations of Simpson's and Scofield's writing that we miss out on resources available to imagine and enact a more just world. By foreclosing the perceived validity of alternative ways of understanding and inhabiting the world, settler colonial power works insidiously to occlude modes of persistence that exceed its systemic structures. This is why the dominant interventions endorsed by the Canadian government and the mainstream media to combat the gender-based violence disproportionately suffered by Indigenous women tend to reaffirm the foundational structures of the Canadian state: greater police presence, stiffer penalties for perpetrators, enhanced education, and greater absorption of Indigenous women into the capitalist economy. The first two naturalize the state's recourse to coercive force through policing while reifying its monopoly on the levying of "justice" in the courts, and the second two reify capitalist individualism as the supposedly natural pathway to gender equality and personal safety for Indigenous women. What remains unacknowledged is how these various technologies of settler colonial administrative policy—systems of law enforcement, justice, education, and economics—are implicated in the production of the very conditions that put Indigenous women at far greater risk of violence than non-Indigenous women.

One consequence of reifying a competitive ecology of gender is that it becomes extremely difficult to view male bodies as anything but impediments to the empowerment of women and non-gender-normative Indigenous people. In what Justice calls the "hypermasculine models of maleness" that we inherit from settler colonialism, he argues that, "if the male body isn't giving harm, it's taking pleasure. . . . It's either penetrative or extractive—either assaultive or extractive. One or the other, there's nothing else" ("Fighting" 145). The metaphor of extraction implies the impossibility of genuine mutuality within such gender models—pleasure is taken *from* another rather than produced dynamically and reciprocally *with* another—foreclosing on both solidarity and creativity. Conceptualizations of gender, like those critiqued by Justice, themselves become "blockades" to intimacy, and as Gwen Benaway reminds us, "for decolonial love, remember that love is a gift, not a transaction." Returning to Coulthard's claim from earlier in this chapter, what if "indigenous masculinities" did not simply need to "vacate" space that could be occupied by "indigenous feminist, queer and trans voices" but could work in solidarity with these other voices to seize more space from settler colonial power while working creatively to generate more space overall? What if space were construed not to be finite and static (a colonial habitat of scarcity) but to be fecund and responsive and alive (an animate ecological web of kinship)? What if, in Simpson's own words, Indigenous men were "to support and assist and to be critically engaged in, but not lead, the dismantling of heteropatriarchy as the crucial nation-building exercise of our time" (*As We* 92–93)? And what if such support and engagement were not simply abstract and intellectual but relentlessly embodied, even at times erotic? In the final section of this chapter, I pursue these lines of questioning through an analysis of Gregory Scofield's erotic poetry from the collection *Love Medicine and One Song: Sâkihtowin-maskihkiy êkwa pêyak-nikamowin*, paying particular attention to depictions of male bodies and the role of consensual vulnerability in creating conditions of possibility for a generative erotic.

## GREGORY SCOFIELD AND EMBODIED MASCULINITY

Métis literary scholar June Scudeler argues that "Scofield posits the body, especially the male body, as a sacred space" (139). The poem "Ceremonies," for example, begins thus: "I heat the stones / between your legs, / my mouth, / the lodge where you come / to sweat" (*Love Medicine* ll. 1–5). Honouring fellatio as ceremony,[20] Scofield draws the reader's attention to the sex organs of the male beloved while simultaneously exalting the embodied experience of the male speaker,[21] whose mouth becomes the metaphorical sweat lodge in which "medicine is sweet, / the love, sacred" (ll. 24–25). The speaker's mouth is not only the architect of the beloved's pleasure but also the locus of sensation as taste, touch, and speech commingle in the multidimensionality of embodied erotics. Scofield emphasizes the voice of the speaker (as he "chant[s] with frogs" and "sing[s]" the beloved "to dreams"), his taste through the "chew[ing]" of "bitter roots," and both smell and touch via the "earth smell / deep in [the speaker's] nostrils, / wetting / the tip of [his] tongue" (ll. 16, 17, 23, 13–15). Heightened by contrast to the darkness of the sweat lodge, the sensory overload of the passage catalyzes the embodied pleasure of both speaker and beloved to a point of transcendence.

The poem "He Is" tracks the journey of the beloved—identified via the masculine pronoun—as he navigates the speaker's body from "lips," "teeth," and "mouth" to "ears," "neck," and "chest," on to "belly," and down "between [the] legs" (ll. 2, 3, 6, 8, 10, 12, 15, 20). Acting with varying degrees of urgency on parts of the speaker's body, the beloved transforms into diverse other-than-human kin: earthworm, caterpillar, slug, moth, snail, spider, watersnake, frog, mouse, grouse, weasel, turtle, mountain lion, and finally spring bear. Cariou describes these "lightning-quick changes" as "more than a succession of simple metaphors in the poem; instead they are a powerful gesture toward Cree transformation stories, in which . . . [t]he ability to transform into an animal is a sign of spiritual strength" (viii). Thus, although Scofield's erotic poetry indeed celebrates male bodies—from the intimate details of "each mole, every fine hair" ("More Rainberries" l. 12) to the totality of the "whole abundant self" ("Ôchîm" l. 11)—it remains attuned to the spiritual dimensions of embodied pleasure and resolutely refuses biological determinism. Scofield indeed honours male bodies without ever conceding such bodies to be stable or fully knowable. "Among the most important themes in this collection," argues Cariou, "are the ideas of transformation and fluidity, which are presented in the largest arc of the story as well as the most minute details of the imagery" (vi). Reaching to interstitial spaces such as muskeg and metamorphic beings such as caterpillars and frogs, Scofield locates beauty and power in boundary crossings—not least in traversing the boundaries between male bodies. My point is not that Scofield elevates *only* male bodies to the realm of the sacred or that the speaker and his beloved are defined *solely* by their maleness; rather, I wish to acknowledge that male bodies have a place of reverence in his poetry, for they are depicted within an animate, sensate universe of differently gendered and embodied beings, and that the relationships among all of these beings can be enlivened through consensual vulnerability (and potentially by erotic intimacy).[22]

Scofield's attentiveness to the corporeality of male bodies is both rare and significant. For example, in hir path-breaking article "Stolen from Our Bodies: First Nations Two-Spirits/Queers and the Journey to a Sovereign Erotic," from which I borrow this chapter's title, non-citizen Cherokee theorist Qwo-Li Driskill writes that "I have been removed from my erotic self and continue a journey back to my first homeland: the body" (53). However, in mapping out this journey back to the body for hirself and for other Indigenous people, it is difficult to find reference to embodied men anywhere in the article beyond the vilification of a "white masculinity" that "murders, rapes, and enslaves" (53). That is not to suggest that the onus is on Driskill to map journeys to embodied maleness specifically but to recognize how such avoidance is characteristic of more general ambivalence toward male bodies in Indigenous queer and two-spirit theory. According to Brian Joseph Gilley's cogent genealogy of the field, "The goal of early studies was to find non-western examples of 'gender-bending' behavior to combat Euro-American assumptions about compulsory heterosexuality, gender essentialism, and the deviance of same-sex relations. The questioning of sexual dimorphism and biological paradigms precipitated a new approach that deemphasized bodily sex, sexual desire, and sexual object choice for an emphasis on gender construction" (123). Early two-spirit theory was productive, in Driskill's view, "because it recenter[ed] discussion onto gendered constructions": whereas "queer too often refers to sexualized practices and identities[,] Two-Spirit . . . places gendered identities and experiences at the center of discussion" in ways that honour Indigenous traditions that "are not necessarily about sexuality" (*Asegi Stories* 71). However, as Gilley argues, this "strategic deemphasis of sexuality" came at a cost, insofar as it precipitated "a certain form of asexual criticism placing desire in a nebulous realm missing certain visceral realities and agentive subjective corporeality" (123, 124–25). If we take "agentive subjective corporeality" to mean the embodied experience of desire, then the implication is that much of the criticism referenced by Gilley is not only "asexual" but also disembodied. In *The Queerness of Native American Literature*, however, settler scholar Lisa Tatonetti suggests that the disembodied and asexual criticism

CARRYING THE BURDEN OF PEACE

lamented by Gilley might, in fact, be gender-specific. Reaching to the foundational critical and creative work of Indigenous lesbian theorists Paula Gunn Allen, Beth Brant, and Chrystos, Tatonetti argues that "The erotic," as a "decolonial imperative . . . that is *situated in the body*," has actually been "here all along" in women's queer and two-spirit theorizing (xx–xxi). Tatonetti quotes Allen's 1986 monograph *The Sacred Hoop*, for example, to explicate "the erotic" as a "'sexual connection' or 'power that women carry within their bodies'" (xxi). Thus, the embodied nature of queer desire has been part of the critical field for quite some time—but tellingly not so much in relation to the experiences of those who identify as male. This absence undoubtedly informs Gilley's ethnographic work with "contemporary Two-Spirit men" to "reignite the conversation about sexual desire and its role in personal and cultural survivability" (125).

Given the history of hypermasculine violence on this continent, as well as anxieties about the spectre of gender essentialism and the threat of co-optation by settler heteropatriarchy, reluctance to seek the liberatory potential in male bodies is logical. These are the same reasons that etienne is initially viewed as a threat in Simpson's story rather than a potential source of emotional and erotic nourishment. Affirmations of biological maleness and celebrations of masculine power risk trading in biological essentialisms and being conscripted into chauvinism and misogyny, especially when masculinity becomes conflated with strength and dominance. Yet the elision of male bodies from critical discourse also represents another form of risk: that is, unconsciously sustaining colonial myths of the body as inherently shameful and thereby naturalizing competitive ecologies of gender that constrain Indigenous futures. Ktunaxa poet Smokii Sumac's evocative question within the context of FTM transition—"without trusting men / how do i become / a man / worthy of trust?" (*You Are Enough* 49)—registers the cost of this conspicuous critical absence.[23] As Scofield explains, "there's such a loathing of historical oppressive maleness. . . . [T]here's still this stigma. There's still an expectation about what denotes masculinity and strength. . . . Until there's a gentleness woven into that expectation, then it's going to be one of those things that's constantly in tension" ("Liberation" 218). In "Stolen from Our Bodies," Driskill invokes the work of Chrystos and Brant to identify "radical Two-Spirit *woman*-centred erotics as tools for healing from colonization" (59; emphasis added).[24] Heeding Simpson's cautions that "Indigenous masculinities" should not be "centred" in resurgence and that Indigenous men should "support . . . but not lead" the "dismantling of heteropatriarchy," I do not wish to argue in this chapter for a radical *man*-centred erotics. Rather, I wish to acknowledge the healing potential of radical *embodied* erotics—whether two-spirit, queer, straight, cis-, trans, or otherwise—in which male bodies might participate. Through analyses of Scofield's poetry and Simpson's prose, I contend that there are places for those who self-identify as Indigenous men (or with Indigenous masculinity) in the embodied, experiential, consensual erotics that will nurture decolonial Indigenous futures, particularly if vulnerability is acknowledged as a source of strength, not weakness, and the dynamic mutuality of relations among diversely gendered people is honoured.

To describe the beloved's desire for the speaker in the poem "Ôchîm ♦ His Kiss," from *Love Medicine and One Song*, excerpted as an epigraph to this chapter, Scofield deploys the metaphor of "maskwa pawing / all his winter hunger."[25] The speaker responds by "yield[ing] up roots and berries / and [lying] back / [his] whole abundant self" (ll. 7–8, 9–11). The erotics of this scene introduce a complicated relationship between sensual embodiment and vulnerability. Although Scofield's speaker demonstrates agency in determining to "lie back" and "yield up" his body—thereby affirming his "whole[ness]" and "abundan[ce]"—he resigns himself to being acted on by the beloved, creating conditions of heightened risk in which he might indeed be devoured. When I asked Scofield about the tensions that arise in "Ôchîm ♦ His Kiss" among physical intimacy, vulnerability, and power, he responded with a metaphor about the carnival that I find instructive:

> In order to experience the absolute and utter jubilation
> of being turned upside down, you need to first of all say,
> "It'll be okay, I think I can be turned upside down. I will
> be grounded again at some point." But really what you've
> done is given yourself permission. You've allowed yourself

to be vulnerable. And in allowing yourself that vulnerability, you've allowed yourself that experience. And allowing
yourself that experience, you've allowed yourself all of the
things that have come with that experience: the terror, the
jubilation, the excitement, the panic. You've allowed yourself all of these amazing emotions which, once you've landed
again[,] permeate, they just radiate throughout your body
and they become a part of your knowing. ("Liberation" 219)

In relation to Scofield's oeuvre, forms of consensual vulnerability like that depicted in "Ôchîm ◆ His Kiss" and in the carnival
analogy generate dynamically embodied relational power. Thus,
rather than offering up the body in a sacrificial manner in which
power—construed in a finite sense—is claimed from the vulnerable speaker by the active beloved, here we see both power and
pleasure portrayed in a mutually generative fashion. Rather than
the "assaultive or extractive" masculinity critiqued by Justice for
"taking pleasure," Scofield depicts the reciprocal creation of sensual
joy. Such consensual vulnerability—or chosen intimate generosity
carrying both risk and reward—can therefore be read as a source
of strength rather than weakness, specifically, in this case, for those
who self-identify as men but certainly for others as well. I argue
that Scofield's evocative twinning of powerful subjectivities, embodied and affirmed as male, with a necessarily *chosen* and *consensual*
vulnerability, thus works to insulate his honouring of Indigenous
masculinities from co-optation by hypermasculine individualism
and patriarchy. In this way, Scofield offers visions of the male body
that transcend the corrosive prescriptions of colonialism critiqued
by Justice. In fact, Scofield seems to provide one of the "alternatives"
that Justice argues "literature ought to offer."
  About Scofield's poetry, Justice has stated that "the vulnerability, the gentleness, the confusion, the uncertainty—all of those are
. . . sources of strength; all of those are . . . powerful ways of reveal-
ing our humanity. Where vulnerability is not weakness; it is being
open to the possibility of change, being open to the possibility of
being transformed by love, by passion, by touch" (McKegney et al.,
"Strong Men Stories" 249–50). It is this transformative possibility

that lives within both Scofield's and Simpson's work that makes it so valuable in terms of decolonial activism. Ultimately, to read Scofield's poetry is to feast and to be nourished by the roots and berries of erotic expression and, in this way, be armed with embodied awareness, intersubjective knowledge, and territorial situatedness. Not only does the poetry explicitly represent alternatives to colonial anthropocentrism, Cartesian dualism, gender dimorphism, and compulsory heteronormativity through its depictions of homoerotic lovemaking within a sensate ecosystemic reality, but it actually enacts an experiential ceremony in which such alternatives become manifest in cadences, rhythms, and images. When I listen to Scofield read from his poetry—an act, I should note, that itself models agentive vulnerability on behalf of community—it becomes impossible to imagine myself as disembodied intellect or as separate from the other-than-human elements of the world by which I am surrounded and of which I am undeniably a part. These are among Scofield's many gifts to Indigenous resurgence and to the invigoration of non-heteropatriarchal Indigenous ecologies of gender.

And, of course, such ecologies have both social and territorial implications. As Scofield argues,

> it's all interconnected. The muskeg, the reeds, the rocks, the smell of the earth, the bogs, all of these things are medicines from the earth, and those are the things that we possess within our own bodies. We don't have to look very far. Parts of our bodies are muskeg. Parts of our bodies, there are frogs there. And [writing *Love Medicine and One Song*] was really just throwing those physical elements up and being able to give them to the spiritual energies where they exist. . . . When you think of these sacred ceremonies—of give-aways, naming ceremonies, fasting—sex and sexuality is all a part of that. You name things on someone's body. You fast those things, you hunger them, you crave them, you sing those things, you dance those things, you taste those things, you feast them. ("Liberation"220)

And it is in such generative feasting—characterized by consent and creativity rather than selfish consumption—that, in the words of Kim Anderson, we "remember the sacredness of men" ("Remembering" 87).

In conclusion, my argument about all of this is really quite simple: if we continue to understand "masculinity" as pertaining to qualities connected in some way with maleness, and we recognize that there are individuals within Indigenous families, communities, and nations who do and will identify *as* male—or *with* masculinity regardless of their biological sex, as Lisa Tatonetti's forthcoming work *Written by the Body* demonstrates—then the concession that "masculinity" pertains only to those negative characteristics inherited from and naturalized by settler colonialism bears stark consequences. It means that the resources available to affirm the subjectivities of those individuals will be constrained and potentially contaminated not only by violent individualism but also by shame (as argued in Chapter 2). If the only way that one's identity as male or masculine can be understood is through a rubric of destructiveness, then I think that we are in trouble. And that is why I consider it imperative to look to the work of Indigenous artists who are always imagining other horizons of possibility: for masculinity, for desire, for ways of being in the world.

In "Recovery and Transformation," Kanien'keha:ka writer Beth Brant argues that "our strength as a family not only gives us tools, it helps *make* tools" (qtd. in Rifkin, *When* 234). Simpson's and Scofield's work, like that of many Indigenous artists, helps to generate decolonial tools through imaginative interventions. It does not simply critique unhealthy and imposed notions of masculinity that have been damaging to Indigenous families and nations, nor does it strictly look back to supposedly authentic models of manhood from cultural traditions prior to colonial interventions. Rather, Simpson and Scofield embolden such critical and reclamatory impulses with a commitment to creating what is needed now: a recognition of the myriad possibilities for positive, productive, and embodied masculinities that will serve the needs of individuals and communities. I consider this a "callout"[26] to Indigenous masculinities studies, and I hope to see the field move in this direction.

# THE
# PEOPLE
# AND
# THE
# GIFT

# 4. DE(F/V)IANT GENEROSITY:
## GENDER AND THE GIFT

Our biology is only a very small part of our humanity; the rest is a process of becoming. —DANIEL HEATH JUSTICE (*Why Indigenous Literatures Matter* 33)

We were told by my mother, my grandmother, my aunts, my uncles, that giving is the only way to be human, that if you don't know that giving is essential to survival, then you don't know how to be human yet. —JEANNETTE ARMSTRONG ("Indigenous Knowledge and Gift Giving" 48)

**S**yilx theorist Jeannette Armstrong explains that there "is no word for 'greed'" in her language. The term employed for one who gives only "in order to get something back" translates into English literally as "swallower or destroyer of giving" (48). Armstrong's teaching is evocative for two reasons. It demonstrates the profound gulf between worldviews that recognize economic exchange as the normative state of existence and those that honour "gift-giving as a basic human principle" (Kuokkanen 31). It also signals the threat that naturalization of the former can pose to the latter: belief that desire for return is always already inculcated in the bestowal of any gift denies the very foundation of gift giving as an expression of humanness—it *destroys* the gesture embedded in the gift itself. In her analysis of Genevieve Vaughan's feminist gift theory, Sami scholar Rauna Kuokkanen notes that "the gift and exchange are two distinct, logically contradictory paradigms with different values and objectives. . . . For Vaughan," she continues,

> exchange—often defined as giving in order to receive—is ego-oriented as well as prompted by self-interest. The exchange paradigm requires that what is given and what is received be of equal value; furthermore, it is based on the values of self-interest, competition, domination, and individualism. Gift-giving, in contrast, is based on the values of care, cooperation, and bonding. It is other-oriented, and gives directly to the needs of others. The gift paradigm is present everywhere in our lives, yet it is not only erased but also viewed as inferior and unrealistic compared to exchange. (30)

In this chapter, I examine the deviant and defiant resilience of the logic of the gift in contexts conditioned by the exchange economics of extractive global capitalism and the impact of such resilience on gender knowledges. I do not take issue with Vaughan's assertions that exchange and gift giving are "logically contradictory" or that the motion of exchange is hegemonic—in other words, that exchange serves not only to displace other economic systems but also to invest them with alternative meanings (such that the gift, for instance, becomes legible as a form of trade). Rather, as elsewhere in this book, I consider how settler colonial aspirations toward Indigenous elimination—*here through the violent imposition of the exchange paradigm*—are met with the vivaciousness and stamina of Indigenous brilliance—*here through the radical persistence of the logic of the gift*. Focusing on the lands and seas of the Pacific Northwest, where Indigenous gift economies have been targeted for elimination by the anti-potlatch policies of successive settler colonial governments, I examine the capacity for the logic of the gift to endure, even in unlikely settings and circumstances. Because economic and gender systems are mutually informing, I consider whether the endurance of the gift can unsettle not only the omnipresence of the exchange paradigm in contemporary society but also the system of heteropatriarchy with which it is entwined. Ultimately, I contend that the gift is a liberatory ethic, in both economic and gendered terms, a hypothesis that I test through an analysis of Haisla-Heiltsuk writer Eden Robinson's literary art.

Raised in Kitamaat Village, British Columbia, Robinson is of two matrilineal nations. By virtue of her mother's Heiltsuk heritage, she should "belong to the Eagle Clan"; however, because "[y]ou aren't supposed to attend a feast or a potlatch without an Indian name and since [her family was] living in Kitamaat Village," her mother agreed for the "sake of convenience" to allow Robinson and her sister to take on "Beaver Clan names at a Settlement Feast" (Robinson, *Sasquatch* 4–5). This anecdote, shared in *The Sasquatch at Home: Traditional Protocols and Modern Storytelling*, registers the ongoing significance of giveaway ceremonies such as the potlatch to Robinson and her community; the dynamic relationship between individual and clan-based identities in Haisla and Heiltsuk cultures; the role of gender in cultural affiliation among northwest coastal Indigenous Peoples; the importance of place to both clan and nation; and the vibrant persistence of sovereign decision making amid the strictures of protocol. I am struck, for instance, by how Robinson's mother expresses her gendered authority, affirming her daughters' connections to territory, community, and culture even as her decision contravenes Heiltsuk matrilineality—and doing so to facilitate their participation in a ceremony central to the Haisla gift economy. Robinson's fiction is unwaveringly attentive to the interface between economics and gender. Set primarily in Haisla territory near Kitimaat or in the traditional, ancestral, and unceded territories of the Musqueam, Squamish, and Tsleil-Waututh Peoples to the south (in what is commonly referred to as the city of Vancouver, British Columbia), her stories illuminate how capitalist exchange conspires with colonial dispossession to produce conditions of oppression designed to engineer specific kinds of gendered subjects. Yet Robinson refuses to deny her characters agency to resist, and a key weapon in this enterprise is the resilience of the logic of the gift.

I begin this chapter by analyzing Armstrong's and Kuokkanen's theorizations of Indigenous gift economies before demonstrating the prescience of the gift to Robinson's work via the short story "Terminal Avenue," in which a father's surreptitious potlatch symbolizes Indigenous resistance to the eliminatory policies of the state. I then consider the consequences of the colonial imposition of the exchange economy on the Haisla gift economy through an analysis of "Queen of the North," with attention to how the naturalization of exchange conspires with heteropatriarchy to endanger Indigenous women. In order to understand how exchange economics come to be reified in settler colonial society, I then turn to Robinson's 2006 novel *Blood Sports*, the bold formal and stylistic innovations of which force readers to reckon with "what's real or not real" (144), in the process suggesting that presumptions about gender and economics in contemporary Canadian society are based on illusions. By depicting both heteropatriarchy and exchange economics as simulacra, the novel opens up alternative possibilities for social formation and gender expression, including as pertains to masculinities. In the latter portion of the chapter, I focus on paradoxes in the characterization of the novel's young protagonist, Tom Bauer, who seems, on the one hand, to concede to the inevitability of economic exchange yet, on the other, to behave in ways that I read as demonstrative of the logic of the gift. At the heart of this tension lies his admission of indebtedness to his sociopathic older cousin Jeremy Rieger, who humiliates and tortures Tom to the point that he "start[s] to believe" that he will "die" (153): "Jer [is] an asshole. . . . But . . . I *owe* him a lot" (50). Tom's legitimation of what the reader recognizes as perversely unfair terms of exchange dramatizes both the improbability of achieving equivalent values amid conditions of inequality and the manner in which notions of debt can be employed to perpetuate subordination. Nonetheless, even as he betrays complicity in his oppression, Tom retains senses of humility, humour, and generosity that insulate him from capitulating to his cousin's violent masculinity. Although in some ways conforming to external pressures, Tom refuses to abandon the logic of the gift, which, I contend, frees him to perform alternative masculinities that persist beyond heteropatriarchy. In this way, Robinson's work shows us that, if we hope to imagine masculinities differently, then we ignore economics at our peril.

## GENDER AND THE GIFT

The assertion that "the gift and exchange are two distinct, logically contradictory paradigms" should not be taken to suggest that they are mutually exclusive. "[A]ll considerations of the gift," Kuokkanen reminds us, "must be careful not to assume the existence of the 'pure' gift or a clear demarcation between the gift and other paradigms" (23). Gifts that exceed the logic of exchange happen all the time within otherwise capitalist contexts—from parents' unbidden attentiveness to the needs of infants to anonymous gifts to simple gestures of kindness enacted out of love with no expectation of return.[1] As Vaughan explains, "in discussing the gift economy we are naming something that we are already doing but which is hidden under a variety of other names, and is disrespected as well as misconstrued" (1). Despite its persistence, the gift economy is devalued precisely because it does not register *as economic* within contexts in which exchange has been reified. Conversely, forms of exchange have always been operative within Indigenous societies that prioritize the logic of the gift. To elucidate the potlatch system, for example, Gordon Robinson identifies "oolachan oil or grease" as the "most desirable material . . . because it [can] be traded or bartered to other Indian tribes" (39).[2] Oolachan proves to be integral to Haisla potlatch ceremonies both because it registers as a valuable gift and because its value persists within systems of exchange. Thus, although they constitute "distinct logics," the gift and exchange are neither antithetical nor discrete; rather, when integrated into the dynamic web of meaning making that constitutes one or another worldview, each comes to be read, understood, and experienced differently—with profound consequences for relations among people and between people and the land.

Kuokkanen notes that "In anthropology the gift is usually treated as a mode of exchange between groups (or individuals representing groups). The gift comes with certain obligations, countergifts, return payments, and debts" (26). The gift is made legible within most Western worldviews[3] through exchange because the presumption of humankind's innate self-interest obfuscates the meaning of gifts devoid of return. For gift theorists following Marcel Mauss, "gifts always signify the social identity of their original owner or owners;

the latter remain spiritually involved in them, and may even retain a claim over them. Thus gifts, even if materially detachable from the person, are inalienable as opposed to alienable objects" (Willmott 14). Even though Mauss marshalled his theorizations to "provide the basis for a radical critique of . . . capitalist modernity" (Willmott 14), his contention that the gift comprises obligations of "giving, receiving, and paying back" (Kuokkanen 26) sustains the logic of the exchange contract. As a result, post-Maussian understandings of the gift fail to register adequately gifts beyond the structural limits of exchange. Pierre Bourdieu, for example, reads the gift as a form of symbolic violence, arguing that "'There are only two ways of getting and keeping *a lasting hold over someone*: debts and gifts'" (qtd. in Kuokkanen 26–27). In this analysis, debts and gifts are two sides of the same coin, with the monetary metaphor apt given Bourdieu's apparent inability to conceive of "the giving and sharing that exist outside the system of indebtedness" (Kuokkanen 27).

The difficulty that theorists such as Mauss and Bourdieu have imagining gifts beyond the framework of exchange comes not from the conceptualization of the gift per se but from the ideological infrastructure in which they imagine the gift to persist.[4] Concepts such as exchange and the gift register differently based on the system of thought in which they are discussed. Although Western anthropological scholarship has sought to theorize Indigenous gift economies as distinct forms of social organization, it has tended to do so without unsettling the dominant Western view of the human as ego-driven, individualistic, and innately self-interested, and as such it risks misrepresenting Indigenous understandings of the gift. Vaughan's choice of title for her introduction to *Women and the Gift Economy*, "A Radically Different Worldview Is Possible," suggests that to actualize the kinds of social change for which she and her co-authors argue requires liberation from the yoke of "Patriarchal Capitalism"; it requires the invigoration of (an) altogether different worldview(s), which Vaughan seeks in feminist philosophy and Indigenous thought. I speculate that this is also why, in her contribution to the volume, Armstrong discusses land, language, leadership, consensus building, gender, and family from a Syilx perspective before turning to the subject of the gift: unsettling the Western worldviews of her audience and immersing those listeners in the Syilx worldview comprise necessary preconditions for rendering understandings of the Syilx gift economy possible.

Armstrong's discussion of Syilx governance, for example, elaborates a radically anti-individualist philosophy that retains respect for autonomy, integrity, and diversity.[5] In the Syilx community, Armstrong explains, "the idea of 'chief' has to do with how well that person hears everyone. . . . Our word for chief means to be able to take the many strands that are moving outward and twine them into one strand" (43). In a manner that resonates with Haudenosaunee leadership, as discussed in Chapter 1, Syilx leaders bear neither coercive authority nor hierarchical leverage over the rest of the community; rather, they are entrusted with honouring diverse community members by weaving their perspectives into a coherent, collective logic and "say[ing] it back to the people" (43). Syilx governance delineates "a very clear process" of consensus building by which groups "speak to and listen to each other . . . to clarify for each other . . . their views" (44). Armstrong explains that

> We tell people: "You're not here to debate or to enforce your own agenda. You're not here to convince me of what you think. You're here to listen, and to hear the most diverse and opposite view to yours, and to understand where it's coming from and why it's there, and why that opinion is important in terms of how we find a solution. You are responsible for doing that. You are responsible for hearing what is the most opposite to your opinion, and finding a way to try to incorporate the other's diversity, the other's difference, and embrace that in terms of what we collectively come up with as a solution, so the difference will no longer be a difference, it becomes part of what we are and who we are." (45)

Consensus is made possible by respect for those with whom we initially appear to disagree and the generosity of spirit necessary to strive to understand them fully. Syilx governance is thus strategically non-adversarial and therefore different from Western governance—often coded as "masculine"—in which decisiveness, persuasiveness, and the ability to impose one's will are valued and in which opposition is to be defeated rather than understood and incorporated.[6]

The Syilx worldview in which "giving is the only way to be human" is thus radically different from Western heteropatriarchy; it does not subscribe to the artificial separation of humans via a hierarchized gender binary or the separation of the people from the land via the assignment of subject status to the former and object status to the latter. "[T]he land is a body that gives continuously," Armstrong affirms, "and we as human beings are an integral part of that body" (42). Settler colonialism, conversely, oriented toward the acquisition and exploitation of land, depends on the illusion of a fundamental separation between human and other-than-human that carries gendered implications. The economics of exchange naturalized within Western worldviews are inflected by "hierarchy, domination, and violence," which, Kuokkanen remarks, are not coincidentally "also elements of the dominant masculine identity" (31). The gift and exchange are not just different economic models—they can function synecdochically in relation to worldviews: one that is Western, settler colonial, and patriarchal and another that is Indigenous, land-based, and, as theorists such as Vaughan and Kuokkanen argue, matriarchal[7] and/or feminist.

## EXCHANGE AND THE COMMODITIZATION OF THE BODY

Eden Robinson's short story "Terminal Avenue" explores tensions between such worldviews through the depiction of a dystopic contemporary Vancouver in which settler colonial rule has descended into apartheid and fascism while the potlatch persists in clandestine form as an embodied expression of Indigenous sovereignty.[8] The story is told through flashbacks in the mind of Wilson Wilson, a Haisla resident of "Vancouver Urban Reserve #2," during the moment when he is advanced upon by armoured "Peace Officers" bent on his destruction. As an officer's "club flattens him to the Surrey-central tiles," Wil focuses on the memory of a secret potlatch held by his father at Monkey Beach before the family moved from Kitamaat to Vancouver: "This is the moment he *chooses* to be in" (546; emphasis added).[9] Against the overwhelming force of the militarized state, Wil "holds fast" to what Anishinaabe critic Grace Dillon calls "the parallel world of what is perhaps his family's most fully 'traditional,' and, therefore, intentionally sovereign moment." Existing in this moment, for Dillon, "[is] not escapist but rather politically and culturally activist and a refusal to simply disappear" (236). Dillon's use of "parallel" here illustrates how the perspectival difference animated by distinct worldviews indexes the same event differently. In "Terminal Avenue," Wil affirms in this moment an alternative moral, legal, and economic order represented by the potlatch—one that foregrounds his family's humanity against the state's regime of dehumanization, one that honours Indigenous futurity at the very moment when agents of the state seek to enact his demise.[10] His memory focuses on his father in ceremony, defying the surveillance planes overhead: "His father puts on his button blanket, rests it solemnly on his shoulders. He balances on the boat with the ease of someone who's spent all his life on the water. He does a twirl, when he reaches the bow of the speedboat and the button blanket opens, a navy lotus. The abalone buttons sparkle when they catch the light. [His wife is] laughing as he poses. He dances, suddenly inspired, exuberant" (546). The energy of the depiction and the pronouns employed stress the father's agency, and the sensuousness of Robinson's diction foregrounds the multi-modal interactions of sea, wind, sun, and sky. Contrasting the sterile tiles of Surrey Central Station and the robotic advance of the "sexless and anonymous" Peace Officers moving "like a machine" (541), Robinson depicts Wil's father dancing his full humanity, honouring relations with his family, the land, the sea, and other-than-human kin—significantly in the present tense, implying a sense of continuance.[11]

Whereas "Terminal Avenue" depicts the violent clash between the exchange economy of patriarchal capitalism and the gift economy of the Haisla potlatch, Robinson's "Queen of the North" depicts members of the Haisla community already mired in a context of economic disparity. "[S]ymbolized by the history and continuing presence of the Alcan Aluminum smelter in Kitimat," "[i]ndustrial capitalism" constitutes, for settler scholar Cara Fabre, "the mechanism that sustains colonization and residential schooling" in Robinson's work (12).[12] The worldview imposed on the Haisla community through residential schooling[13] and other colonial policies such as the potlatch ban not only reifies exchange economics but also complicates the meaning of the gift, causing it to signify differently. As Armstrong argues in relation to the Syilx gift economy, the capitalist perversion of giving only "in order to get something back" contaminates the gift itself. "Queen of the North" centres on two acts of gift giving, neither of which appears to be legible as an instantiation of the Haisla gift economy: one involves "gifts" given to the protagonist, Karaoke, in order to buy her silence regarding ongoing sexual abuse by her uncle, and the other involves her "gift" to her abuser of clotted menstrual fluid presented as an aborted fetus in effort to halt the abuse and punish its perpetrator.[14] In the first example, Uncle Josh exploits gift giving as a coercive instrument designed to mask and sustain victimization, and in the second, while intervening creatively in such victimization, Karaoke draws symbolically from the anti-futurity of intergenerational death as a disciplinary action that rests uneasily against theorizations of Indigenous gift economies offered by Armstrong and Kuokkanen. The gift, in "Queen of the North," is denied the capacity to express "how to be human" because the context is conditioned by Indigenous dispossession, patriarchal capitalism, and intergenerational trauma. Economic exchange has been reified as the normative terrain of existence in ways that constrain the gift's signifying resonance. "[L]and and bodies are commodified as capital under settler colonialism and are naturalized as objects for exploitation," argues Michi Saagiig Nishnaabeg theorist Leanne Betasamosake Simpson, which is why "sexual violence has to be theorized and analyzed as vital, not supplemental, to discussions of colonial dispossession" (As We 41).

The Syilx expression for giving only to receive—"swallower . . . of giving"—proves to be pertinent to "Queen of the North," in which consumption symbolizes how exchange can exacerbate vulnerability to violence. In the story's first depiction of sexual violation, the mouth is associated with the satiation of individualistic desire as Karaoke, still young enough to be watching *Sesame Street*, explains that "When it's over he'll have treats for me. It's like when the dentist gives me extra suckers for not crying, not even when it really hurts" (190). The connection between transactional gift giving and the simile of the dentist registers a tension between appearance and reality; because of the horrific imbalance of the exchange, the reader wonders whether Karaoke, and not the treats, is actually being consumed. Later in the story, Robinson returns to images of consumption in an exchange between Karaoke and a "middle-aged red-headed man in a business suit" (206). Like Uncle Josh, described as having "perfect pouty lips and bleached white teeth" (186), this man has "teeth so perfect" that Karaoke wonders "if they [are] dentures. No, probably caps. I bet he [takes] exquisite care of his teeth" (208). The exchange occurs at a powwow as Karaoke is making fry bread to raise money for Helping Hands. Although she tells the man that she has made her "last batch" and is therefore done for the day, he "slap[s] a twenty-dollar bill on the table" and insists that she "[m]ake another" (207). As she objects, he places "five twenty-dollar bills on the table" (207), betraying confidence in his entitlement to her labour, which she begrudgingly supplies.[15] Because the baking is for charity, the performative "overpayment" seems to be designed by the man to be a type of gift, yet that gift is laden with an expectation of repayment. Robinson lays bare the sexualized nature of his intentions when he asks, "'How should I eat these?'" After thinking to herself "With your mouth, asshole," Karaoke explains, "'Put some syrup on them, or jam, or honey. Anything you want,'" to which he replies "'Anything?'" and stares "deep into [her] eyes" (208). The innuendo implicated in his sexually charged use of "'Anything?'" betrays a sense of entitlement not only to Karaoke's labour but also to her body, which he eroticizes through his gaze—"he was still standing there, watching" (208)—and exoticizes through his expectations regarding Indigenous femininity. After inquiring "'Are you Indian then?'" (207) and "'Why're you so pale?'" he asks Karaoke to "'shake [her] hair out of that baseball cap'" and insists that "'You should keep it down at all times'" (209). Here economic, generational, and gendered privilege is catalyzed by white settler entitlement, manifesting in the man's expressed claim to her body and his desire for that body to conform to his imaginings of sexually available Indigenous womanhood.

In these ways, "Queen of the North" dramatizes how economic disparities produced by capitalism inform vulnerabilities to exploitation that come to be exacerbated by exchange itself. And readers cannot help but recognize the gendered nature of this process, as evidenced by the man's symbolic consumption of Karaoke (whose sweat has dripped into the batter that he is eating [207]), by Uncle Josh's efforts to purchase her silence,[16] and by the ominous implications of her mother's economic dependence. Twice during the story, Karaoke implies her mother's knowledge of the abuse. First, in the midst of an argument, Karaoke wonders "what she'd do if I came out and said *what we both knew*. Probably have a heart attack. Or call me a liar" (196; emphasis added). Later, when she acts on a plausible suspicion that her uncle was abused in residential school and confronts him by saying grace "out loud" at the breakfast table, Karaoke opens her eyes to find that

> Mom was staring at me. From her expression *I knew that she knew*. I thought she'd say something then, but we ate breakfast in silence.
> "Don't forget your lunch," she said.
> She handed me my lunch bag and went up to her bedroom. (213; emphasis added)

When I teach this story, this scene never fails to elicit condemnation from students, who react strongly to what they perceive as the mother's failure to protect her daughter. Although I have no interest in exonerating the mother, it is crucial to recognize that Robinson takes considerable care to illustrate how her capacity to parent is constrained by economic conditions, leaving her reliant on Josh for both financial support and child care. Whereas Josh "dresse[s] his long, thin body in clothes with expensive labels—no Sears or Kmart for him," Karaoke's mother is "broke" (186). When Karaoke asks for the coveted Barbie Doll speedboat for Christmas, her mother declares it "a toss-up between school supplies and paying bills, or wasting . . . money on something I'd get sick of in a few weeks" (186), leaving the door open for Josh to purchase the toy as an exchange commodity masquerading as a gift.[17] The point here is not to imply that the mother is blameless but to recognize that the economic and gender inequities embedded within capitalist exchange conspire to compromise relations between mother and daughter and to exacerbate the vulnerability of each to exploitation. Furthermore, the reification of exchange economics as natural and inevitable within the community depicted in the story causes the gift to signify differently, becoming a gift that is not a gift, as epitomized by Uncle Josh and the man at the powwow. The mother's statement "'Don't forget your lunch'" therefore becomes symptomatic of the gift's contamination: the gift of a "lunch bag" registers as so inadequate a gesture of support, given the profundity of Karaoke's disclosure, that it seems the gift can no longer nourish and nurture—it has become that which it was not.[18]

With relation to masculinities, Robinson's depictions demonstrate how economically dominant men can conscript exchange in campaigns to satiate their predatory appetites. Utterly divorced from the sacred erotic celebrated in Gregory Scofield's poetry above, "Queen of the North" depicts intimate encounters that are assaultive and extractive (to borrow Justice's terms), corrupting sexual intimacy into violation.[19] Here we see masculinities untethered to community, to reciprocity, to roles and responsibilities—masculinities that bely the agentive vulnerability championed by Scofield and Simpson in the previous chapter, functioning conversely to coerce vulnerability in others. Furthermore, Robinson's work illuminates the deterritorializing nature of such predation. These assaults fracture and fragment the humanity of Karaoke, alienating her from her full, embodied self, as evident in her response to the "gift" of the speedboat toy: "My mouth smiled" (187). Her mouth, the instrument of not only taste but also speech, no longer expresses her emotional reality; it is alienated as a tool similar to the alienated body of Nitotem in Louise Halfe's poem discussed in Chapter 2. Directly after this exchange, Robinson cuts to a scene of Karaoke herself engaging in lateral violence in a group attack against a lone female victim: "I want to say I'm not part of it, but that's my foot hooking her ankle and tripping her while Ronny takes her down with a blow to the temple" (188). Again Karaoke's body acts in a manner divorced from subjectivity and will. The point here is that violent and predatory masculinities assault her integrity; they work toward her deterritorialization by *dis*integrating her embodied, emotional, and cognitive self, on the one hand, and by disrupting her integration into the kinship community, on the other, by contaminating relations with her mother, sister, and uncle. These acts of deterritorialization, I contend, are embroiled with what Robinson reveals to be assaults on the integrity of the gift, as it functions within the Haisla gift economy.

## SIMULATING PATRIARCHY, REIFYING EXCHANGE

Like "Queen of the North," Robinson's novel *Blood Sports* portrays a contemporary social terrain in which exchange appears to be ubiquitous. The novel focuses on the life of economically disenfranchised protagonist Tom Bauer as it is thrown into disarray by the arrival of his wealthy, sociopathic older cousin Jeremy, who moves into the small apartment that Tom shares with his alcoholic mother in Vancouver. The story moves back and forth between Tom's adolescence—the period when Tom is tormented by Jeremy in efforts to force his compliance with an elaborate system of masculine control orchestrated via drug money, horror films, performative sexualization, and sadistic violence—and his early adulthood, the novel's temporal present, in which he, his common-law partner Paulie, and their infant daughter Melody are kidnapped by a former business partner seeking to extort from Jeremy "hundreds of thousands of dollars" (194). Tom's struggles to break free from his cousin's influence in the novel's earlier time frame mirror his efforts to escape the physical prison in the later one, with symbolic resonance in each case to his longing for liberation from the heteropatriarchal expectations of Jeremy's performative hypermasculinity. Jeremy models a virile individualist masculinity built upon violence that is highly visible and productive of social capital within the novel's dominant milieu; Tom, conversely, appears to be both incapable and undesirous of accessing such levers of legible masculinity. In these ways, the novel considers how exchange economics come to be naturalized over other modes of sociality in contemporary Canadian society and the impact of such naturalization on gender, this time through the depiction of white settlers rather than Indigenous characters. I read Robinson's novel as an extended rumination not on Indigenous *experiences* per se but on the necessity of revitalizing Indigenous *values*—in particular, Indigenous ethics of the gift—to liberate even mainstream society from economic and gender imperatives that destroy lands and relationships.

Robinson describes *Blood Sports* as "an homage to the original *Hansel and Gretel*, the version in which Hansel uses a finger bone from a previous victim to convince the witch he's still too skinny to eat" (279). Robinson is fascinated by the relationship between appearance and reality, particularly how economic conditions come to be treated as inevitable and ongoing—as *real*. She dramatizes concerns that such conditions might be based on illusion as Tom wanders the streets of Vancouver's Downtown Eastside suffering from amnesia, telling himself when confronted by others "Wonder if they're real. . . . Ask, 'are you real?' just in case you are standing on the sidewalk staring back at nothing" (144). His anxiety about the reliability of his perceptions is then seemingly dismissed by a character, identified only as "Eyepatch," who insists, "Don't get hung up on what's real or not real. . . . That's just another straight jacket'" (144). This directive anticipates my central concerns in this section. Robinson's novel interrogates not only how structural inequities embedded within capitalist exchange are based on myths and illusions ("what's . . . not real") but also how the coercive engines of reification and naturalization condition us not to question their veracity ("don't get hung up on [it]"); furthermore, this process quarantines and contains (like a "straight jacket"), delimiting our capacity to identify otherwise, including within the arena of gender. To be clear, I am suggesting that *Blood Sports* not only denies the legitimacy of systems of power such as economic exchange and heteropatriarchy by exposing them to be based upon illusion but also, just as importantly, makes legible to readers the socializing processes through which such illusory systems come to be treated as *real*, thereby illuminating the processes of social engineering through which oppressed characters such as Tom are conditioned to accept their marginalization—and, often, the suffocating prescriptions of gender that they inherit.

In *Simulations*, postmodern theorist Jean Baudrillard explains that "Simulation . . . is the generation by models of a real without origin in reality: a hyperreal. The territory no longer precedes the map, nor survives it. Henceforth, it is the map that precedes the territory—Precession of Simulacra" (2). As Baudrillard is aware, the conditions of settler colonialism lay bare the politicized nature of the hyperreal.[20] The settler colonial project of Indigenous elimination works first by imagining *the Indian* and then by imagining the Indian's inevitable demise through "benevolent" absorption or "tragic" obliteration.[21] As Vizenor argues, "The simulation of the *indian* is the absence of real natives—the contrivance of the other in the course of dominance" (vii). Indians are the copy without an original, simulations that bear critical consequences because their proliferation and coercive application serve to naturalize conditions of oppression as inevitable rather than as consequences of policies, actions, and attitudes. In relation to masculinities, these are the imaginings of an "impossibly masculine race" critiqued by Choctaw scholar Brian Klopotek (251) that inform the stereotypes of "masculindians" discussed in Chapter 1. The precession of settler colonial simulacra constructs the Canadian nation-state as natural and enduring; patrilineal nuclear family social structures as natural and enduring; extractive capitalism and exchange economics as natural and enduring. Meanwhile living Indigenous Peoples are simulated as no longer natural, anachronistic, and fated for absorption or elimination. Robinson mobilizes stylistic innovations[22] throughout *Blood Sports* not simply to expose the inaccessibility of the real but also to track the processes through which simulacra come to be wielded in the authorization of one worldview over another—particularly as relates to gender and economics. As such, *Blood Sports* alerts readers to the possibility of interpreting both reality and its representations in other ways via worldviews that settler colonialism has placed under erasure; Robinson arms readers with weapons to invigorate other ways of inhabiting space, of engaging in social relations, of expressing and experiencing gender.

The third chapter of *Blood Sports*, entitled "Jag," uncannily illustrates the "successive phases of the image" through which Baudrillard's precession of simulacra unfolds (11). The chapter consists of transcripts to home movies taken by Jeremy, which Tom's mother, Christa, entrusted to a private investigator in the hope of lengthening Jeremy's prison sentence and thereby protecting herself and her son from his violence. Baudrillard's first and most naive phase of the image—"it is the reflection of a basic reality" (11)—is evident in the premise of Christa's enterprise: that films can provide evidence for an extrarepresentational *reality* of illegal activity and thereby convince legal authorities of Jeremy's criminal culpability. His performativity as "filmmaker" then implies the second phase of the image—"it masks and perverts a basic reality" (11). For example, after the taping has concluded for a homemade pornographic film and the performers appear to have passed out, the transcript reads thus: "From the camera angle, it appears as if [Jeremy] suddenly and repeatedly stabs [one actor], but he stabs beside her. Mr. Rieger makes sound effects for the knife entering her stomach and for agonized screaming" (73).[23] Here the private investigator attempts to read back across perspectival manipulations toward an unmediated reality, with the "basic reality" principle remaining intact. He intuits a disjuncture between the appearance of violence and a supposed truth—"but he stabs beside her." Baudrillard's third phase of the image—"it masks the *absence* of a basic reality" (11)—is implied by the form of the chapter itself: transcripts to lost recordings, copies of copies. Despite Christa's desire to trace the films back to a tangible core of criminality and the private investigator's desire to make that "reality" legible through written language, the endeavour is futile. In the letter to Detective Pritchard with which the chapter begins, Christa writes, "George seemed like such a nice private investigator, and he had such lovely offices. Honestly, he charged so much money to keep the tapes in his safe, I never thought he'd go out of business!" (61). Readers are aware from the outset that the videos are lost, that the private investigator is absent, and that appearances ("seemed") have not yielded predicted outcomes ("I never thought"). Unable to marshal representation in the service of verifiable *proof*, Christa is left grasping at the extrarational: "I *pray* that you find a way to keep my nephew in prison" (61). Ultimately, the reader is led to ruminate on Baudrillard's fourth and final phase of the image: "[I]t bears no relation to any reality whatever: it is its own pure simulacrum" (11).

*Blood Sports* illuminates the consequential nature of the precession of simulacra by demonstrating how copies without originals come to be treated as authentic, thereby conditioning expectations about behaviour and worth—processes exacerbated under conditions of settler colonialism. Two areas in which such processes become legible in Robinson's novel involve the naturalization of exchange economics over the logic of the gift, which I will discuss in the subsequent section, and the naturalization of heteropatriarchy over other models of social organization through the valorization of the nuclear family, to which I now turn.

Heteropatriarchy itself, of course, is a simulacrum, yet its naturalization undergirds the social infrastructure of settler colonial societies, including the urban Canadian setting depicted in *Blood Sports*. Robinson alerts her readers to the specious foundations of such infrastructure through two extreme examples of patriarchal violence located spatially in the underbelly of the nuclear family home. In the first example, Tom's eventual partner Paulie struggles to liberate herself from a familial setting in which male and female offspring are valued disparately: "[B]orn last . . . after three brothers . . . [Paulie] never got any birthday parties" (278). "[A]ll the boys [got] a new car when they graduated," Paulie explains. "Nothing fancy. Toyota hatchbacks, Honda Civics. . . . The only thing keeping me in that house going to school like a good little girl was the promise of a new car to take off in. Instead, I got a purse and a set of granny underwear with the days of the week embroidered on the front" (172). The ludicrous imbalance between gifts of vehicles for male siblings and "a purse" and "granny underwear" for Paulie betrays pedagogical intentionality by the parents, with feminine identity being constrained within the household to prescriptive sexual standards implied by "the days of the week"—standards that Paulie confesses strategically to placating by "going to school like a good little girl." The double standard embedded within her parents' teachings plays out in the vehicular mobility afforded to the brothers compared with Paulie's subjection in the passenger seat to her father's sexist victim blaming: "Dad used to drive me down the worst alleys in East Hastings to show me the junkie prostitutes and the people who feed off them.[24] This is what sin gets you. . . . You are going to end up on skid row if you fuck boys" (179). Like the insidious pedagogies of gender wielded in residential schools (and discussed in Chapter 2), Paulie's father's lessons displace responsibility for sexual violence onto women as the corrupting cause of their own violation while obfuscating the culpability of predatory men and the structures of exchange through which they often operate. The undeniably patriarchal social engineering depicted here is exposed by Robinson to be built on illusion—not just Christian platitudes of "just desserts" and "God's will" but also quotidian posturings of familial functionality and cohesion. The "two-storey" Mazenkowski home presents an outward face of affluence and stability, yet Paulie's alcoholic parents routinely binge in its basement so as not to damage their antiques when their drinking sessions inevitably erupt in violence. Robinson implies that the heteropatriarchal family unit, modelled by the Mazenkowskis, is built upon a foundation of voluntary narcosis (drunkenness), hidden away in the symbolic subconscious of the home. The hypermisogyny that conditions Paulie's experience is betrayed as a simulacrum but one with direct and damaging implications for her subjectivity. And in case readers have missed the colonial implications of this process, Robinson reminds them with the Mazenkowskis' address: 1492 Empress Drive.

Whereas the Mazenkowski home betrays the heteropatriarchal nuclear family unit as something of a façade, a second basement in the novel illustrates even more graphically the role of such simulations in the reproduction of violence—precession of simulacra. When Tom, Paulie, and Melody are kidnapped, they are held captive in a basement prison that resembles "'a daycare or something'" or "'[m]aybe a play room.'" It boasts a "mural [of] . . . happy bunnies" on one wall and is separated from the rest of the basement by "thick, solid [metal bars] painted the same colour as the floor, pastel green, a colour beloved of old hospitals and mental wards" (263–64). The room's institutional feel reinforces its socially reproductive purpose: like hospitals, mental wards, and daycares, prisons are designed to discipline particular forms of docile subjects. In this case, the disciplinary program is expressly patriarchal insofar as the prison has been constructed to impose the unencumbered law of the father. As Tom's kidnapper explains,

"I helped a friend build this place. . . . He believed in the End of Days. But his wife got sick of milking cows and plucking chickens while they waited for the Apocalypse, so she took his three kids and moved back to Surrey. My friend turned the basement into his own little prison. Snatched his kids first. Caught his wife in the parking lot when she came to pick up the kids. Not one person noticed they were gone.

"Then one day he went out to get some firewood just over there beside the stream. Tree fell on him. He died. By the time I dropped in to ask him a favour, his wife and the three kids were puddles of fat and piles of bone. Took forever to get the stink out." (196)

Unwilling to endure affronts to his authority, the husband in this story manufactures a model of domesticity designed to condition obedience while constraining the possibilities for self-expression within an imposed nuclear family paradigm. Although the nuclear family has been naturalized to some degree as a structural building block of Canadian society, here it is exposed as unnatural, contingent on masculine violence, and perversely oriented toward false futurity. The daycare theme of the "play room" might indeed suggest social reproduction, but the father's zealous belief in "the End of Days" locks the family into a horizon of death that plays out in the collateral losses of the wife and children after the father's happenstance demise. This calamity begins in fiction, through the story of "the End of Days," which conditions particular modes of behaviour and relations that come to be entrenched disciplinarily via the basement prison, which subsequently leads to collective death—a self-fulfilling prophecy, precession of simulacra, map preceding the territory. In this way, Robinson reveals how power dynamics built upon illusion manifest brutally in the lives of her characters. As Anishinaabe writer Kateri Akiwenzie-Damm asserts, also in relation to misogyny and violence, "These ways of thinking don't just remain in people's fantasies without having any impact in the real world. They do impact our reality, they absolutely do" ("Affirming Protectorship" 181).

The spatial orientation of these two contexts of violence does not appear to be accidental: the drunkenness associated with the Mazenkowski basement implies that the family's patriarchal configuration is built upon a narcotic illusion rather than anything inherent in the human condition, and the layout of the basement prison extends this critique to suggest that heteropatriarchy's reification is intentional and strategic rather than a simple accident of history. Furthermore, the prison resembles not only a daycare, hospital, or mental ward but also a theatre. With brick walls on three sides and a mural on the back wall, the prison becomes a proscenium stage upon which roles are coerced and performed. The bars mark an imaginary fourth wall as Paulie and Tom are directed to conform to expectations insisted on by their kidnappers while their daughter is reared under the surveillance of masculine control (the kidnappers being violent men). Heteropatriarchy is a copy without an original that is treated as authentic, enforced strategically and violently, and then performed as the norm against which behaviours and identities are valued. And, as the fate of the home's original occupants suggests, the consequences of delimiting gender knowledges in this way are catastrophic.

## MASCULINITY AND THE RESILIENCE OF THE GIFT

Given the meticulous tracking of the relationship between economics and gender in *Blood Sports*, Tom proves to be an intriguing case study because, though he appears to endorse the legitimacy of the dominant system of economic exchange, he simultaneously resists conforming to the dominant gender mores of heteropatriarchy. I argue in what follows that such resistance is made possible by his resilient affection for the logic of the gift. Although the gift economy is seemingly overwhelmed in the novel by the pressure of economic exchange, Tom holds fast to the gift *as an ethic*—even in the hypercapitalist context of the drug trade—which enables him to perform masculinity in ways that defy dominant models. Whether conceived as reward, punishment, or repayment, indebtedness is a primary engine of action throughout the novel. In fact, the kidnapping that forms the novel's structural backbone is based on debt.[25] "'[Jeremy]

Rieger owes me a lot of money,'" explains Firebug. "'We're talking hundreds of thousands of dollars, Tom'" (194). The novel catalogues myriad attempts to even scores. For example, Jeremy enlists Paulie to seduce his younger cousin in order to avenge the latter's theft of his "silver 1992 Jaguar XJS coupe" (153). Jeremy describes his reasoning in this way: "'[P]ayback's a bitch and you are her stand-in'" (174). And to avenge a beating that left him with a broken leg, Willy Baker and his brother attack Paulie's mother according to a logic of "tooth for a tooth, leg for a leg" (163). Unsurprisingly, each of these events prompting "payback" is itself a response to perceived prior violations—stealing the Jag is imagined as revenge for Jeremy's sadistic intrusions into Tom's life, and the beating of Baker is conceived as punishment for his involvement in the theft—thereby implying the improbability of tracing instances of violent exchange back to originary sources. The infinite regression of indebtedness,[26] combined with the novel's spectacularly perverse instances of "repayment,"[27] implies the illusory nature of exchange economics: like heteropatriarchy, it is its own pure simulacrum.

The specific terms of Tom's indebtedness are defined by Jeremy, who declares, "'I'll help with rent and food and bills and all you have to do is one itty-bitty thing. . . . I want you to be good.'" "'Define "good,"'" Tom responds. "'You listen to me when I tell you what to do. No arguing. No debates. No whining'" (78). Jeremy equates paying for "rent and food and bills" with the vague behavioural imperative of "be[ing] good," which he elaborates as requiring unquestioned obedience. The scene dramatizes both the improbability of equivalent values in incidents of exchange between disparately empowered parties and how systems of indebtedness proclaimed to foster the return to balance ultimately exacerbate subordination. Tom certainly receives something of value here—financial stability amid the tumultuous terrain of poverty—but what is claimed in return is acquiescence to perpetual indebtedness, which imprisons him in a relational structure designed for his disempowerment. The extent to which Tom is affected by such coercion is evident later in the novel when, abandoned in the forest and handcuffed to a steering wheel, he contemplates that "[I] could get [Paulie and Melody] killed if [I do] something stupid. [I] could get them killed if [I do] nothing.

[I] could sit here and *be good* and hope for the best" (124; emphasis added). The reiteration of Jeremy's vague imperative to "be good," even under conditions in which Tom's "life literally depend[s] on it" (124), suggests how effectively Tom has been convinced of the legitimacy of indebtedness as arbitrated by his cousin.[28]

*Blood Sports* depicts graphic violence, physical and psychological torture, sexual domination and rape, and sadistic punishment that borders on the grotesque. Yet among the most perplexing aspects of the novel is not the brutality of its depictions but that in their wake its protagonist remains convinced of his indebtedness to his sociopathic tormentor. Tom endures various forms of humiliation and abuse by Jeremy: his long blue hair is shorn, his favourite clothes are burned, and he is forced to lose his virginity on camera with a sex worker; Jeremy strategically seduces the woman with whom Tom is infatuated in order to enflame the latter's jealousy; and Jeremy tortures him with such ferocity at one point that Tom actually "start[s] to believe" that he will "die" (153). However, despite all of this, Tom confides in a friend, "Jer was an asshole. . . . But he was there for us when no one else could be bothered. I owe him a lot" (50). I consider the concession "I owe him a lot" terrifying because it suggests that Tom ultimately concedes to the system of exchange set up for him by his (tor)mentor—it suggests that this system registers to him as legitimate. Tom's friend's response—"Fair *enough*" (50; emphasis added)—is illuminating because it works backhandedly to draw into question the very possibility of fairness within contexts of such inequality, reading less as agreement than as concession to perpetual conditions of unfairness—conditions that Tom ultimately seems to accept.

Somewhat surprisingly, Tom's concession of indebtedness does not carry with it a sense of obligation to conform to the model of masculinity that Jeremy demands. Given that Tom lacks various forms of social capital boasted by his cousin—from wealth to good looks to confidence to the capacity to wield violence—it would make sense were he to envy Jeremy and seek to emulate his behaviours. After all, whereas Tom confesses to being "invisible" and "under the radar in high school," "Jer stuck out" (176, 52, 166). When she first met him, Paulie describes Jeremy wearing a sleek black Armani suit, his shirt casually unbuttoned at the top. Light tan on his face except for a faint outline of sunglasses. His dark brown hair had that just-stepped-off-my-yacht, didn't spend a lot of time (yes, I did) on my hair look. . . . He even looked good nose to nose. . . . Jer had beautiful skin, the kind you want to lick when it glistens. Ripped body, sinews moving as we moved. I couldn't stop touching him. . . . His hair, his muscles, his skin. (166–67)

Despite the siren pull of Jeremy's masculine visibility, Tom actively resists his teachings about gender. Tom eschews the trappings of material wealth that his cousin flaunts; he remains contemptuous of the "rotating series" of yuppie "friends" by whom Jeremy is surrounded; he shows no desire for the dominative sexual relationships that his cousin boasts with women; and he rejects the hypermasculine violence so central to Jeremy's authority, autonomy, and self-worth. If the goal of the social engineering enterprise is to remake Tom in Jeremy's image, then *Blood Sports* exposes it to be an unmitigated failure. However, if the goal is not to make Tom into Jeremy but to consolidate the latter's authority by instilling in the former a sense of obligatory, ongoing subservience (and a belief that this is more or less just), then it appears to succeed. Robinson demonstrates how the semiotics of luxury and power mobilized to promote individualist notions of masculine dominance in mainstream culture do not, in fact, propel individual marginalized men such as Tom to the realm of the privileged elite but work, more insidiously, to normalize their oppression. The novel thus depicts—I think courageously—the potential costs of reifying capitalist fictions of the neutral and impartial market as *the* system to which marginalized men (as well as others) must conform to access power.

But why, when Tom so candidly consents to his indebtedness (and therefore the system of exchange for which his abuser stands), is he able to resist conforming to Jeremy's model of masculinity? Jeremy repeatedly pressures Tom to engage in acts legible according to dominant rubrics of hypermasculinity (e.g., having sex with a sex worker[29] and shooting Firebug at the novel's end); Jeremy even inscribes masculine violence on Tom's body, "lower[ing] the cigarette" until "the tip touches . . . skin" (153). Yet Tom remains resolute in enacting his gender identity in ways that deviate from his cousin's example and, I argue, are liberated in significant ways from settler heteropatriarchy. The discrepancies between the cousins' performances of masculinity are particularly evident in relation to sex and intimacy. Within Jeremy's hyperindividualist worldview, sex bears meaning solely in relation to his own pleasure, while sexual partners are dehumanized as vehicles for his own gratification. Robinson portrays this gruesomely as Jeremy assaults Paulie in a restaurant bathroom, "rub[bing] the head of his cock along [her] jaw," his "mouth opened jaw-cracking wide as if he was the one pinned to the floor" (173). His miming of the actions that he seeks to menace from his victim dramatizes the horrific selfishness of rape: the feedback loop of his "jaw-cracking wide" mouth in relation to his weaponized penis indicates how the encounter is all about him while Paulie's humanity and free will are constrained and disavowed.

Tom's relationship with his own sexuality could scarcely be more different. Although Tom has been infatuated with Paulie for years at the time, he resists her invitation to join her in the bath tub when she is detoxing in his apartment: "Lengthy, awkward pause where he dropped his eyes to the floor. 'You don't have to do that, Paulie. . . . I don't need a pity fuck'" (175). Whereas sex for Jeremy is either transactional or forced, Tom refuses the inevitability of sexuality's embeddedness within systems of exchange. As he explains,

> "When me and Mom moved to Vancouver, we didn't know anybody. . . . We didn't have anything. She hooked up with any guy that would give us a roof and regular grub. The guys that would take us in were always these assholes who treated her like a blow-up doll. I hated them so much it felt like I was breathing hate, like it was running through my veins. You're hot, Paulie. You know you're hot. But . . . I dunno. If all you need is a crash pad and company, then stay." (175)

For Tom, sexuality is not an exchange commodity within an individualist habitat of scarcity but a sensual opportunity for intimate generosity.[30] I believe this to be made possible by what I will call his *resilient commitment to the logic of the gift*, even in contexts conditioned by capitalist exchange. This commitment becomes legible to readers via his ethics of generosity, protectorship, and forgiveness, which inform his embodiment of masculinities that I interpret as beyond heteropatriarchy.

Tom's generosity is showcased humorously by his method of conflict resolution when a group of "skater kids" turns the downstairs apartment into "a skate park" (47). Unlike his friend Mike, who wants to "go down" and threaten the kids with violence, Tom opts to arrange with his neighbours the "slightly out of sync" playing of Celine Dion's "The Power of Love" "on three different stereo systems" in the building (47). "Any of the divas are skater-repellents," he explains, "but no one can touch Celine" (47). The scene provides much-needed comic relief, yet a comparison of Mike's and Tom's actions suggests that there is more to it. Whereas Mike escalates the conflict by leveraging the threat of masculine violence[31]—yelling "'I'll kick your ass into tomorrow, you little punk!' . . . his face going heart-attack red" (48)—Tom deflects the youths' postured animosity with humour, intentionally misinterpreting their jeers as expressions of affection for Dion's music (and thereby aligning himself with performative femininity). The point here is that liberation from the yokes of hypermasculinity and individualism enables Tom to place himself in the skaters' shoes, reminding Mike, "Five years ago, everyone was calling us the punks. Now we're the grown-ups" (48). "They're good kids," Tom explains. "They're just acting out" (49). His affirmation of common humanity with the skaters reveals that the two groups are not truly in conflict, which resonates with the Syilx strategies for consensus building articulated above by Armstrong. Tom strives "to hear" and "understand" views that on the surface appear to be contrary to his own, recognizing the bridging of "oppositional dynamics" across generations as a "responsibility" with community-building dimensions.

Tom's adherence to the logic of the gift is further elaborated in his efforts to protect Paulie and their daughter. Akiwenzie-Damm argues that "We have to reclaim what's good about men having a protective role, being the protectors in the community. I believe that's a legitimate male role and a positive role that helps our families and our communities to stay safe and be healthy" ("Affirming Protectorship" 182). Within a context conditioned by heteropatriarchy, however, gendered protectorship—as Akiwenzie-Damm is aware—runs the risk of denying women agency and naturalizing male authority over others.[32] It also risks emphasizing the identity of the protector over responsibilities to the protected. In *Blood Sports*, Robinson crafts Tom's acts of protectorship, however, in ways that guard against the perpetuation of patriarchy. In one instance, while on respite from "the oven they [call] their apartment," Tom allows Paulie and Melody, who have fallen asleep, to slumber "as long as he [can]" before "walk[ing] them home and, despite Paulie's protests, right up to their apartment," even though he is late for work (40–41). In a second, as the family travels on a bus "packed with kids with snowboards and skis[,] . . . [and] Mel clutche[s] Paulie in the front seats, Tom [stands] over them so the skis and snowboards [won't] fall and hit them" (111). And in a third, while he and Paulie are watching Canada Day fireworks from a dinghy on the ocean, Tom "pull[s] out a glow stick . . . lean[s] over . . . lift[s] up Paulie's hair . . . [and] snap[s] it in place around her neck. 'So that the boats will see us,'" he says (243). The thread running through these examples is Tom's care for the safety of his loved ones without such vigilance being marshalled in the service of his own ego. Tom engages in these acts irrespective—rather than because—of how they will inform others' perceptions of him: in the first example, he deems being late for work of less importance than the safety of his loved ones—"Lucky Lou's won't fall apart without me" (40); in the second, he maintains his stance although it provokes others' ire—"Tom refused to move, even though he got dirty looks" (111); and in the third, he applies the glowsticks even though he and Paulie are in the early phase of their courtship and doing so risks making him appear overly safety conscious and thus potentially less attractive. Tom undertakes these actions not to look good, to claim authority, or to "win the girl" but out of commitment to others' well-being.

Unlike Tom, others in the novel have difficulty conceiving of a world in which self-interest is not the natural condition of being human. When he explains to his mother that Paulie has been "trying to help," for instance, "Her lips [become thin] and she [sits] up, ramrod straight. 'Herself. She was trying to help herself, Tommy'" (213). Christa's refusal to entertain the possibility of aid untethered to personal interest betrays an underlying denial of the logic of the gift. Acts identified in the novel as "forgiveness" trace the contours of such denial. After Jeremy tortures Tom in punishment for his theft of the Jag, he "opens his wallet and hands [Tom] some bills," declaring, "'I'm forgiving you, you dumbass'" (102). Within the individualist worldview shared by Jeremy and Christa, however, true forgiveness is an impossibility, as evident in Jeremy's elaboration: "'I'm giving you credit for balls. So I'm letting you off the hook. For now. But you're going to be good, Tom. If you fuck up again, I won't be so forgiving'" (102–03). Here the qualifiers "if" and "for now" constrain and then overturn the gesture of forgiveness, leading to further threats designed to sustain Tom's subordination. Through the lens of heteropatriarchy—signalled by the lauding of "balls"—forgiveness transforms into a coercive tool; if forgiveness, for Jeremy, is a species of "gift," then it is an "inalienable gift," according to Maussian logic, upholding the social standing of its giver and thereby his power over the receiver. In contrast, Tom, who I am arguing retains ethical attachment to the logic of the gift, is shown by Robinson to forgive differently. Significantly, his foremost act of forgiveness is narrated from the point of view of its recipient, implying its resonance beyond "the social identity of [its] original owner" (Willmott 14). Paulie writes in her atonement letter to Tom that "No one's forgiven me for anything. You are the first. I didn't even ask you to. You just did. It should feel better than it does. I guess. You are supposed to feel good when someone forgives you. Right? Maybe it's the newness that's weirding me out. Is that a word? Newness?" (179). Again Robinson's stylistic choices evocate: the letter cuts off at the word *newness* with neither a valediction nor an elaboration, leaving the reader with a sense of potentiality framed as a question. Forgiveness, as practised by Tom, is indeed "new" within the context of the novel because individualism, heteropatriarchy, and exchange economics have become so naturalized as to seem inevitable. Yet Tom forgives Paulie not because it will gain him favour but because it is what he understands her to need. He just does it. It is not a social play to gain power. It is what it purports to be.

## LIBERATORY MASCULINITIES BEYOND EXCHANGE

Kuokkanen argues that whereas "Markets are founded on the principle of scarcity . . . a gift economy is founded on abundance" (30). As Armstrong explains, the gift economy of the Syilx Nation nonetheless "has a lot to do with scarcity":

> In a land where there is not a lot of abundance, where the fragility of the ecosystem requires absolute knowledge and understanding that there must be care not to overextend our use of it[,] . . . we have developed a practice, a philosophy and a governance system . . . based on our understanding that we need to be always vigilant and aware of not over-using, not over-consuming the resources of our land, and that we must always be mindful of the importance of sharing and giving. (41)

Thus, the logic of the gift, while militating against constraint through the principle of mutual generativity, can survive and even flourish, according to Armstrong, amid seemingly inhospitable conditions. From a hyperindividualist perspective like that epitomized in the novel by Jeremy and Christa, conditions of scarcity seem likely to prompt the anxious policing of wealth rather than "mindful[ness]" about "sharing and giving" as modelled in Syilx, Haisla, and other Indigenous gift economies. Yet from the clutches of poverty in Vancouver's Downtown Eastside, Tom acts resolutely according to an ethic of generosity. Although he explicitly concedes to his own indebtedness, thereby acknowledging exchange economics and the naturalization of his own oppression via transactional violence, his behaviour remains expressive of other possibilities. Rather than allowing the reification of exchange to "swallow" and "destroy" the act of giving, Tom retains deviant and defiant affection for the logic of the gift, and therein lies his resurgent potential.

The majority of the critical writing on *Blood Sports* contends with the novel's refusal to portray characters identifiable as Indigenous and therefore the implications for the novel's study as Indigenous literature.[33] This has not been my interest in this chapter. Yet the novel's interrogation of the relationships among individualism, heteropatriarchy, and exchange economics is nonetheless instructive in this regard. "Transformation," according to Kuokkanen, "will require the dominant culture to change its values as well as the thinking and behaviour guided by those values" (161). Through her depiction of a relationship between two disparately empowered white settler cousins, Robinson exposes dangerous deficiencies in the dominant culture's thinking, behaviour, and values concerning gender and economics, and she offers alternatives that I contend are expressive of Haisla sensibilities through their valorization of the logic of the gift. Simpson argues that, "If we accept colonial permanence, . . . our rebellion can only take place within settler colonial thought and reality" (*As We* 153). *Blood Sports* is about thinking and living differently, about recognizing, cracking open, and breathing life into alternative ways of being in the world. By showing that individualism and economic exchange (as well as the gender system of heteropatriarchy with which they are embroiled) are neither natural nor inevitable through her concerns with simulation in the novel, Robinson opens up other possibilities, which I call *masculinities made possible by the logic of the gift*. I intend this not as a crude Marxist exercise in which understandings of gender constitute inevitable by-products of particular modes of production but as recognition of the mutually informing nature of gender and economics, legible as worldview. The enterprise of invigorating masculinities liberated from heteropatriarchy and attuned to Indigenous ways of knowing therefore means *thinking economy differently*. To radically reimagine "masculinity" requires efforts to unshackle the enterprise from individualism and the economics of exchange reified in settler colonial society. Tom's plight reveals both the difficulty and the urgency of this enterprise.

# 5. MASCULINITY AND KINSHIP

Just before I became a father, I asked my dad, "Do you have any advice?" . . . And he goes, "Three things: Listen to your elders. Listen to your kids. Take care of your fucking shit." —TERRANCE HOULE ("Deeper than a Blood Tie" 154)

And so I know that I like to write about men a lot. . . . I have three brothers, and I have two fathers, . . . and my best friends are men and they're beautiful men, gentle men, hard men, and men who are fathers and brothers themselves—so I think that that fellowship, that tribe of man medicine that I'm involved with all the time with the uncles I've adopted and me listening at their supper tables or over the phone or through e-mails. I'm grateful that I have that in my life. Yes. —RICHARD VAN CAMP ("Into the Tribe of Man" 184–85)

I n the short story "The Night Charles Bukowski Died," Tłı̨chǫ[1] author Richard Van Camp grapples with the perilous allure of seemingly *just* violence. Faced with the bullying of a mentally ill member of their dorm community, the story's narrator and a friend orchestrate a plan to "roll" Mikey's tormentor, thereby hoping to end the harassment while gifting Mikey with courage to stand up for himself in the future.[2] "Everybody in this dorm knows [Scott] bullies Mikey," the narrator laments, "but nobody does anything / Nobody" (34).[3] Through the use of stream of consciousness, Van Camp registers the intensity of the revulsion of the narrator at

147

this injustice as he stammers through a series of revenge fantasies: "I wanted Mikey to *take this take this* roar in his head take a black shotgun and light this whole dorm up just grab Scott gut peel and skin him and *go just go* til he hits the province line *and and . . .*" (32; emphasis added). The immediacy of the interior monologue form implies that the narrator believes genuinely in the righteousness of the plan: that by attacking Scott the young men will not only right a terrible wrong but also create conditions in which the mental illness that afflicts Mikey might be healed and "he will put his scream away" (33).[4] However, when the co-conspirators leap from the bushes and begin raining blows down on their antagonist, "Mikey just stands there . . . crying like a cat," repeating "I want to go home / I want to / go home I / want to go / home" (35–36). Never does he confront his oppressor with justified anger and achieve desired liberation. The story ends with Mikey crying into the narrator's chest with the narrative's frantic pace slowing—possibly in resignation or defeat— its final statement drawn out over seven lines:

> I
> throw
> back
> my
> head
> and
> roar (36)

I begin this final chapter with Van Camp's short story because it illuminates the ambivalence of *just* violence as a pillar of naturalized masculinity in contemporary North American society. The circular nature of the story—which begins with Mikey crying in the shower and ends with him crying in the narrator's arms and in which the failure of efforts to get Mikey to put "his scream away" is betrayed by the narrator's own climactic "roar"—suggests the inadequacy of violence as a liberatory instrument when the context of oppression is steeped in toxic masculinity. Rather than charting a pathway *out*, violence appears to lock the young men *in*, leading them to replicate the very behaviours that they purport to reject. When he recognizes that Mikey has not joined the attack, for instance, the narrator is outraged and uses language that echoes the bullying that he seeks to avenge: "Come on man MOVE! But Mikey just stands there. . . . [T]hen it hits me he's crying standing there stupid fucking RETARDED . . ." (35). The narrator's reaction, given Mikey's failure to conform to the desired model of masculine behaviour that the young men have been trying to instill in Mikey, is to deride and belittle—to "other"—him. Yet, even in light of manifest failures to escape toxic masculinity and to achieve something resembling "justice," Van Camp's story, in my reading, refuses straightforwardly to condemn the narrator's desire to intervene in this way. I refer to this as the ambivalence of *just* violence because it seems to me that, although fraught, the narrator's longing to marshal violence in a campaign to protect the vulnerable is portrayed as a very human response—if a naive one—to what the narrator in Van Camp's novel *The Lesser Blessed* (1996) calls "acts unforgiveable" (1).[5] As Van Camp told Sylvie Vranckx in an interview, "I can't stand bullies or when people are made to suffer so I enlist my gladiators to help in my fiction" ("'I Carve'"). His work, as a whole, shows remarkable sensitivity to the attractiveness of certain characteristics and behaviours that might stereotypically be coded "masculine" and be subject—in books like the present one—to critique, even as his work seeks to complicate heteropatriarchy and make room for alternative gender knowledges.[6] The confession of Van Camp's protagonist in *The Lesser Blessed* to feeling simultaneous attraction and revulsion to the hypermasculinity of a high school bully (who resembles Scott from the short story in many ways) is demonstrative of such even-handedness by the author: "I'd be a liar if I told you he didn't scare me, but something about guys like Darcy always intrigued me. I knew he had had his share of drugs, booze and fights. He was everything I wasn't. He was bad news, but still . . ." (36).

I turn to Van Camp's literary art here because it helps to address a limitation in this volume: my reluctance, thus far, to engage explicitly with the naturalized features of dominant masculinities in contemporary North American culture—what Billy-Ray Belcourt calls "the putative givenness" of dominant ideas about masculinity ("Can the Other"). In seeking to pursue radical alternatives to "common sense" masculinities—alternatives made possible by intimate generosity, by the logic of the gift, by what Ty P. Kāwika Tengan calls "embodied discursive action," and by other creative means—in *Carrying the Burden of Peace* I thereby risk disregarding experiences and perspectives that remain vital; I risk alienating Indigenous readers for whom masculinity takes on more tangible, explicit, and enduring constellations of forms;[7] I risk implying that all expressions of masculinity naturalized within dominant culture are negative (or antithetical to Indigenous resurgence) and that Indigenous persons who identify with such expressions are doomed to perpetuate heteropatriarchy.[8] Van Camp's writing provides nuances to these discussions, grappling with manhood and masculinity in ways that are celebratory and critical with the same stroke, greeting readers where they are on their journeys. It speaks not only to those invested in radically rethinking gender but also to those with more conventional gender understandings that veer toward the mainstream. "The Night Charles Bukowski Died," for example, plays on the reader's cultivated desire to witness the tormentor's comeuppance in a manner legible through codes of masculine heroism, but then it illuminates the potential for other ways of conceiving masculinities by implicating the reader in the failure of such heroism—"I want the bad guy to get his just desserts, but the narrator's roar shows that it's not so simple, so perhaps my desire here is part of the problem." The author explains this technique as "welcoming people with a stereotype": that is, getting their attention with something comfortable and familiar such as the stereotype of "Cowboys and Indians"; however, "keep reading," Van Camp says, "and I'll tell you stories about how an eagle has three shadows or how frogs are the keepers of rain. . . . There's magic here if you're willing to look past the stereotypes" ("Into" 186). And that magic is often concerned, in his work, with what it means to be a good man—a good lover, a good friend, a good father, son, uncle, and brother.

In this chapter, I examine the development of Van Camp's Dogrib/Tłįchǫ protagonist Larry Sole, from the novel *The Lesser Blessed*, who struggles to negotiate his place in an often hostile high school context in the fictional town of Fort Simmer, Northwest Territories, all the while engaging with, trying on, longing for, critiquing, and imagining through narrative various models of masculinity. Among the key tools to which he turns in this process of becoming is storytelling, and among the key ethical systems through which Van Camp arbitrates the legitimacy of Larry's steps along the way is kinship. As independent scholar Mareike Neuhaus argues, "Stories carry knowledge, but in order for them to do so they need to take shape; they have to be formed, crafted; otherwise the knowledge communicated in the stories remains but the memory in someone's mind rather than the collective memory that can be shared by a family, tribe, or people. So just how stories create and define relationships, hence performing kinship, is a vital question" (127). Larry employs storytelling to pursue imagined futures in which kinship is functional and enduring, and Van Camp embeds those stories within a novel that traces the parameters of relational ethics. In the shadow of unspeakable trauma and removed from his nation's traditional territory, Larry, like many characters discussed in this book, labours to develop and retain a sense of personal integrity while making accommodations in thought and behaviour to make possible his integration into potentially hostile social spaces. Mentorship regarding the viability of performances coded as "masculine" within the Fort Simmer high school community constitutes a crucial and volatile part of this process. Ultimately, I argue that prioritizing Tłįchǫ ethics of kinship causes particular expressions of masculinity to gain prominence, for Larry, while causing others to recede and exposing even others to be, in fact, anathema to his development, to his family's well-being, and to Tłįchǫ continuance and flourishing—some deterritorialize while others allow him to be who he is.

In the pages that follow, I first consider Van Camp's retelling of the Tłįchǫ creation story as a narrative tool for decoding the novel's perspectives on both gender and kinship, thereby picking up on discussions of ecologies of gender from Chapter 1. Then I examine depictions of Larry's father, whose performative dehumanization registers the tactical fracturing of bodily integrity, territorial continuance, and kinship relations in residential schools discussed in Chapter 2. In the following section, I consider Larry's Métis friend Johnny Beck as an alluring model of individualist hypermasculinity, resonant with the characterization of Jeremy from Eden Robinson's

*Blood Sports* discussed in Chapter 4. I conclude by reflecting on the generative power of intimacy as a decolonial ethic, as discussed in Chapter 3, through an analysis of Larry's ethics of kinship with his mother, his surrogate father Jed, and his beloved Juliet. In these ways, Van Camp's novel allows me to pick up a number of argumentative threads from throughout *Carrying the Burden of Peace* and to braid together possibilities for generative masculinities in relation to kinship. I begin, however, with a conversation between Larry and Johnny in which the former mobilizes creative artistry to comple-ment his limited cultural knowledge in order to welcome his friend into conditions of intimacy while simultaneously guarding from exposure vulnerable elements of his traumatic past.

## CREATION STORIES AND KINSHIP

"So tell me about being fool blood," he said.

I sat down. "Whattaya wanta know?"

He got up and handed me a cigarette. He was saving the joints till later.

"Well, what tribe are you? Chip? Cree?"

"Dogrib."

"I thought they were from around Yellowknife."

I got a little nervous. "Yeah."

"What's the scoop?"

"Well, Jed told me that our tribe came from a woman who gave birth to six puppies." I eyed him while I said that because I knew some people would laugh. He didn't, so I continued.

"Well, she had to live by herself in the woods so she could raise her pups. One day she left her hut so she could check her snares, and when she came home she could see human footprints in the snow and ashes."

"No shit," Johnny said.

"Yeah . . . so one day she went out like she was going to check her snares but she snuck back and watched her hut. She could hear her pups yapping like this: Yap! Yap! Then she could hear them laughing like children. After a while she could hear kids running around the hut and choo! Out from the hut run six kids, all naked."

"Whoah!" Johnny said.

"Yeah! So she watches them and they're playing in the snow all laughing and having a great time. She runs out of the bush and chases them back into the hut. They all make a run for the bag she used to leave them in. Three make it and turn back to pups. A girl and two boys don't. She catches them. They stay human and they're the first Dogribs. She raised them to be beautiful hunters with strong medicine."

"Hunh. Wait a minute," Johnny interrupted. "What happened to the three that made it back to the bag?"

"Humph. I don't know. Jed never told me that part."

"Better find out."

—RICHARD VAN CAMP (*The Lesser Blessed* 51–52)

Van Camp positions the telling of his nation's creation story at the intersection of race and performance. Johnny's inquiry into the experience of "full bloodedness" connects biology with identity by suggesting that Larry's sense of self might be informed by racial background. However, by articulating his query in the irreverent lingo of the two teenaged friends' multi-ethnic social sphere in the isolated town of Fort Simmer and replacing the antiquated colonial categorization "full blood" with "fool blood," Johnny concedes the mediation of identity by discourse and social performance. Larry's rendering of the Dogrib creation story is itself performative insofar as it masks as well as reveals, dramatizing the origins of the group in part to protect its vulnerable teller from providing unwanted access to his own narrative of personal trauma. To shield himself from questions regarding his displacement from traditional Dogrib territory near Yellowknife that might solicit painful family history, Larry crafts his response to Johnny's "What's the scoop?" as a depiction of the origins of the Dogrib People, thereby obfuscating his personal experience as a young Tłįchǫ man while placing that experience within a mythic narrative of nationhood. Yet, as the anxious pause after the sacred tale's opening line suggests, sharing the creation story nonetheless carries social risk (through its articulation of a form of truth claim) and provides both Johnny and the reader with significant information about Larry that transcends the racial inflections of blood quantum.

Larry's storytelling emphasizes cultural distinctiveness by seeking to illustrate to the Métis audience what it means to be Dogrib, but it also fosters intercultural dialogue and alliance through the intimacy of its articulation; Larry invites Johnny (and thus the reader) *in* through story. In this manner, Larry's understanding of what it means to be "fool blood" is not so much racial as relational; it is an expression not of insurmountable difference but of relational indebtedness and potential kinship. As Cree scholar Shawn Wilson states, "Identity for Indigenous peoples is grounded in their relationships with the land, with their ancestors who have returned to the land and with future generations who will come into being on the land. Rather than viewing ourselves as being in relationship with other people or things, we are the relationships that we hold and are part of" (80). Relationships, for Wilson, constitute the very terrain through which Indigenous Peoples persist—the medium of their being. The source for Larry's understanding of the story above reinforces the importance of relations and kinship in the scene; Slavey surrogate father figure Jed shares Larry's Dene heritage but is neither a member of the Dogrib Nation nor a biological member of Larry's family.[9] Far from rendering suspect or inauthentic the cultural knowledge that Larry accrues, Jed's tribal background and role as surrogate father indicate how bonds of kinship that unite not only biological families but also broader relations can participate in the continuance and prospering of Indigenous nations. As settler scholar Ellen Bielawski asserts, the Dogrib term for one's blood relations, "Sehóti ('my people')," is also the term for "one's larger grouping," one's "hunting band," the "group one travel[s] with," and "one's settled community" (503). Daniel Heath Justice clarifies what is at stake in understanding Indigenous nationhood through kinship or through lineage and biology: "Kinship is adaptive; race, as a threatened constitutive commodity, always runs the risk of becoming washed out to the point of insignificance" ("'Go Away, Water!'"

151). The foundation of Indigenous survival for Justice, conversely, is "our relationships to one another—in other words, our kinship with other humans and the rest of creation. Such kinship isn't a static thing; it's dynamic, ever in motion. It requires attentiveness; kinship is best thought of as a verb rather than a noun, because kinship, in most Indigenous contexts, is something that's done more than something that simply is" (150).

My objectives in this chapter build in important ways upon Justice's theorizations, which is why I focus on how Larry mobilizes cultural knowledge and storytelling to weave together a viable kinship network amid conditions of loss and exile. I concede, however, that my attraction, as a settler scholar, to Justice's work on kinship might be influenced by its calibration toward ethics of inclusivity. If kinship is conceived as a network of reciprocal responsibilities among humans, the land, the ancestors, other-than-human kin, and the cosmos, then an aspirational sense of potential belonging therein might obtain for settlers like me. If Indigenous kinship systems are figured as concentric circles rippling outward, then a desire might persist among settlers to imagine themselves as eventually being taken into that relational system as a kind of manufactured belonging in stolen territory—what settler scholar Terry Goldie calls "indigenization" and constitutes what Eve Tuck and K. Wayne Yang call a "settler move to innocence" (1). I wish to name this insidious aspirational possibility here so that my arguments can be assessed in relation to it. I nonetheless read *The Lesser Blessed* as an examination of the comparative utility—for Indigenous youth, like Larry, grappling with the legacies of genocide—of Indigenous relational ethics of kinship versus more granular modes of community formation, adaptation, and dissipation that carry currency within the individualist mainstream. Through the depiction of Larry's struggles to find and nurture a sense of community amid conditions of exile in a remote but urban high school setting (and his occasional willingness to sacrifice personal integrity to satiate individualist desires), Van Camp illuminates the dangers of failing to honour kinship ties as ongoing and dynamic responsibilities, dangers made all the more perilous through the social sanctioning of self-interested and violent masculinities by his high school peers.

By foregrounding the movement from isolation to community, first through the breaking of the mother's solitude by the puppies' birth and then by the metamorphosis of three puppies into the first Dogribs, Larry's rendition of the Dogrib creation story emphasizes communal values, including those of kinship. As they develop into "beautiful hunters with strong medicine," the first Dogribs illustrate the nation's dependence on their performance of social roles and responsibilities, here the provision of physical nourishment through hunting and of spiritual nourishment and healing through the administering of medicines.[10] Here Van Camp does not distinguish by gender among the first Dogribs in terms of their roles in the community. All three are described as "beautiful hunters with strong medicine," which troubles simplistic gender binaries by wedding the putatively feminine ideal of beauty with the supposedly masculine act of hunting and the putatively masculine ideal of strength with the supposedly feminine acts of nurturing and healing. Van Camp thus implies the inseparability of masculine and feminine while suggesting that aspects of both are necessary for individuals to develop their gifts in ways that truly benefit their communities.[11] The taking up of communal roles involves a process of maturation in which the puppies evolve into children who then grow into beauty and strength. The creation story is thus concerned with the treacherous terrain between childhood and adulthood, in which adolescents negotiate commitments to and places within various communities by making choices for which they must ultimately take responsibility. Larry and Johnny, for instance, are faced with establishing their places in Fort Simmer's high school community, in families (like that of the first Dogribs) headed by single mothers, and in evolving kinship relations with each other and with Juliet Hope, with whom Larry is infatuated and whom Johnny dates in the story. Such negotiation is seldom easy, and the invigoration of kinship responsibilities often comes at a cost. For example, the newly human children "playing in the snow" and "having a great time" in the creation story seek to avoid absorption into the fully human world of adult responsibility (represented by the mother, who supports the family by trekking daily to her trapline) by retreating into the hut and the womb-like bag that their mother "used to leave them in"; they seek a place of perceived safety in which they imagine that they can retain the freedom of childhood (represented by their reversion back to puppies). So though the "girl and two boys" who become "beautiful hunters with strong medicine" and the first Dogribs offer one horizon of possibility for Larry, Johnny, and Juliet, in which they might accept kinship responsibilities and thereby take up places of value within the larger community, alternatively the three might replicate the frantic escape from responsibility enacted by the remaining puppies/children.[12]

The late Anishinaabe writer Basil Johnston has lamented "the loss of a sense of duty" in many Indigenous communities, arguing that "the whole emphasis is on rights. 'My rights are being violated,' 'My rights are being infringed upon.' There's not a word about duties. To us, a right is *debnimzewin*. But each right is also a duty. . . . And so we've got to go back to some of these values: responsibility, duty, right" ("Young Men" 45). Justice concurs, arguing that Indigenous nationhood depends on an understanding of the "common social interdependence within the community, the tribal web of kinship rights and responsibilities that link the People, the land, and the cosmos together in an ongoing and dynamic system of mutually affecting relationships" ("'Go Away, Water!'" 151). The relationship between Larry and Johnny provides an opportunity to assess how particular models of masculinity foster and/or corrode the kinship bonds that Justice identifies as crucial to Indigenous continuance. In particular, I question below whether the model of masculinity embodied by Johnny—which privileges individual freedom over communal responsibility—offers a viable future for socially disenfranchised characters such as Larry and whether the type of social capital that Johnny boasts translates into a meaningful role within the various communities in which the two young men persist. In essence, I ask in this chapter whether Johnny's masculine persona, obviously valued as cool and desirable within the high school setting, fosters empowerment and continuance through its strength and beauty (like the qualities of the first Dogribs) or whether it exacerbates alienation by trapping individuals in states of arrested development (like the imprisoned puppies at the close of the creation story).

## MODEL OF MASCULINITY 1: THE LAW OF THE FATHER

In *Elder Brother and the Law of the People: Contemporary Kinship and Cowessess First Nation*, Robert Innes examines "the importance of kinship relations in the maintenance and affirmation of individual and collective identity for members" of his home community in southern Saskatchewan (6). His research brings to light how Cowessess members have "undermined the imposition of the *Indian Act*'s definitions of Indian by acknowledging kinship relations to band members who either had not been federally recognized as Indians prior to 1985, or were urban members disconnected from the reserve" (6–7).[13] Innes argues that traditional Elder Brother stories elucidate "principle[s] of inclusion" that are "linked to . . . kinship patterns found in the Law of the People" (198). Remarkable in his findings is "the persistent adherence to the values in the Law of the People by Cowessess members, even by those who have not actually heard the stories" (8). In other words, Cowessess members have continued to practise culturally specific ethics of kinship, which defy the settler colonial impositions of heteropatriarchal social organization and inheritance, *even* in the absence of the stories by which such ethics are informed. Echoing discussions in Chapter 4 regarding how the logic of the gift is embedded inextricably within Pacific Northwest Indigenous worldviews and therefore can persist in the face of the economic interventions of capitalism, here practices of kinship embedded in the worldview of Cowessess First Nation obtain, in action and in thought, without requiring explication via the stories.

In *The Lesser Blessed*, Larry finds himself in similar circumstances, seeking to negotiate kinship geographically distanced from the traditional territory of the Tłı̨chǫ and with tenuous access to the stories that express the Tłı̨chǫ worldview. Because of his father's death, his mother's prevailing silence, and his disconnection from other members of his nation, Larry seldom receives cultural knowledge that might explicate male roles and responsibilities within a traditional Tłı̨chǫ system of kinship. The teachings that he acquires are either incomplete, like the initial rendering of the Dogrib creation story by Jed,[14] or compromised by the ferocity of their teller, like the introduction to "the drum" that he receives from his abusive biological father. At the same time, Larry is denied a functional associative system in relation to which he might position himself because his family is fragmented by alcoholism and violence. In fact, after his father's death, Larry expresses a desire for his mother and Jed to "get together" as a "family" because he "really needed some stability. I know that sounds lame, but it's true" (3). In a vacuum of cultural context and domestic cohesion, Larry is profoundly uncertain of his place in the family, the Tłı̨chǫ Nation, and the social environment of his high school. When asked to draw a self-portrait early in the story, he hands in "a picture of a forest." To his therapist's response that "there is no one," Larry states, "Look, there. I am already buried" (1). The drawing betrays suicidal ideation emerging from the despair of non-recognition through a potent metaphor for Larry's inability to envision his place in the world. Like Tom Bauer in Eden Robinson's *Blood Sports*, as discussed in the previous chapter, Larry shares a sense of his own invisibility. Because society offers few models of healthy masculinity that he might emulate and those around him generally fail to validate his existence, he imagines himself under erasure beneath the earth, symbolically re-enacting his earlier unsuccessful attempt at self-immolation by lighting the gasoline that he and his cousins are sniffing.

To elucidate the sorrow underlying this desperate act, Larry declares of himself and his cousins, "We wept because we knew we had no one. No one to remember our names, no one to cry them out, no one to greet us naked in snow, to mourn us in death, to feel us there, in our sacred place. We wept because we did not belong to anyone" (79). His poetic lament betrays a sense of personal deficiency conditioned by a rupture of integration—to "not belong to anyone" is to *not belong*, to not experience the validation of one's full humanity as a sense of *integrity*; in this way, Larry and his cousins are deterritorialized. Such unbelonging has gendered valences as well. With the social and familial fabrics that might have enveloped their lives tattered and torn, Larry and his cousins are wounded by isolation; they have "no one" because they feel abandoned by their parents, the broader community, and the Canadian nation, leaving no dynamic relational space in which to negotiate empowered identities (masculine or otherwise). Not only are they denied validation, in this context, but also the cousins are denied senses of purpose

CARRYING THE BURDEN OF PEACE

and meaningful roles. As Justice asks, "what [does it mean] to have a masculinity that belongs and is in service to kin and community rather than a masculinity that exists solely as personal expression of self?" (personal communication, 4 June 2020). With "no one to remember [their] names" and thereby acknowledge their person-hood, each child comes to believe that she or he is unworthy of remembrance, which fuels the desire for narcosis through fume sniffing or death by fire.

Unlike settler colonial conceptions of identity formation (where, among other things, individuation is generally achieved through one's attainment of independence from a group), most Indigenous conceptions of identity formation involve one's progressive integration into the collective—often celebrated through ceremonies of initiation.[15] Thus, whereas mainstream Canadian understandings of identity tend to focus on and distinguish the individual, in most Indigenous nations, as Shawn Wilson argues, identity is *only* discernible in relation to the group. The isolation figured in Larry's surname, Sole, thus marks the insinuation of colonial ideologies into the Tłı̨chǫ community, which threatens to sever the threads of interdependence that enable a nation's continuance. Larry's surname, of course, also has the capacity to resonate with Tłı̨chǫ values of self-sufficiency and personal integrity, as "integrity" is theorized in the introduction to this volume; building upon the work of anthropologist Jean-Guy Goulet, Kristina Fagan identifies "among the Dene 'the highest regard for one another's autonomy,'" which informs the "reluctance to interrupt, interfere with, or even instruct one another" (212). However, without the requisite cultural knowledge, "Sole" risks becoming untethered from communal re-sponsibilities and marking a radical individualism averse to Tłı̨chǫ values. Denied integration into a network of communal roles, Larry is unclear not only about his identity but also about appropriate masculine behaviours.

Although absent from the temporal present of *The Lesser Blessed*, Larry's biological father provides a dysfunctional model of masculin-ity compromised by colonialist violence. A product of residential schooling, Larry's father asserts his masculinity through domina-tion and sexual violence. The three most explicit depictions of his behavior in the novel are acts of sexual violation portrayed as performances for his son. In the first case, Larry peers in a window after returning home late to discover his aunt "passed out" and his "dad fucking her" (88). Viewing the incident like a silent film, Larry sees his father deny the bodily autonomy of another for the gratification of his own sadistic desire. In an even more explicit lesson, Larry is "called . . . out of [his] room" by his father—who is "speaking French," which he "learned . . . in the residential schools" and only spoke "when he drank"—to find his mother "passed out on the couch . . . in her bathrobe" and his father "laughing." "Spread[ing] her legs," the father violates Larry's mother with a "yellow broomstick" (58), thereby dramatizing the supremacy of male sexual privilege through the derogation of the female body while rendering rape and physical assault a joke for the eyes of the male child. The father engages in a form of performative humiliation that echoes the tactical assault on Indigenous gender systems and kinship relations (discussed in Chapter 2) in which shame was wielded in residential schools to compromise relations between Indigenous men and women, between Indigenous Peoples and the land, and between individuals and their embodied selves. The father is depicted as having learned these lessons horrifically well, disavowing with laughter Larry's mother's pain (and indeed her humanity) and instructing the son about the supposed deficiency of womanhood through violence—teachings that undoubtedly complicate Larry's relationships with women in the novel while assaulting his own sense of responsibility as a witness.

The toxic model of masculinity enacted by Larry's father betrays the legacies of attempted genocide. Residential schools' envisioned destruction of Indigenous societies and families is implied to be ongoing as the father's sexual tyranny leads to his oral rape of Larry, who reacts by attempting murder-suicide. Forcing his penis into his son's mouth, Larry's father dehumanizes the child as a vehicle for sexual release, inscribing in Larry a sense of worthlessness in his father's eyes. By murdering his father, Larry implicates himself in this doomed masculinist cycle, which augurs its own demise by placing the desires of one generation over the survival and well-being of the next. This is why Larry claims that "it is every parent's dream to watch his child burn" (10). Absolute hierarchies, unlike radically democratic kinship relations, create their own usurpers because empowerment in such systems requires another's loss of power (much like what I referred to as competitive ecologies of gender in Chapter 3); power must be seized because it will never be shared willingly and because it is conceived in finite terms rather than as mutually generative. Thus, Larry's default model of masculinity in a biological sense—his father—overturns itself, fracturing Larry's vulnerable sense of place while foreshadowing the destruction of the broader community through one generation's violation of its successor. Seemingly locked into a cycle of violence that affords him no future, Larry adopts the role of "Destroying Angel," holding aloft lit matches in a propane-filled room, "screaming, 'Let's die! Let's die! Let's die!'" (79–80).

## MODEL OF MASCULINITY 2: INDIVIDUALIST ADOLESCENT MACHISMO

In the shadow of suicidal despair, Larry exemplifies the precarious identity formations emergent from colonial attacks on Indigenous gender and kinship systems: he enters high school with only tenuous access to his Dogrib heritage and no immediately accessible male role models because of his father's death and Jed's absence. Adding to his perplexity, Larry boasts no physical characteristics recognized by his peers as desirably masculine. With "spaghetti arms and daddy-longlegs," he is not considered "a threat to anyone and, in turn, people just [look] past [him]" (22). This glossing re-enacts the non-recognition that Larry laments before the fire and leads him to seek models of masculinity noticed (and thereby potentially respected) in the high school environment. Unlike Tom Bauer in Robinson's *Blood Sports*, who actively resists such highly visible models of masculinity, Larry covets them. The allure of social validation is actuated in the novel by Johnny Beck, a Métis student with the looks, the defiance, and the demeanour to seize the kind of public recognition that eludes Larry. Johnny manifests several qualities identified within the teens' predominantly non-Indigenous social circle as masculine and therefore desirable to the socially disenfranchised. Describing his first view of Johnny in the school foyer, Larry reports that "His hair was feathered and long, his eyes piercing and blue. . . . [T]he thing I remember about Johnny was the look on his face. He looked like he didn't give a white lab rat's ass about anything or anybody[,] . . . like he was carrying the weight of Hell. All the girls were saying, 'What's his name? Find out his name!'" (2). Johnny's detached bearing becomes an ironic catalyst to social inclusion as the "look on his face," which suggests indifference to "anything or anybody," incites efforts to discover his name that thereby validate his performed identity. The empirical command to "Find out his name!" offers the desired antithesis of the perpetual non-recognition that Larry and his cousins lament prior to the fire with "no one to remember [their] names." Unlike Larry, Johnny achieves popularity in his new school because his behaviours are perceived by that community as both masculine and "cool." For example, when Johnny defies the authority of Mister Harris and rearranges the entire classroom as a gesture of non-conformity and resistance, Larry lauds on behalf of the student body, "We had our hero" (12). Johnny is enticingly rebellious, "handsome . . . in a lost sort of way" (49), effective as a fighter, and sexually alluring—all qualities that lead him to be perceived as "the hottest commodity to come to Fort Simmer in a long time" (24) and render him a potentially useful model of masculinity toward which Larry can aspire.

As the two young men become fast friends, readers recognize that Johnny's detachment, apparent indifference, and propensity toward violence have roots in a neglected and transient home life. In fact, his performance of "not giving a white lab rat's ass about . . . anybody" masks the nurturing affection that he displays in private toward his younger brother, Donny, for whom he feels responsible and whom he treats more like a son than a sibling. To the complaint that their father had permitted Donny to avoid doing homework "if [he] didn't want to," Johnny responds in a raised voice, "You don't listen to him, okay? You listen to me." He then asks Larry in an exasperated paternal fashion, "Man, what am I gonna do about that kid?" (48). Johnny is forced into a surrogate parental role because of poverty's attendant instabilities and the neglectful nature of both of his parents, which informs, at least partially, his burgeoning desire for freedom from responsibility. Outside the fractured domestic space, however, Johnny is careful to hide the nurturing and conscientious elements of his personality and to mobilize something akin to what bell hooks theorizes in the African American context as "cool pose": a performance of masculine self-interest and capacity for violence that black men are encouraged to "front" or "fake" in order to "mask true feelings" and achieve facades of social dominance that hooks exposes as illusory and ultimately counterproductive (148).[16] Johnny's cool public persona becomes a beacon for Larry in his efforts to gain social capital. By teaching Larry the rules for fighting, smoking drugs, and avoiding venereal disease, Johnny endeavours to pass on elements of this cool persona, willingly accepting the position of mentor that Larry seems to desire.

Van Camp encourages the reader of *The Lesser Blessed* to view the relationship between Larry and Johnny as a form of surrogate brotherhood through a critical scene in which the two encounter ghostly incarnations of their potential adult selves. The nameless spectral characters are referred to as "Rasp Man," whose "voice was haunting, as if he were a face screaming without a throat" (60), and "the Boxer," who "shadowbox[es] his fists about his brother's head" (61) throughout the scene. Significantly, Larry refers to Rasp Man and the Boxer as brothers despite providing no corroborating evidence for this assertion. Given Johnny's status as a pugilist, Johnny bears an implied connection to the Boxer, and Larry's history of suffering burns all over his body, his earlier description of "swallowing fire" (37), and his cryptic drug-induced declaration "I am my father's scream" (38) associate Larry readily with Rasp Man. Larry's interpretation of the two as brothers therefore gestures toward a familial hunger, a longing for kinship that strikes the reader as rational given Larry's father's tyranny, his mother's emotional distance, his status as an only child, and his earlier description of weeping "because he had no one." The mirroring of a brotherly relationship between Larry and Johnny, however, appears to be both alluring and dangerous given the image of the Boxer and Rasp Man standing "like lovers in an incredible dance" before "the Boxer thr[ows] his brother on the ground and proceed[s] to smash his sneakers into him" (62). Affection and even attraction clearly persist between Larry and Johnny,[17] yet the mediation of the relationship by a hypermasculine gendered economy without rigorous commitment to mutual responsibility renders it vulnerable, like that of the ghostly "floater" siblings, to collapse beneath the weight of the young men's troubles and recourse to violence.

Although the masculinity modelled by Johnny does not approach the ferocious malevolence of Larry's father, it remains dangerous because it seems to endorse a primary foundation of self-concern. Johnny's detached demeanour, which Larry and others find so attractive, portends the emotional detachment that Johnny ultimately betrays in his relationships with Larry and Juliet, the latter of whom he treats like an anonymous vessel for his own sexual gratification. When asked why he moved from his hometown, Johnny replies that "there was no one left to fuck" (23); although this cheeky statement can be dismissed as jocular teenaged posturing, the lack of worth that it ascribes to intimate partners is echoed in Johnny's flippant description of sex with Juliet, with whom Larry is infatuated: "A bit too bony for me. She did this thing with her hips when she was riding me . . . man, that hurt. But other than that she was okay. . . . [I]f she gives me the clap, I'll kill her" (43). Johnny's performative willingness to disavow Juliet (and violently)—augured in the phrase "I'll kill her"—ultimately manifests in his abandonment of her on learning of her pregnancy (a consequence, like the venereal disease mentioned above, that Johnny fears will impinge on the freedom that he, like the puppies in the Dogrib creation story, is desperate to retain). Johnny explains his departure in words reminiscent of the perpetual adolescent Peter Pan—"I want to be beautiful just a little bit longer'" (117)—betraying a heightened sense of self-interest exacerbated by fear of diluting his individualist identity within ongoing relational commitments such as parenthood. Johnny instead forgoes intimate and ongoing responsibilities, beyond his connection to Donny, thereby replicating his own father's painful absenteeism. Although he does not dehumanize others to the extent that Larry's father does (showing uninterest rather than brutality), Johnny similarly denies the restrictive influence of women on his own masculine autonomy and thereby suppresses responsibilities inherent in the "rights" and "duties" discussed by Johnston and the kinship relations theorized by Justice above. Furthermore, Johnny renders implausible the intimate generosity celebrated as sacred erotics by poets such as Qwo-Li Driskill and Gregory Scofield.

Despite being appalled by Johnny's casual disregard for Juliet in his sexual tale-telling, Larry cannot readily shake his mentor's appeal. Even after calling Johnny a "fucking asshole"—silently, of course—and admitting to no longer being able to "see the Jesus in Johnny," Larry still exclaims the night of Johnny and Juliet's consummation "What a guy!" (44). He is unable to deny the ongoing attractiveness of Johnny's individualist masculinity because it offers the social recognition that Larry covets and therefore an ironic sense of belonging despite its reliance on detachment. He desires to emulate Johnny in order to gain analogous notoriety, which is why—when he is told that he has been "brought into a circle . . . for fighters" like Johnny—Larry is "smiling inside" (61) and why—if he could "perform an autopsy on him"—Larry would "steal his eyes" (49). He longs to co-opt Johnny's perspective, which leads him at one point to actually pose as Johnny in order to grope Juliet. In a darkened laundry room while she is unaware, Larry runs his hands over her body—exulting, "I guess she thought I was Johnny. Haha!" (94)—thereby echoing in muted fashion both his father's assaults on unconscious women and his father's masculinist laughter. No longer treating Juliet with the "respect and awe" (29) that he exhibits in the novel's opening, Larry literally performs Johnny's persona and in doing so adopts a similarly self-interested masculinity that disregards Juliet's bodily autonomy—as well as his responsibility, as Tłı̨chǫ, not to interfere with another. Yet, unlike Johnny, he remains delegitimized socially because it all takes place in the dark; Larry thus compromises sincere interpersonal bonds with both Juliet and Johnny without ever accessing the social capital that he might have expected Johnny's model of indifferent sexual self-interest to bring.

The attempted replication of individualist masculinity fails because Larry becomes neither the envied ladies' man nor the admired fighter. In fact, the only time that he achieves the status of spectacle is when he is beaten to the point of hospitalization with Johnny looking on and refusing to intervene. Johnny's seemingly cruel restraint as Jazz the Jackal punches and kicks Larry into submission at once teaches him the consequences of entering the circle of fighters

(a perverse life lesson in performative masculine codes) and dramatizes the tenuous nature of the bond of kinship between Larry and
Johnny since it is unaccompanied by a sense of responsibility for
(and to) the other—roles detached from responsibilities. The model
of masculinity through which Johnny gains respect and admiration
thus leaves Larry alone and vulnerable, abandoned and broken. As
an intervention in the social disenfranchisement of Indigenous
youth like Larry, the model of Johnny Beck proves to be attractive
but illusory. It offers the outcast an image of empowerment while
locking him into cycles of violence and neglect. Larry's emulation
of Johnny heightens his alienation by encouraging Larry to shun
meaningful and ongoing interpersonal relationships while continually failing to facilitate his social recognition. He thus gets no closer
to clarity of his social role in the Fort Simmer community, and the
dynamic meanings of responsible citizenship in the Tłįchǫ Nation
are further obscured. In this way, Larry dramatizes the dangers
of turning to individualist models of masculinity that deny the
prescience of kinship concerns. As his wounding under Johnny's
neglectful gaze portrays, although such models appear to facilitate
both status and community, they can alienate young Indigenous
men from other viable sources of identity, strength, and self-worth.

## INTIMATE GENEROSITY AND THE FREEDOM OF RESPONSIBILITY

To return to the Dogrib creation story, readers are encouraged to
evaluate Johnny in relation to the first Dogribs, both because of
the relationship of triangulated desire with Juliet and Larry and
because of the repeated attention drawn to his beauty and strength
(two qualities revered in the "beautiful hunters with strong medicine"). However, his resistance to the roles and responsibilities of
kinship, championed in the creation story through hunting and
healing, suggests alternatively that Johnny (and by extension Larry
and Juliet) might relate symbolically to the puppies/children who
revert back to animal form only to be recaptured by their mother.
Johnny's efforts to retain his freedom after Juliet becomes pregnant,
for instance, elicit an ironic imprisonment similar to the doomed
attempt to escape by the puppies/children when his own absentee

father, who has returned to take Johnny away from Fort Simmer, throws his son forcefully into his pickup, slams the door, and speeds off (118). Larry's final image of Johnny, trapped in the truck "crying" and unable to "get away" (118), eerily resembles the confinement of the three remaining puppies and bespeaks the delimiting nature of the purportedly liberatory masculinity that Johnny has endorsed throughout the novel. As masculinity scholar Michael Messner notes, "rather than liberating men," "pursuit[s] of . . . masculinity" like those undertaken by Johnny (and to a lesser extent by Larry) tend to "lock men into self-destructive behaviors and into oppressive, hierarchical, and destructive relations with women and with other men" (78–79). As feminist scholar Genevieve Vaughan puts it, "patriarchy [is] founded on males' rejection of their own (feminine) humanity" (2). Jed's revelation late in *The Lesser Blessed* that the children who "made it back to the bag" and "turned back into pups" were killed by their mother (105) implies the stakes of such supposedly liberatory pursuits, particularly those in which freedom for the self is imagined as a higher value than the well-being of others.

We must caution ourselves, however, against considering Johnny's transgressions encapsulated entirely by the act of child abandonment and therefore assuming that an attempt by Johnny and Juliet to forge a nuclear family unit would constitute an optimal final scenario for the novel. Returning to the words of bell hooks, such a reading "buy[s] into the romantic myth that if only there was a . . . man in the house life would be perfect" and neglects "the evidence that there are plenty of homes where fathers are present, fathers who are so busy acting out, being controlling, being abusive, that home is hell" (102). Larry's relationship with his biological father clearly fits into the latter category. hooks stresses that "the father-hunger" felt by children such as Larry "is as intense as the father-hunger children in fatherless homes feel" (102). In *The Lesser Blessed*, Van Camp troubles the reader's longing for nuclear family domesticity by depicting the prelude to Johnny and Juliet's first sexual encounter as the play-acting of parental roles, with the two flirting in the domestic space of the kitchen before Juliet leads Johnny off to the bedroom with the words "Let's go check on the kids. . . . I gotta go check on the kids" (39). Larry's comment that "it was like a movie, only real" (39), recognizes astutely how Johnny and Juliet are dramatizing parental roles portrayed in popular cultural media such as film as natural, even inevitable, and thereby, in Mark Rifkin's words, casting Indigenous ethics of kinship "as aberrant or anomalous modes of (failed) domesticity" (*When* 37). Yet their performance is ironic because Johnny has no intention of settling into a parental role (and presumably, at the time, neither does Juliet). What Larry sees as "real" is illusory, which suggests that the naturalization of the nuclear family as the dominant mode of social organization is itself a construct, as illustrated by the discussion in the previous chapter of the daycare prison in *Blood Sports*, a suggestion corroborated by the number of dysfunctional biological families depicted throughout *The Lesser Blessed*. Van Camp's focus on kinship relations indicates the inadequacy of narrow biological conceptions of the family, independent of the interwoven threads of communal obligations. Thus, the naturalization of the nuclear family as "real" is exposed in the novel as potentially dangerous: it risks devaluing the larger social sphere in which roles and responsibilities can be modelled by those invested in the community's continuance, while encouraging competitive social relations in which those outside the immediate family fail to be recognized as one's relations, as kin.

Van Camp provides alternatives to both Johnny's individualism and the idealization of nuclear family domesticity in the relationship among Larry, his mother, and Jed, all of whom identify as kin despite differences in tribal background and biological lineage. Like the puppies/children from the Dogrib creation story, this relationship involves "a girl and two boys," but unlike the relationship among Larry, Johnny, and Juliet it is characterized by commitment to mutual well-being and growth.[18] Sitting on a hospital bed after his beating, Larry "softly [takes] Jed's hand and place[s] it on [his] mom's," such that their "arms ma[k]e a perfect triangle" (82). It is "perfect" because none of the three attempts to assert her or his will over the others; they gain strength through interpersonal commitments, in stark contrast to the self-concern of Johnny—who, on the following page, is described as "walk[ing] behind us, apart from us" (83)—and the tyrannical individualism of Larry's biological father, whose past violence resonates in the scene via the mother's wounded tear duct, which the "father had destroyed [and] would never work again, so even though she made the sounds of crying, nothing came" (82). Overcoming his past performances of individualist masculinity that conform to the model of Johnny, here Larry intervenes in his family's history of violence through an act, reminiscent of the strong medicine of the first Dogribs, that recognizes the relational nature of healing: "My left hand touched my face where my tears ran hot and wet. I held my wet finger to my mother's right cheek and ran a wet trail where her tears should have been. We cried together" (83). By sharing this emotional response, Larry subdues the urgency of his own immediate pain, diffusing it within a collective grieving process that privileges solidarity, interpersonal commitment, and communal responsibility over the primacy of individual convalescence. In fact, here Larry acknowledges that true healing for the individual demands the strength and well-being of the group—and that sense of sacred responsibility is reciprocated in his mother's nurturing. The scene thus resonates, in my reading, with the ceremony of condolence envisioned by Aionwahta (and discussed in Chapter 1), in which his own despair is transcended through an agentive responsibility to ease the grief of others: the active attentiveness to others' well-being generates a reciprocal sense of purpose that serves the integrity of the condoler. Counter to a belief in personal healing according to what Lauren Vedal calls "an individualist, masculinist formula" (115), here Larry, his mother, and Jed adopt a therapeutic approach "that emphasize[s] community harmony and integration" (Fagan 113)—an approach in which healing, like sensual intimacy, is neither competitive nor finite but mutually generative. This too is decolonial love. By recognizing the pain of another as his own pain and the healing of another as a source of his own strength, Larry thus steps into a dynamic kinship role and embraces the responsibilities that the role calls into being.

In my reading of *The Lesser Blessed*, Van Camp seems to be calling for models of masculinity committed to radically democratic principles of Indigenous kinship while critiquing the naturalization of individualist masculinities—like those pursued by Johnny—steeped in settler colonial imperatives of capitalism and heteropatriarchy and offering illusions of integration while perpetuating violence and neglect. Discussing Van Camp's work in relation to that of Métis writers Gregory Scofield and Warren Cariou, Justice remarks

> If only these were the visions that were dominant: the vulnerability, the gentleness, the confusion, the uncertainty. All of those are also sources of strength; all of those are also powerful ways of revealing our humanity. Where vulnerability is not weakness; it is being open to the possibility of change, being open to the possibility of being transformed by love, by passion, by touch. . . . And the work here gives me hope for much, much better opportunities, and models of powerful men who are gentle men, who are loving men, who are generous men. (McKegney et al. 249–50)

Like many of the authors whose works are surveyed in this volume, Van Camp's writing actuates what Johnston champions as the vital dynamism between "rights" and "duties" and what Justice honours as "the tribal web of kinship rights and responsibilities," suggesting that in *The Lesser Blessed* only masculinities built upon the freedom *of* responsibility, rather than the freedom *from* responsibility, will foster empowered individual identities and meaningful Indigenous continuance.

Van Camp concludes the novel with a poetic reversal of the isolation that informed Larry's attempted suicide:

> And I wept because I knew I had someone
> someone to remember my name
> someone to greet me naked in snow
> someone to mourn me in death
> to feel me there
> in my sacred place (119)

This celebration of connection rejects both the forced isolation of Larry's youth and the individualist entitlement enacted by Johnny. Larry commits at the novel's end to pursuing sincere relations capable of informing the expression of empowered masculinities that refuse domination and dehumanization—that refuse to mine empowerment parasitically from others. However, his pledge "in time" to "find one to call *my own* / *mine* to disappear in / to be . . ." (119; emphasis added; ellipsis in original), suggests the ongoing difficulty of nurturing non-dominative masculinities in contexts conditioned by settler heteropatriarchy. Although Larry's spoken vow and the ellipsis with which the novel concludes demonstrate commitment to Indigenous futures through intimate generosity, the reliance on a possessive vocabulary ("to call my own") suggests the insidious resilience of masculinist heteronormativity; it is strikingly different from his earlier longing to "belong *to*" someone. Vedal, for example, argues that "Larry's story follows a masculinist coming-of-age formula structured by rivalry with, and betrayal by, male peers. This formula concludes with Larry losing his virginity to Juliet." For Vedal, "the primary problem of healing in the novel" is that Larry "achieves emotional independence—from male peers as well as Juliet—and a restored sense of wholeness" because of "a single sex act" that constitutes his "initiation into manhood" (115). Reading this love scene in *The Lesser Blessed* through the lens of kinship rather than heteronormative Western individuation, however, I consider the sensual intimacy between Larry and Juliet to be less about his own "emotional independence" and more about a "sense of wholeness" made possible by interpersonal responsibilities. During their coital encounter, Larry tells Juliet, "'Look at me. . . . Look into me, just look at me.'" When she returns his gaze, he proclaims, "I wasn't alone / I wasn't forgotten / . . . / I wasn't bad I was clean" (110). The perspectival exchange between the two young adults, which requires Juliet to choose both physical and emotional connection by looking *into* her sexual partner, suggests something beyond the radical autonomy that Vedal fears. It suggests a "dynamic mutuality," like that discussed in Chapter 3, that exceeds the scriptures of heteropatriarchy. Although the repetition of the first-person pronoun throughout the passage emphasizes Larry's experience, we cannot forget that Juliet calls Larry to her home, initiates the sexual encounter, and is portrayed as agentive throughout the scene.[19] Also, as Vedal notes, "That *The Lesser Blessed* is a young adult novel matters" (113). To return to the discussions with which I began this chapter, Van Camp speaks to an audience of young men (among other constituencies, of course) with neither condescension nor placation, recognizing the omnipresence and prescience of sexual desire and sexual anxiety in adolescence; however, he mobilizes that audience's anticipated hyperconscious desire for individual sexual gratification—what Justice calls a "touch that is . . . a taking touch" rather than "a giving touch" ("Fighting" 145)—in order to build toward a constellation of sensual possibilities enacted via kinship responsibilities.

Recalling teachings from traditional storyteller Louis Bird regarding "untangling the meanings of sexual relationships," Warren Cariou notes that the Cree Elder

> was very specific about the role of the man. The role of the man is to understand that giving pleasure is the primary thing, not receiving it. It was interesting because he felt, I think, that he didn't have to explain that to the women, but that the men needed that knowledge because they had forgotten it, or it had been forgotten somehow. And he saw this as not just an experience or something that you're wanting to do, but actually this is your role. This is a responsibility to give pleasure and if you're not doing that you're not fulfilling your role as a man. (McKegney et al. 261)

In *The Lesser Blessed*, Larry charts a story map of sensual intimacy that is mutually generative and, in my reading, liberated from settler heteropatriarchy even though such intimacy is celebrated between a cis-hetero male and a cis-hetero female and occurs in the context of a high school environment conditioned by masculine privilege. This is a gift that Van Camp gives us with his writing. It is neither easy nor without risk, but I contend that the literary art analyzed throughout *Carrying the Burden of Peace* shows us the necessity of such gifts, illuminating their vitality within our efforts to imagine, enliven, and express masculinities that are worthy of claiming.

# NAKED AND DREAMING FORWARD:
## A CONCLUSION

What I vision, . . . it's something that I can realize and what I have to honour is the distance. . . .

I have to build up earthwork underneath the dream until that dream is resting on the earth, and that's the reality that we've come to. . . . The past, it has a strong influence on the future, but it doesn't own the future. —JOANNE ARNOTT ("Intimate Like Muscle and Bone" 196)

Elucidating how he "untangled" himself from "the crushing roles and responsibilities of what it means to be a man," Anishinaabe theorist Randy Jackson told me some years ago that "[it's] not really about gender; it's how do I as a person contribute to the well-being of my community" (interview). Maybe what I am talking about in *Carrying the Burden of Peace* need not be labelled "masculinity." Maybe what I am talking about is more fully encapsulated by *integrity*: territoriality, chosen vulnerability, intimate generosity, ecologies of gender made possible by the logic of the gift. Maybe I am talking about being responsible, accountable, loving, and selfless, about what it means to express one's full humanity in defiance of settler colonialism's tireless deterritorializing assault. Yet, as the visionary narrative art curated in this book demonstrates, settler colonialism is and always has been a gendered enterprise—violently so. And its dispossessive machinery has been calibrated to impoverish many things, including our understandings of what "masculinities" can mean, how and by whom they can be embodied and expressed, and to what ends. The deterritorializing imperatives of settler colonialism are designed to force individuals, communities, and landscapes to become what they are not, in the process obfuscating Indigenous ecologies of gender replete with other knowledges and possibilities, ecologies of gender in which non-dominative masculinities persist through the dynamic interplay of autonomy and responsibility—in which personal integrity is a principal value and "each right is also a duty" (Johnston, "Young Men" 45).

If Indigenous men and boys—as well as those who identify otherwise yet for whom masculinities retain value—cannot see the sacred within themselves, then we are telling the wrong stories. If "sacred masculinities" reads like an oxymoron, then there is emotional, intellectual, embodied, and creative work yet to do. The one-page poem "Sacred" by Driftpile Cree writer and theorist Billy-Ray Belcourt, which tracks the suffocation of its queer speaker's recognition of the sacred in himself/themselves,[1] illuminates the urgency of such work while delineating the care required to perform it to decolonial ends:

> a native man looks me in the eyes as he refuses to hold my hand
> during a round dance. his pupils are like bullets and i wonder what
> kind of pain he's been through to not want me in this world with
> him any longer. i wince a little because the earth hasn't held all of me
> for quite some time now and i am lonely in a way that doesn't hurt
> anymore.

The "native man's" refusal to take the speaker's hand enacts a performative disavowal of the latter's humanity, the violent nature of which is affirmed by "pupils . . . like bullets" that betray a longing to make the target of the gaze disappear. It is a look that actively unsees and, in that unseeing, works to compromise the speaker's ability to see himself/themselves. At the outset of this book, I quoted Michi Sagig Nishnaabeg writer Leanne Betasamosake Simpson, who stresses the "responsibility of figuring out a meaningful way to live in the world that is consistent with [one's] most intimate realities" (As We 120). Through his refusal of embodied connection, the "native man" compromises the interface between the speaker's "intimate realities" and "the world," conditioning *in*consistencies that encourage the speaker to fail ultimately to recognize himself/themselves.

The speaker's concession at the close of "Sacred," "i know i am too queer to be sacred anymore," though harrowing, thus comes as little surprise. The speaker has been subject to settler colonialism's deterritorializing assault, here manifest in a dehumanizing gaze that *dis*integrates in ways analyzed in Chapter 2. The speaker's "arm hanging . . . like an appendage [his/their] body doesn't want anymore" suggests coerced alienation from integrated embodied experience; the speaker's recognition that "the earth hasn't held all of me for quite some time now" suggests coerced alienation from integrated territorial kinship; and "the gap" that "keeps getting bigger" between the two dancers suggests coerced alienation from the community itself. The poem thus lays bare how the deterritorializing forces of heteropatriarchy, here replicated within an intimate ceremonial space, work to compromise bodily integrity, land-based kinship, and communal belonging—and not just for the speaker. The speaker's speculation that the "native man" has "been through" some "kind of pain" that informs his desire to disavow the speaker's humanity suggests that he too has been made into that which he is not; in this sense, "a native man"—especially one depicted as static, unchanging, and visibly legible—is an invention, what Anishinaabe theorist Gerald Vizenor might call a "manifest manner" in the service of empire.[2] The repetition of "anymore" in the poem, therefore, refers not simply to an individual life path in which burgeoning queerness comes to be read as rendering one ever less sacred but also more significantly to the forced deanimation of Indigenous ecologies of gender such that kinship, respectful non-interference, and mutual responsibility are no longer operative. In such contexts—which might remind readers of Cree author Louise Bernice Halfe's poem "Nitotem" analyzed in Chapter 2—it becomes possible to no longer recognize one's community as kin. The ceremonial circle is thus broken for the "native man," too, and his constrained vision of Indigenous masculinities ensures that "the gap . . . keeps getting bigger."

Belcourt's poem expressly implicates hegemonic masculinities in Indigenous deterritorialization. The discrete gendered construct with which the poem begins—"a native man"—returns in its final stanza as the speaker recalls "the time an elder told me to *be a man* and to decolonize in the same breath" (emphasis added). With "the same breath," Belcourt illuminates a contradiction: the Elder's diminution of the myriad possibilities of what it might mean to be "a native man" into a demand for compliance that would discipline deviance and necessitate disavowals of intimate realities is betrayed by the poem as incompatible with decolonization. It is a capitulation to competitive ecologies of gender that serve the reproduction of settler colonialism rather than Indigenous resurgence. However, the speaker refuses to concede to such impoverished masculinities and to inherit passively such a deterritorialized world. I begin my conclusion with "Sacred" because I read the poem ultimately as aspirational, as "a protest" that works in the service of the decolonial world that its speaker is denied. The poem's final lines read thus: "and even though i know i am too queer to be sacred anymore, i dance that broken circle dance because i am still waiting for hands that want to hold mine too." Despite the protracted longing of "still waiting," Belcourt's speaker refuses to give up the embodied agency of the dance, imagining in the process the very community of which he wishes/they wish to be part. The sovereign desire of the speaker, expressed in dance, is mirrored by the anticipated desire of another through "hands that want to hold mine too"; the poem thus cultivates community by imagining a ceremony of (re)integration—of coming together—that respects as an imperative the autonomy of the other (which contrasts strikingly the demands of the Indigenous man and the Elder for conformity and compliance). Like the ceremony of condolence envisioned by Aionwahta and discussed in Chapter 1, here the speaker's healing is catalyzed through reciprocity and dynamic mutuality. Although the decolonial community anticipated in the poem remains in a process of becoming, such *reterritorial-ization* is celebrated as possible by the poem's reanimation of the sacred. The poem itself is a ceremony—a "backward and forward" visioning[3]—that casts light on the sacredness of one shadowed by heteropatriarchy's naturalization.

## GATHERING THREADS, VISIONING FORWARD

Emboldened by the aspirational vitality of writers such as Belcourt, I have no desire to tie up neatly the various argumentative threads of this book in the present conclusion. Rather than close things off, I intend to open things up. *Carrying the Burden of Peace* builds upon the premise that conversations about Indigenous masculinities, although risky, are important: *they matter*. I have sought to honour such conversations, to partake in them, and to provoke even more. I turn in these final pages to a source that, though allowing me to reflect on significant elements of this book, prompts future-oriented considerations of what Indigenous masculinities studies ought to aspire to and guard against, of what meaningful, responsible, ethically rigorous, and ultimately liberatory Indigenous masculinities studies should resemble. Heiltsuk-Kanien'keha:ka filmmaker Zoe Leigh Hopkins's 2013 short film *Mohawk Midnight Runners* provokes such considerations through the story of Grant, a young Kanien'keha:ka man, played by Cree actor Cody Lightning, who deals with the death of a friend by adopting his practice of late-night streaking. The film is gentle and generous, funny and powerful. It is irreverent and vulnerable and celebratory of diverse male identities and bodies. It welcomes viewers wherever they are on their journeys of gender knowledge and opens space for growth and change. I consider it a film that welcomes as audience members both those, like Belcourt's speaker, who refuse the hegemonic undertow of dominant masculinities and those, like the "native man," who are swept up by it entirely. It is a story that speaks in a "masculine" vernacular yet allows its male-identified characters the freedom to express selfhood and relationality in ways that are both vulnerable and empowered—a dynamic combination, generative of myriad expressive possibilities.

I turn to *Mohawk Midnight Runners* here for a few reasons: as a film adaptation of the short story "Dogrib Midnight Runners" by Richard Van Camp, it is fundamentally collaborative and resonates with the final chapter in the body of this book; by reimagining Van Camp's story in the context of Mohawk Territory at Six Nations of the Grand River, the film is both territorially and culturally alert in ways that resonate with this project's reliance on Haudenosaunee knowledge; it is generically complex in that it expands narrative art as discussed in this volume to include the audio/visual; and, most importantly, it demonstrates creative sovereignty insofar as the film refuses to let settler colonialism dictate the terms of its engagements with gender. *Mohawk Midnight Runners* is a story of Indigenous strength, resilience, and imagination, not deficiency; it is a work of vision and beauty that transcends both settler simulations and colonial masculinities. I hope that the following reflections provoked by the film offer guidance for future directions in Indigenous masculinities studies.

## PROVOCATION 1: THINKING THE BODY DIFFERENTLY

As Daniel Heath Justice argues, within the ideological scape inherited from settler colonialism, "the male body is seen as capable . . . only of violence and harm," and, "if the male body isn't giving harm, it's taking pleasure" ("Fighting" 145). The reduction of masculine embodied potential to poles of violence and sexual extraction—as well as their collapse in "violent sexuality"—serves the cause of Indigenous elimination by denying Indigenous men and others their full humanity while delimiting avenues of relationality. *Mohawk Midnight Runners* refuses such diminution. Although portraying the naked bodies of Indigenous men on screen for more than half of the film's fifteen-minute running time, Hopkins depicts no overtly sexual or violent acts, encouraging viewers to think the body differently. As Anishinaabe theorist Niigaanwewidem James Sinclair argues, artists such as Van Camp (and, by extension, Hopkins) push "the idea of what beautiful and healthy male relationships look like. In so many depictions of male interactions in fiction we get violence, and, if it's anything else, critics quickly label [it] homoerotic. [Van Camp] resists these safe . . . strategies and instead challenges the reader" (231). Hopkins and Van Camp refuse to allow Indigenous male bodies to be reduced (or reduc*ible*) to instruments only of violence or sexual conquest. Without denying the protracted influence of colonial gender violence on Indigenous lives, the film centres diverse Indigenous bodies in all their expressive potential, opening horizons of possibility for the individuals, communities, and nations that the film represents.[4] With Grant's declaration that "I want something more, you know? I just want more," the film witnesses desire not for satiation but for possibility, for visions of the future that exceed the territorial, political, and gendered confines of a settler colonial present. In Sinclair's words, the film asks "How can we have discourses about male love that are . . . irreducible to just bodies and sex and instead about embracing our inheritances and responsibilities as men, as fathers, and as brothers?" (231).

*Indigenous masculinities studies should honour bodies in all their diverse beauty while guarding against biological determinism and the suffocating imperatives of the colonial gender binary. These studies should work to "ensure every Indigenous body, honored and sacred knows respect in their bones" (Simpson, As We 51), including those who identify as Indigenous men and boys but never in ways that exclude those who identify otherwise.*

## PROVOCATION 2: NON-INTERFERENCE AND SOVEREIGN INTENTIONALITY

The exploration of masculinities in *Mohawk Midnight Runners* is prompted by the suicide of Justin, a non-Indigenous resident of Six Nations played by Ryan Scott Greene, who, in Grant's words, appeared to have "it all." The "wild card in our deck," Justin was known to strip naked and run through the reserve on nights of drinking when the song "Come on Eileen" by Dexy's Midnight Runners played on the radio. This peculiar habit, which earned Justin the nickname "The Six Nay Streak," sticks in Grant's mind in the wake of his death, along with a memory of the night that they "caught [Justin] naked down on the River Road, running." Grant is haunted by the latter instance because it fails to align with a singular explanatory narrative: "That night was different, man. He was sober, you know? He wasn't fuckin' around. And I remembered this look on his face that he had. And, I don't know, man, if you could just see that look that he had." Unlike incidents in the bar—influenced by the "glow" of intoxication, prompted by the stimulus of a song, and, in a way, performed for an audience of patrons—the time along River Road is solitary, enacted for Justin and Justin alone. Mentioning twice the "look" that he had, Grant stresses his intentionality: Justin seemingly pursued this action with purpose and meaning, yet such meaning remains inaccessible to the onlooker. It is, in effect, sovereign. The "look" frustrates because it illuminates just how much has been going on in Justin's life that has been hidden even from his intimates. And as Justice notes above, the male body is *supposed* to be legible—its motivations identifiable, its desires finite. The "look" is troubling because of its opacity: it alerts the viewer to pain that can persist beneath a strong, beautiful, even funny exterior, something that Hopkins accentuates through camera effects that turn Justin's green-blue eyes into cavernous black holes. However, the "look" is simultaneously liberatory: it signifies that myriad possibilities for masculine expression and experience persist beyond social codes and expectations, that the story we have been told about the male body is not the whole story; it honours the intricacies of masculine experience that settler colonialism would deny.

Grant's fixation on Justin's memory manifests in an undeniable urge to run naked himself. Having been locked in a cycle of avoidance since his friend's death, depicted in a montage of solitary drinking, smoking up, and gaming, Grant turns to face his grief through streaking. In contrast to a prior state of alienation from the body—demonstrated to the viewer through images of glazed, vacant eyes, confinement to a chair, and absorption by a TV screen—his streaking is presented as an active, embodied endeavour: Grant is filmed lovingly and whole, silhouetted in moonlight as he runs naked with purpose on Six Nations land. Like Randy Jackson, who explains "That's why I used to run, because I was fully present in my body when I did that. . . . [R]unning was a way for me to stand still, if that makes any sense," Grant reawakens his selfhood by putting his body on the land. As he begins to activate his body through exercise, he engages in what Gregory Scofield calls "a liberation through claiming." "Coming to my own masculinity," Scofield explains, "began with me having to work to be in touch with my own body. . . . I started working out, I started building up parts of my body. I started feeling the places where I was physically strong. And there was a kind of liberation within that process" ("Liberation" 214). Grant undertakes a similarly liberatory praxis, envisioned as a journey back to the body; he fosters his own sense of personal integrity by reintegrating mind, body, and spirit. And he does so, like Justin, in a sovereign manner expressive of his own autonomy and Haudenosaunee ethics of non-interference (as theorized by Kanien'keha:ka psychiatrist Clare Brant and discussed in Chapter 1). Yet, because Grant runs in isolation, at this point in the film, it remains unclear whether his heightened sense of autonomy and purpose will calcify into individualism and self-interest or act as a catalyst to social and territorial integration; it remains unclear whether his chosen vulnerability in streaking will enable him to find peace and community in a way that Justin could not.[5]

*Indigenous masculinities studies should value, theorize, and remain responsive to individual autonomy and personal integrity while working to ensure that they are not co-opted by the corrupting influences of capitalism and individualism. As Anishinaabe Elder Basil Johnston instructs, "we have to go back to some of these values: responsibility, duty, right" ("Young Men" 45).*

## PROVOCATION 3: CONSENSUAL VULNERABILITY AND (RE)INTEGRATION

In my reading of *Mohawk Midnight Runners*, the pathway to well-being initially charted by Grant through streaking is not made fully navigable until two friends, Clarence and Brutus, spy him running. At this moment, his growth seems to hang in the balance between potential validation and flourishment, on the one hand, and denial and relapse, on the other. Hopkins depicts the two friends bursting into Grant's home, laughing hysterically at what they have witnessed—"Why were you running naked with Chris Maracle's dog?!"—and cheekily mocking Grant's hairy physique: "Dude, what's up with all the hair?! You look like you're wearing a sweater vest made outta shag carpeting!" Yet there is gentleness in this ridicule, as signified by Brutus's subtle placement of the gift of a soda on the table next to Grant as they talk and Grant's fairly swift participation in the collective laughter. In fact, the jocular atmosphere appears to foster the sense of connection required for Grant to share his feelings and aspirations rather than prevent it. Directly on the heels of this ribbing, he reveals the depth of his grief for Justin and his desire to make changes in his life: "I want something more, you know. I just want more."

What makes this scene so significant, in my reading, is its use of humour and a typically masculine vernacular to open up space for sharing and support. The scene does not deny the simplistic posturing involved in male socialization but commandeers it in the service of positive change. The mockery becomes not a weapon of exile but a tool of integration because it occurs within what Simpson calls a "constellation of care." Humour, in this scene, is not a form of avoidance but a vehicle for engagement—it enables one to tend closely to the fire without being burned. In the Indigenous Hawaiian context, Ty P. Kāwika Tengan refers to the kind of dialogue that occurs among intimates in this scene as "talking story," arguing that "in the larger context of the group . . . this is what creates . . . a shared identity because you're having and engaging in this communicative event, this modelling of personal stories after collective stories. Making these emotional, personal, and collective connections, that's what solidifies a sense of community" ("Talking Story" 117). Hopkins's film provides a paradigmatic model of such community building: jocularity creates conditions of comfort in which Grant allows himself to be vulnerable; he shares stories about Justin and his own grieving process, which then become layered over by the stories of his friends; these "emotional, personal, and collective connections" inform the mutual decision to continue midnight streaking not in solitude but collectively; the three young Haudenosaunee men then proceed to imagine ways in which to marshal their consensual vulnerability—stripped bare both literally and metaphorically—in the service of their land, community, and nation.

*Indigenous masculinities studies should celebrate how consensual vulnerability generates space for intimacy, dynamic mutuality, and community building while guarding against coerced vulnerabilities of all kinds. In the words of Scofield, "The pathway back is for men to know their own bodies, to know the vulnerability that lives within their bodies, and to honour that vulnerability" (McKegney et al. 261).*

## PROVOCATION 4: ROLES, RESPONSIBILITIES, AND RETERRITORIALIZATION

Reflecting on data from community-based working groups on Indigenous masculinities, Robert Innes, Kim Anderson, and Jonathan Swift identify "a general feeling" among participants "that creating men's spaces [is] a good place to begin rebuilding relationships and responsibilities" and that such spaces can constitute "a beginning of building a community of men who are being and becoming healthy by supporting other men" (302–03). *Mohawk Midnight Runners* celebrates one such space as Grant's efforts to bring himself back to balance through consensual vulnerability and what Tengan calls "embodied discursive action" (*Native Men Remade*) are supported by other men within a "constellation of care." However, as Innes, Anderson, and Swift's stress on *beginnings* implies, the symbiotic relationship between individual healing and group support eventually requires movement beyond the homosocial sphere in order to prove genuinely world building. In other words, "men's spaces" cannot remain strictly inward facing but must ultimately attend to relationships beyond the "in group" in order to serve the territory and the nation. Hopkins demonstrates this spatially via the men's physical movement beyond the fence of Grant's home and throughout Six Nations Territory and narratively via the relational tenor of the men's "agreed-upon ritual":

> Monday night was run for your ex night.
> Tuesdays, we ran for our parents.
> Wednesdays, we ran for everyone on the reserve.
> Thursdays, we ran for our ancestors.
> Fridays was "happy hour"—you could run for whoever you wanted.
> Saturdays was run for no cancer or diabetes.
> And Sundays we ran for the Creator and all our blessings.

Each of these dedications registers commitment to relations that extend beyond the community of runners themselves, relations with political, spiritual, ecological, and gendered valences. Such attentiveness to the contours of kinship also characterizes the choices of whom the men will run for during the final night of streaking depicted in the film. Acknowledging that "we've been running for a week now," Grant suggests, "I think it's only best we pay respects to Justin and his family." Brutus decides to run for a former lover named Beth. "I really screwed her over," he explains. "I just want her to be happy." And Clarence shares that he will be running for his on-again-off-again girlfriend Belinda, who, he then discloses, has that day informed him that she is pregnant. Although Clarence confesses, "I'm not ready to be a dad, man," Grant exclaims, "Clarence, this is great. We're gonna be uncles now!"

With this exchange, the men begin to grapple with their roles and responsibilities, doing so in decidedly heteronormative terms: futurity is augured through Clarence's procreative union, Brutus claims responsibility for transgressions committed in a bygone heterosexual romance, and Grant asserts identity in masculine terms through the familial marker of "uncle." Yet, on closer examination, there's more going on here. Brutus's homage to a former lover falls outside a patriarchal framework of masculine possessiveness insofar as Brutus wishes not for reunion but for Beth's happiness in her current relationship. He honours her autonomy and decision making: "I hope they have a good life together, you know?" Similarly, Grant's jubilant response to Belinda's pregnancy is not a simplistic endorsement of nuclear family social organization and biological succession but a gesture of communal commitment to the next generation,[6] a gesture that nonetheless validates the fraught emotions that Clarence is experiencing. Although this scene trades in masculinist language—even concluding with a penis joke about what it means to "*swing* by" Belinda's house—I believe that it does so to open up for both its characters and its audience potentialities *beyond* dominant regimes of gender. To borrow from Métis scholar Warren Cariou, to "change the script" of problematic gender codes (Cariou and Calder 127), one must first know it, and *Mohawk Midnight Runners* is able to rehearse and then transcend the script of putative masculinity in the service of change. In these ways, the film illuminates how homosocial spaces and masculine posturing might be marshalled in the service of imagining and embodying Indigenous masculinities beyond heteropatriarchy—perhaps even *against* heteropatriarchy.

*Indigenous masculinities studies should theorize roles and responsibili-*
*ties as fertile vehicles for activating senses of purpose through which full*
*humanity might be actualized while guarding against the ossification of roles*
*as themselves identities. As Ngāti Pūkenga theorist Brendan Hokowhitu*
*instructs, "look for complexity . . . as opposed to the simplistic answers. The*
*thing to keep in our minds is the risk of pathologizing Indigenous masculin-*
*ity. It is easy to pick holes at—thinking it's history and we're just products*
*of that history—but we also need to look for those moments where . . .*
*Indigenous men are interacting with those discourses and either challenging*
*them or using them for their own purposes" ("Embodied Masculinity" 108).*

## THOSE WHO CARRY THE BURDEN OF PEACE

As the "gap" between the dancers grows in Belcourt's "Sacred," symbolizing the community's *disintegration* because of the naturalization of heteropatriarchy, the speaker determines to "fill it with the
memories of native boys who couldn't be warriors because their
bodies were too fragile to carry all of that anger." Far from the
ethics of the Rotiskenrakéh:te, whom Kanien'keha:ka activist Ellen
Gabriel describes as those who honour, respect, and practise "peace
in their daily lives but [have] the ability to protect the people and
the land when a threat to their safety is imminent" ("Those"), or
the ethics of the okihcitâwak, whom Cree activist Colin Naytowhow describes as those who are "here to help" and ensure that "the
camp [is] kept safe" (qtd. in Smoke), warriorhood, as it is expressed
here, is divested of meaning and overdetermined by rage. In fact,
"all of that anger" appears to corrupt male bodies into mere vessels
of violence, denying other expressive possibilities. Warriorhood
appears to ossify into a simulated image resonating more with the
"bloodthirsty savage" image of masculindians than with the needs
of communities. Once again, however, I stress that such delimited
understandings—the products of settler colonialism's constricted
vision of the world—are not the only ones available to us. In fact,
by refusing to conform to entrenched stereotypes of warriorhood
and masculinity, the male children welcomed into the circle by the
speaker's memories imply that other expressive realities are possible.

**Image 10:** Still from *Mohawk Midnight Runners*: (left to right) R. Douglas Hutchison, Cody Lightning, and Jon Proudstar. Credit: *Mohawk Midnight Runners*, dir. Zoe Leigh Hopkins (Big Soul Productions, 2013). Distributor: Vtape.org.

*Mohawk Midnight Runners* gifts its audience with inspired reimaginings of Indigenous warriorhood, as the young Haudenosaunee men pursue responsibilities as nurturers, caregivers, and protectors, and of Indigenous masculinities. The film does more than reimagine: it offers depictions of masculinities that precede, succeed, and exceed colonial limitations; masculinities that are embodied yet spiritual, empowered yet vulnerable, hilarious yet deadly serious; masculinities that nurture both the full humanity of Indigenous persons and the empowered futures of Indigenous nations. Hopkins refuses to concede to the impoverished iconography of inherited simulations of Indigenous masculinity. She refuses to concede to the naturalization of heteronormativity and Indigenous dispossession. At the same time, she refuses to deny men communities of jocular posturing and laughter that can create conditions in which sharing and mutual support become possible. *Mohawk Midnight Runners* thus constitutes a creative intervention that is as practical as it is visionary, as epitomized by Grant's simple assertion: "I want more."

Indigenous masculinities are more than what settler colonialism has told us they are. The hegemonic masculinities developed through European men's participation in colonial atrocities and inculcated in mainstream North American society (what Scott Morgensen calls "colonial masculinities"), the simulations of Indigenous masculinities propagated to naturalize the settler state (what I call "masculindians"), and the socially engineered, subordinate masculinities disciplined through residential schooling and the *Indian Act* (what I theorize above via "the false promise of patriarchy")—they are not, nor have they ever been, the only masculinities available to us; these profound failures of imagination exist to quarantine and contain our gender knowledges. Indigenous literary art offers more generative and world-building possibilities: it reaches to and participates in what Qwo-Li Driskill calls a "much larger memory that stretches all the way back" (*Asegi Stories* 138); it interrogates the systemic violence through which that memory, in many cases, has been rent from our knowing, and it generates new memories still, via stories armed to nurture a more just and balanced world.

# GRATITUDE

To the artists, activists, academics, and Elders whose wisdom is shared in *Masculindians*, I am forever grateful for your generosity and will continue to work to be worthy of the trust that you placed in me. The present volume represents some of that labour.

This project has taken well over a decade from conception to publication, and during that time it has been buoyed by inspiration gleaned from the brilliance of many people. I express my gratitude to several of them below.

To the practitioners of Indigenous masculinities studies who struggle in the service of more nuanced and generative understandings of gender: Kim Anderson, Bobby Henry, Brendan Hokowhitu, Rob Innes, Shane Keepness, Lloyd Lee, Lisa Tatonetti, Ty Tengan, and others.

To the mentors who have challenged and guided me, taught me and taken me to task: Eugene Arcand, Louis Bird, Jo-Ann Episkenew, Louise Bernice Halfe, Basil H. Johnston, Janice Hill Kanonhsyonne, Bonita Lawrence, and Thomas Kimeksum Thrasher.

To my ILSA family for providing the generative spaces and supportive relationships in which vigorous critical work can be nurtured: Allison, Armand, Aubrey, Daniel, Deanna, Heather, Jesse, Jordan, June, Kaitlin, Keavy, Kristina, Maddie, Marie-Eve, Michelle, Niigaan, Pauline, Renate, Rick, Sarah, Smokii, Sophie, Svetlana, Warren, and many others.

To the IHRN team for continuous inspiration and insight, including the Advisory Council—Eugene, Kelly, Mandi, Marion, Mel, Rick, and Sam—and the researchers—Alex, Andrew, Bobby,

Dallas, Darren, Devi, Davina, Jamieson, Janice, Jeremy, Jordan, Kalley, Michael, Mike, Shane, and Taylor.

To the research assistants whose tireless labour and welcome critical insights have strengthened this project in manifold ways (its weaknesses, of course, remaining my own): Abbey Cressman, Cara Fabre, Jennifer Hardwick, Marshall Hill, Ky Pearce, and Jamieson Ryan.

To the graduate and undergraduate students at Queen's University whose engaged conversations in Indigenous literature classes over the past several years have challenged and invigorated this work.

To the colleagues and friends on whom I rely for guidance and mentorship in the Department of English and throughout Queen's University in the territories of the Haudenosaunee and Anishinaabe Peoples.

To the University of Regina Press team for direction and support during the publication process for this volume, including Kristine Luecker, Karen Clark, Kelly Laycock, David McLennan, Duncan Campbell, and Dallas Harrison. Thanks, as well, are due to the University of Arizona Press team for support of the co-publication.

And to the brilliant, rigorous, and generous reviewers of the manuscript, I am forever indebted to the rare sensitivity with which you approached this project, made immeasurably stronger for your criticisms and recommendations (its weaknesses are again my own).

To each of you and many others, I am grateful.

And to the women whose laughter, wisdom, and kindness animate my joy and illuminate the future toward which I aspire—my wife, Sherrie, our daughters, Caitlyn and Kyara, and my mother, Bubbles—and to my father, Ian, who has consistently shown me the strength arising from nurturing masculinities, I am rich from your many teachings.

# ACKNOWLEDGEMENTS

**P**arts of Chapter 1 were originally published in "Warriors, Healers, Lovers, and Leaders: Colonial Impositions on Indigenous Male Roles and Responsibilities," *Canadian Perspectives on Men and Masculinities: An Interdisciplinary Reader*, edited by Jason A. Laker, Oxford UP, 2011, pp. 241–68, and in "Writer-Reader Reciprocity and the Pursuit of Alliance in Indigenous Poetry," *Indigenous Poetics in Canada*, edited by Neal McLeod, Wilfrid Laurier UP, 2014, pp. 43–60.

Parts of Chapter 2 were originally published in "'Pain, Pleasure, Shame. Shame'—Masculine Embodiment, Kinship, and Indigenous Reterritorialization," *Canadian Literature*, vol. 216, 2014, pp. 12–33, and reprinted in *Arts of Engagement: Taking Aesthetic Action in and beyond the Truth and Reconciliation Commission of Canada*, edited by Dylan Robinson and Keavy Martin, Wilfrid Laurier UP, 2016, pp. 193–214.

Parts of Chapter 5 were originally published in "'Beautiful Hunters with Strong Medicine': Indigenous Masculinity and Kinship in Richard Van Camp's *The Lesser Blessed*," *The Canadian Journal of Native Studies*, vol. 29, nos. 1–2, 2009, pp. 203–27.

I am indebted to the University of Manitoba Press for the publication of *Masculindians: Conversations about Indigenous Manhood*, 2014, since the interviews housed therein have informed my thinking for this project in myriad ways.

Work on this project has been made possible by grants from the Social Sciences and Humanities Research Council of Canada.

# NOTES

## BURDENS AND BUNDLES: AN INTRODUCTION

1    In his blog post entitled "'Just Make Me Look Like Aquaman': An Essay on Seeing Myself," Ktunaxa transmasculine writer and scholar Smokii Sumac describes such recognition's impact on personal integrity in a narrative about the time that his two-spirit identity was acknowledged and affirmed in a ceremony by a Choctaw medicine woman. "[F]or me," Sumac writes, "it wasn't until she saw me—really saw me, that I began to learn what it meant for me to carry and honour my role." Importantly, Sumac's feelings of nourishment and self-worth are here articulated through the language of roles: his sense of self being honoured and supported by another is expressed through a sense of purpose and duty. This, in my understanding here, is integrity.

2    Brant refers in this passage to the awakening of her awareness "in the thirty-third year of [her] life" that she could "love women sexually, emotionally, and spiritually—and all at once" (56–57), arguing that this realization enabled a sense of wholeness of benefit not only to herself but also to her community. Although she refers specifically to her sense of integrity as a "whole woman," her championing of gender and sexual diversity implies that such wholeness can be experienced by others throughout the gender spectrum provided that the gender systems in which they function do not police their desires or coerce forms of fragmentation and denial. For this reason, and to show how this argument is also relevant to those who self-identify as men (or as other-than-women), I have altered "woman" to "person" in this quotation. I have changed "whole woman" to "whole [person]" not to diminish gender difference (in one's experiences and one's worldview) but to open up who is able to experience such wholeness.

3    I stress that these are the objectives (conscious or otherwise) of settler colonialism—an adaptable structure bent on Indigenous disappearance in the service of resource exploitation and the accumulation of land and

capital for non-Indigenous populations. These are not the inevitable experiences of Indigenous persons. As I will argue throughout this book, settler colonial policies and practices from the *Indian Act* to residential schooling to mainstream curricula to hiring practices to mundane or everyday racism have consistently targeted gender to deny the full humanity of Indigenous people. However, I do not wish to imply the perverse "success" of colonial technologies of erasure via the pathologization of Indigenous populations. The resilience, resistance, and resurgence of Indigenous individuals, families, communities, and nations are both demonstrated and fostered by the critical and creative voices upon which I draw in this book.

4    This definition of "masculinities" is a revised version of the one that I first expressed in *Masculindians: Conversations about Indigenous Manhood* ("Into" 7). Furthermore, I should note that "masculinity" in common usage tends implicitly to mean white masculinity, which tends to be taken as the norm from which other masculinities deviate. White masculinities are usually tied to wealth (upper- and middle-class masculinity) or physical labour and toughness (lower-class masculinity), each of which is bound, therefore, to settler colonialism. My enterprise in this book is to denormalize and decentre white masculinities by engaging with bountiful alternatives emergent in Indigenous literary art.

5    For example, Robert Innes, Kim Anderson, and Jonathan Swift note that many participants in their study of Indigenous masculinities "struggled with the concept of 'masculinity,' equating it typically with hegemonic, patriarchal, or hypermasculine identities that they were . . . trying to escape" (287); the authors thus note that several Indigenous participants identified "'masculinity' as a behavior to recover from" (289).

6    Pêyahtihk is translated from Cree in the collection as "to walk softly, to give something great thought or consideration" (4).

7    These works include Tłı̨chǫ writer Richard Van Camp's *The Lesser Blessed* (1996); Cree writer Tomson Highway's *Kiss of the Fur Queen* (1998), which explores similar matters through the relationship between biological rather than surrogate brothers; Cherokee-Greek writer Thomas King's *Truth and Bright Water* (1999); then understood to be Irish-Scottish-Métis writer Joseph Boyden's *Three Day Road* (2005); and Haisla-Heiltsuk writer Eden Robinson's *Blood Sports* (2006). I discuss Van Camp's novel and Robinson's novel in Chapters 4 and 5 of this volume.

8    Hokowhitu's articles published at this point include "Tackling Maori Masculinity: A Colonial Genealogy of Savagery and Sport" (2004) and "Sport, Tribes, and Technology: The New Zealand All Blacks Haka and the Politics of Identity" (co-authored with Steven J. Jackson 2002). Kim Anderson's *A Recognition of Being: Reconstructing Native Womanhood* (2001) and Paula Gunn Allen's *The Sacred Hoop: Recovering the Feminine*

*in American Indian Traditions* (1986) are examples of Indigenous feminist works that consider male roles and responsibilities within the context of Indigenous women's empowerment. The work that I refer to here by Duran and Duran is *Native American Postcolonial Psychology* (1995). Those works concerned with settler representations of Indigenous masculinity include Elizabeth Cromley's "Masculine/Indian" (1996) and Brian Klopotek's "'I Guess Your Warrior Look Doesn't Work Every Time': Challenging Indian Masculinity in the Cinema" (2001).

9    When I noted to Stó:lō writer Lee Maracle that, compared with Indigenous feminist work and Indigenous queer and two-spirit work, the body of knowledge on Indigenous masculinities is relatively sparse, she clarified that "there's not a book on it; that doesn't mean there isn't bodies of work. A body is a person. There's lots of men who can speak to this issue. They just haven't been published" ("This" 34).

10   I am particularly grateful to the late Métis scholar Jo-Ann Episkenew for her support and encouragement in this regard. Not only did she stress to me the importance of initiating conversations about masculinity, but also she insisted that these conversations be made public to enable Indigenous readers to participate in the collaborative generation of knowledge on this topic. I am forever indebted to Jo-Ann for her mentorship, guidance, and friendship.

11   These gatherings included "Gender and Decolonization: A Resurgent Gathering," an event organized by the Kahswentha Initiative at Queen's University in February 2015; "Amiqaaq: A Symposium on Indigenous Masculinities," put on by the Faculty of Native Studies at the University of Alberta in December 2015; and a gathering on the subject of "Indigenous Masculinities" held prior to the Native American and Indigenous Studies Association conference at the University of Hawaii, Honolulu, in May 2016.

12   Further analysis of the gift as a philosophically charged vehicle for fomenting social cohesion, fostering reciprocity, and creating conditions for masculinities worthy of claiming is supplied in Chapter 4 of this volume.

13   As I wrote some years ago, "As much as intellectual empathy and ethical commitment can pervade the work of a scholar with neither biological nor immediate social connection to Indigenous communities, the consequences of that individual's work cannot be experienced personally with the same intensity as one whose day-to-day lived experience is being Indigenous. Although I endeavor to be as sensitive and respectful as I am able, as a non-Native critic I simply do not stand to inherit the adverse social impact my critical work might engender, and this, it seems to me, impacts the way my work functions and is something about which I must remain critically conscious" ("Strategies" 57). Although the article from which this quotation is excerpted is more brazen than it needed

to be, indicating my immaturity as a scholar at the time, I still stand by its central premises. The article also provides a more fulsome elaboration of my thoughts on the ethical responsibilities of settler scholars of Indigenous literatures.

14   *You Are Enough* forms something of a cadence or mantra throughout the collection, affirming its speaker's progress toward expressing, internalizing, and practising self-love. The collection thus balances a scathing critique of an untenable settler colonial present with a vibrant ethos of becoming. As Sumac writes, "when you survive genocide / everyone left / is family" (43).

15   Sumac's work also remains relentlessly attuned to the urgency of embodied experience. His untethering of masculinities from solely cis-male bodies in no way diminishes the collection's celebrations of embodied intimacy and recognition of affective and bodily knowledge. As Sumac writes, "our trained bodies know" (49). I gratefully acknowledge that my thinking in relation to Sumac's poetry has been profoundly influenced by settler scholar Lisa Tatonetti's forthcoming study of non-cis Indigenous masculinities and the affective transit of knowledge in literature, film, and art entitled *Written by the Body: Gender Expansiveness and Indigenous Non-Cis Masculinities*.

16   After declaring that "my first time was good," Sumac's speaker offers the qualification "the consensual first time / the one that i count." When, at the beginning of the poem's third section, the speaker introduces "the other first time," the reader is conditioned to anticipate, therefore, the elaboration of a non-consensual "first time"; however, the passage that follows depicts a beautiful scene of sensual intimacy made possible by "sweet green apple / consent" (29). Here the term "other" refers to the speaker's first sexual encounter with a woman. In a powerful act of refusal, the speaker denies the reader access to "the bad sex," to sex weaponized via toxic masculinity and violence, instead focusing poetic attention on a celebration of sensual intimacy that nourishes both speaker and audience—"a gift of learning / reciprocity" (29).

17   Such radical autonomy is theorized within the Haudenosaunee worldview by Kanien'keha:ka psychiatrist Clare Brant as the "ethic of non-interference," as I will discuss in Chapter 1.

18   In conversation with Laura Coltelli, Anishinaabe theorist Gerald Vizenor states that "I touch myself into being with my own dreams and with my imagination. I am what I say I am, and I emphasize I am a state of being, and I gather all those words that feed and nurture my imagination about my being" (Coltelli 159).

19   According to its website, 'Aha Kāne's vision, purpose, and mission are "To nurture a healthier Native Hawaiian male population by eliminating psychosocial, health, and educational disparities through activities

founded on traditional cultural practices that build sustainability in the community . . . [t]o increase our awareness and empower Native Hawaiian males to fulfill our roles and responsibilities amongst ourselves, as well as within our families and respective communities . . . [and] [t]o strengthen the Native Hawaiian community through nurturing and perpetuating the traditional male roles and responsibilities that contribute to the physical, mental, spiritual, and social well-being of Native Hawaiian males, their families, and communities."

20    My recollection of the response, for which I was present, is that the speaker argued that some queer and two-spirit Hawaiians "flaunt" their sexuality unnecessarily.

21    This incident illuminates tensions at play in grappling with Indigenous men's issues through the critical lens of masculinities studies. The representatives of 'Aha Kāne were invited to speak at the gathering because of the important work in which they engage pertaining to the revitalization of Indigenous Hawaiian culture and the fostering of self-knowledge and self-worth among Hawaiian men and boys. Their voices and experiences were of considerable value to the objectives of the gathering even though one representative of the group demonstrated homophobic intolerance during the discussion. On the one hand, Indigenous masculinities studies risks obfuscating the voices of more conservative individuals who do not yet have the language to think through gender in fluid, pluralist ways but nonetheless have significant cultural knowledge to share; on the other hand, the inclusion of voices that would cast homophobia as "traditional" places queer and two-spirit people at risk through the disavowal of their humanity and cultural legitimacy. Distressed by the apparent lack of safety afforded to queer Indigenous youth at the gathering, Daniel Heath Justice announced in his final comments on that day that he would no longer participate in critical discussions of Indigenous masculinities after the Honolulu event.

22    According to its website, the Indigenous Governance Program, the first of its kind in North America, was founded in 1999 to advance four key objectives: "1. An Indigenous learning environment based on a foundation of Indigenous world views, knowledge and scholarship; 2. Educating and training students (Indigenous and non-indigenous alike) to be transformational leaders, with a commitment to personal decolonization; 3. Working with Indigenous communities and organizations to assist and contribute to the development of governance capacity; and, 4. Supporting the struggle of Indigenous nations to restore their land bases and ensure respect for their inherent and treaty rights" ("Indigenous Governance Programs"). The review was conducted by Madeleine Kétéskwew Dion Stout (a retired professor and specialist in Indigenous health, racism, lateral violence, and trauma) and Jamie Chicanot (a partner with the

firm ADR, which specializes in workplace conflict resolution). The independent Victoria newspaper *The Martlet* quoted an anonymous former student stating that "What the report said was true. . . . It is a traumatic and unsafe environment for many so I'm glad another year of students won't be exposed to that" (Dodd and Fagan).

23 When I began to explore this subject matter, Alfred was the first scholar whom I consulted back in 2007. Part of that initial discussion is included in our interview published in *Masculindians* (Alfred, "Reimagining"), coupled with another conversation from 2011. Alfred's own expressions of masculinity have come under considerable scrutiny in recent years and been tied to the unhealthy environment identified in the Indigenous Governance Program. In an interview regarding his departure, Alfred stated that, "'If you're asking me if I'm hyper-masculine, well, I'm Mohawk from Kahnawake. . . . I'm Mohawk from Kahnawake and that's who I am'" (qtd. in Rowe).

24 Glen Coulthard's arguments in *Red Skin, White Masks: Rejecting the Colonial Politics of Recognition* regarding male behaviour are prescient here. "Although many Native male supporters of Idle No More have done a fairly decent job symbolically recognizing the centrality of Indigenous women to the movement," he argues, "this is not the recognition that I hear being demanded by Indigenous feminists. The demand, rather, is that society, including Indigenous society and particularly men, stop collectively conducting ourselves in a manner that denigrates, degrades, and devalues the lives and worth of Indigenous women in such a way that epidemic levels of violence are the norm in too many of their lives. Of course, this violence must be stopped in its overt forms, but we must also stop practicing it in its more subtle expressions—in our daily relationships and practices in the home, workplaces, band offices, governance institutions, and, crucially, in our practices of cultural resurgence. Until this happens we have reconciled ourselves with defeat" (179).

25 To reckon with this complicity, I aspire to an abiding sense of caution in the present volume, as well as citational sensitivity.

26 Jesse Rae Archibald-Barber is Métis, Cree, and Canadian from Regina and a professor of Indigenous literatures at the First Nations University of Canada. Walsh is non-Indigenous. As Walsh notes in his response to an article by Alicia Elliott, he was "the only self-identified LGBT2S+ person who is director of a university press in Canada" at the time of the controversy ("Response to 'We Need to Talk'"). He indicates that URP responded to the signatories' concerns "by offering more space in the anthology, highlighting their voices and the issue of violence against women and Two-Spirit writers. We also offered an anthology devoted to their writing. They declined." There were many reasons to consider in retaining McLeod's work, including (1) the fact that the anthology aimed

to be comprehensive, including all published Indigenous writers from Saskatchewan, (2) the slippery slope of exclusion for antisocial conduct and how such conduct might plausibly be found to apply to several other authors, (3) the potential utility of work by perpetrators in efforts to combat gender-based violence, and (4) the influence of McLeod's critical and creative writing on Saskatchewan-based Indigenous writers and on the field of Indigenous literary studies in Canada. Archibald-Barber notes in an "Editor's Post" on his personal Facebook page from October 19, 2017, that the anthology "emerged directly out of the roots of the Saskatchewan Indigenous writing community," in "careful consultation with the writers" themselves. He states that, "From the start, I chose not to exclude any writer" and, as such, "could not satisfy [the] demand" that a "writer be removed from the historical record." I wish to clarify that I do not disagree with Archibald-Barber's commitment to including in the collection all published Indigenous authors (including McLeod) from the lands commonly known as Saskatchewan. Although I counselled a different course of action when consulted by the press in the aftermath of the initial "open letter," I am confident that Archibald-Barber made his decision based on ethical principles and extensive community consultation under extremely difficult circumstances. I have collaborated extensively with Archibald-Barber in our capacity as past presidents of the Indigenous Literary Studies Association and have always known him to be a scholar of integrity, generosity, and wisdom.

27   Nixon elaborates these issues evocatively, conceding that "I have no idea what 'me too' and 'I believe you' mean in the context of a normalized culture of abuse among Indigenous peoples or any idea of what's next. I only know that we need to continue having these conversations and making space for Indigenous truths."

28   Walsh argues along similar lines that "Walking with a man on his path towards healing does not mean abandoning the needs of women" ("Publisher's Response").

29   In contrast to others who have sustained their public personae in the aftermath of being accused of violent and predatory behaviour, McLeod has retreated from public life entirely in recent years.

30   In her discussion of "the cost of calling out abuse within marginalized communities," published by the CBC, Elliott argues that Walsh's response to the open letter "uses phrases like 'academic freedom' and 'censorship' as a sort of shorthand non-Native people can both understand and get self-righteously furious about." In a rebuttal of aspects of her argument published a few days later, Walsh rejects her interpretation and endeavours to clarify his use of those phrases ("Response"). Ironically, the sentence with which Elliott follows her critique reads, "After all, everyone knows there's nothing that fires up a certain type of Canadian

more than the idea that they should ever stop talking and start listening."
Walsh's insistence on publicly clarifying his meaning risks betraying the
very traits about which Elliott is speaking. Given the dynamics of the
*kisiskáciwan* controversy, I have struggled with the propriety of publishing
*Carrying the Burden of Peace* with URP, with which it had been originally
contracted. However, with assurances about the press's objectives and
priorities moving forward and thoughtful consultation with current
press staff, I have agreed to the present publication arrangement with
URP and the University of Arizona Press.

31     In "'Just Make Me Look Like Aquaman,'" Sumac argues that, "having
experienced 'both sides,' the world needs to treat women better. We all
do. (Yes, ALL men. Yes, ALL women.)"

32     Please note that the lands surrounding what is commonly referred to as
Kingston on the northern shore of Lake Ontario are also the traditional
territory of the Anishinaabe Nation.

33     Heeding the insights of Simpson and others, I do not ultimately seek
in the chapter to pursue "man-centred" erotics but more accurately to
consider the place of Indigenous men specifically in the generative erotics
that might make decolonial futures possible.

34     See Hokowhitu ("Death"); Klopotek; and Valaskakis (*Indian Country*).

35     In his dedication within *You Are Enough*, Sumac declares the volume
"for the warriors," and, like the collection that the term inscribes, those
"warriors" are replete with possibilities that transcend the gender binary
and putative understandings of warriorhood proffered by settler society.
The term "warriors," in the context of Sumac's poetry, can apply to those
many-gendered creative voices of Indigenous artists, activists, visioners,
water walkers, land protectors, medicine people, and scholars referenced
and honoured throughout the volume.

36     In some cases, this was entirely my responsibility because of the specific
questions that I asked, which guided the interviewee toward discussing
warriorhood. In others, warriorhood came up organically within the
discussion.

37     Acceptance is important here because it indicates a sense that the role
exceeds the individual. As Shana, an Indigenous high school student
interviewed in *Wasáse: Indigenous Pathways of Action and Freedom* (Alfred),
argues, "it's important to look at who designates himself as a 'warrior,' or
who is designated as a warrior. They serve the people, so they should be
chosen by the people. A lot of times, people self-designate themselves,
and maybe they're not serving the interests of the main community" (260).
Sumac discusses a similar understanding of the term "two-spirit": "For me,
like the term Elder, it seemed something that the community conferred
upon you. Something that was witnessed within you and acknowledged,
rather than a title I could give myself" ("'Just Make Me'").

# 1. INDIGENOUS MASCULINITIES AND STORY

1    My use of the terms "territoriality" and "deterritorialization" in this
     project thus deviates from the theorizations of Gilles Deleuze and
     Félix Guattari in *A Thousand Plateaus: Capitalism and Schizophrenia*. For
     Deleuze and Guattari, "movements of deterritorialization and processes
     of reterritorialization" are "relative, always connected, caught up in one
     another" (10). Territoriality and deterritorialization, for these theorists,
     allow us to understand "'race, sexuality, and gender as concatenations,
     unstable assemblages of revolving and devolving energies, rather than
     intersectional coordinates'" (qtd. in Tatonetti 146). According to these
     understandings, deterritorialization can prove to be liberatory; in fact,
     Deleuze and Guattari entreat their readers to "Write, form a rhizome,
     increase your territory by deterritorialization, extend the line of flight
     to the point where it becomes an abstract machine covering the entire
     plane of consistency" (11). Nikos Papastergiadis argues that deterritori-
     alization, in this mode, enables "'a critical sensibility of innovation and
     improvisation'" through which "'the deterritorialized subject both devel-
     ops a more dynamic relationship between past and present, and offers
     new interpretations of the flows in the world'" (qtd. in Tatonetti 156).
     In her analysis of Koyangk'auwi poet Janice Gould's work, Lisa Tatonetti
     traces the empowering potential of deterritorialization, arguing that
     Gould "actively constructs alternate knowledge to deterritorialize—or
     'carry . . . away'—damaging understandings of self" while employing the
     erotic as "a creative force that deterritorializes settler colonial under-
     standings of sexuality to engender Indigenous visibility and voice" (156,
     161). According to this understanding, to territorialize is to solidify, to
     achieve momentary stasis, and therefore to yield to disciplinary power
     (e.g., of the settler state), and deterritorialization is to escape from such
     power through "line[s] of flight." To the contrary, I employ territorial-
     ity in this project to register the natural ways through which identities
     are cultivated via relationality and territorial persistence. Territoriality
     is place-based selfhood nested within mutually generative reciprocal
     relations. Deterritorialization refers to settler colonialism's assaults on
     Indigenous identities, languages, kinship systems, systems of governance,
     et cetera—assaults designed to fragment individuals and families and
     force them off their lands. Crucially, however, deterritorialization, as I
     use it in this book, is not a perverse end point pitched toward the irre-
     coverable; deterritorialization becomes recalibrated by resurgent action
     toward reterritorialization, in the senses not only of revitalized relations
     with human and other-than-human kin but also of land reclamation and
     redistribution—of non-metaphorical decolonization.

2    As Hokowhitu argues in "The Death of Koro Paka: 'Traditional' Māori
     Patriarchy," "To buy into the notion that [Indigenous] culture can be

'authenticated' is to align with the colonizer" (133). This is why he endeavours to use "culture" as a living signifier rather than "traditional culture" ("Beyond Masculinities").

3    In "Warriors, Healers, Lovers, and Leaders: Colonial Impositions on Indigenous Male Roles and Responsibilities," I argue that, "Without even addressing the arbitrary imposition of national borders on the pre-existing Indigenous nations of Turtle Island . . . or the enforcement of Eurocentric notions of land ownership on Indigenous persons who may or may not self-identify as 'Canadian,' 'Indigenous Canadian masculinity,' as a category, lumps together the unique traditions and worldviews of hundreds of Indigenous nations from the T'lingit, Nuu'chah'nulth, and Haisla on the Pacific coast to the Mi'kmaq, Penobscot, and Naskapi on the Atlantic coast to the Inuvialuit, Gwich'in, and Igloolik Inuit on the Arctic coast to the Iroquois, Anishinaabe, and Blackfoot in between. If the question were narrowed to a tribal-specific designation like 'Cree masculinity,' the problem of generalization endures: are we referring to the Woodland Cree of Lac La Ronge or the Swampy Cree of Red Earth or the Plains Cree of Peepeekisis? Each of these communities has its own linguistic idioms, its own oral and written histories, its own traditional songs and stories, its own customs and social systems" (241). I argue further that "the desire to absorb various aspects of living, breathing Indigenous societies beneath an essentialist banner of the 'Indian' betrays a colonial approach to non-European cultures that treats as 'authentic' only those characteristics associated with imagined pre-contact purity, thereby denying Indigenous societies the capacity to adapt, grow, and evolve without forfeiting their distinct identities. As Sioux intellectual Vine Deloria Jr. argues, 'Unlike many other . . . traditions, tribal [traditions] . . . have not been authoritatively set 'once and for always.' Truth is in the ever-changing experiences of the community. For the traditional Indian to fail to appreciate this aspect of his heritage is the saddest of heresies. It means the Indian has unwittingly fallen into the trap of Western religion, which seeks to freeze history in an unchanging and authoritative past'" (242).

4    As Simpson argues, although such citizenships "may not be institutionally recognized," they are "socially and politically recognized in the everyday life of the community, and people get called out on them" (175). This is not work that I, as a settler scholar, can undertake effectively. Fortunately, such work is being done by Indigenous men's groups such as Kizhaay Anishinaabe Niin, community-based scholarly initiatives such as Biidwewidam: Indigenous Masculinities, and scholars such as Ty P. Kāwika Tengan, in relation to Kanaka Maoli culture in *Native Men Remade: Gender and Nation in Contemporary Hawai'i* (2008), and Lloyd L. Lee, in relation to Diné culture in *Diné Masculinities: Conceptualizations and Reflections* (2013).

5    The concepts of refusal, full humanity, and doing gender differently are informed by my reading of the scholarship of Simpson, Justice, and Tatonetti, respectively.

6    Ktunaxa writer Smokii Sumac discusses concerns that emerged for his mother regarding roles and responsibilities through the terrain of FTM transition: "When I talked to her about transitioning, the thing she worried about most was my role in our family, in our story, and in our ceremonies. She was always thinking about how we learn our roles. She wanted to make sure I knew how I would learn what it meant to be son, brother, nephew, uncle, maybe one day, even dad" ("'Just Make Me'").

7    Driskill notes that "*gender* itself is from the Latin word genus, a species/sort/kind" (*Asegi Stories* 167).

8    Among these mentors, I include Janice Hill Kanonhsyonne, Marlene Brant Castellano, Vanessa McCourt, Bonnie Jane Maracle, Daniel David Moses, Rick Monture, Kandice Baptiste, Theresa McCarthy, and Audra Simpson. The lands to which I refer here are also the territory of the Anishinaabe Nation. The area along the northern shore of Lake Ontario around Katarokwi, which would come to be known as Kingston, was inhabited at the time of European arrival in the early 1600s by Haudenosaunee, Huron-Wendat, and Anishinaabe Peoples. In 1783, the Mississauga—a member nation of the Anishinaabe—"ceded Kingston and the surrounding territory to the British Crown . . . with the signing of the Crawford Purchase" (Queen's University). Many Anishinaabe and Haudenosaunee continue to live in this territory, as do Métis, Inuit, and other Indigenous nations from throughout Turtle Island, while the Tyendinaga Mohawks of the Bay of Quinte sixty kilometres to the west of Kingston live in "the only government-recognized [Indigenous] territory within the Kingston region" (Queen's University).

9    As Monture indicates, "The Haudenosaunee . . . have been one of the most widely written-about groups of Indigenous nations in North America" (xi), and my intervention here is not intended to divert attention away from the rigorous analyses of Haudenosaunee society by Haudenosaunee scholars and artists. Several recent works by Haudenosaunee scholars offer indispensable culturally informed critical discussions that far exceed in scope, objective, and accomplishment what is being pursued here, including Monture's *We Share Our Matters: Two Centuries of Writing and Resistance at Six Nations of the Grand River* (2014), Audra Simpson's *Mohawk Interruptus: Political Life across the Borders of Settler States* (2014), Theresa McCarthy's *In Divided Unity: Haudenosaunee Reclamation at Grand River* (2017), and Susan Hill's *The Clay We Are Made Of: Haudenosaunee Land Tenure on the Grand River* (2017).

10   I believe that the term "ecologies of gender" offers a useful elaboration of "gender systems," in this context, because it not only signals the

organic relationship between worldviews and gender structures but also acknowledges philosophically that gender exceeds relationships between humans and extends to human placedness within geographic territories and in the universe more broadly.

11   In discussing these stories, I do not mean to suggest an unbridgeable gap between the spiritual systems implicated in either. Nor do I wish to imply that Porter's telling represents the beliefs of all Haudenosaunee people or that this particular version of Genesis represents the beliefs of all settlers—many Indigenous people do not consider themselves spiritually traditional, many non-Indigenous Canadians do not consider themselves Christian, and many Indigenous and non-Indigenous people bring these spiritual traditions together in their own belief systems. Rather, I want to consider how specific differences in the ways that the two creation stories imagine the world might affect gender relations. I am using previously published versions of both creation stories (from Haudenosaunee and Christian sources, respectively) to avoid co-optation. I am neither Haudenosaunee nor Christian, and I wish to respect those for whom these stories are sacred. I do not intend in this section to deny the sacred power of these stories; rather, I examine them critically to unearth some of their many possible ideological implications, not to supply definitive interpretations.

12   I use the term "traditional" here to distinguish between the band council systems of governance that have been imposed by the *Indian Act* and those governance structures that preceded settler colonialism and have survived it.

13   The traditional system of governance for the Haudenosaunee values balance through "consultation and compromise" (Miller 59). It avoids combative partisanship in efforts toward adaptive consensus at the level of the clan, the nation, and the Confederacy. As Miller suggests, the decisions of the Confederacy have "to be unanimous. Lengthy periods of speech-making and consultation [are] required to reach a decision with which all the nations of the League [think that] they [can] live" (59). In this way, the Haudenosaunee struggle to ensure that, in the words of Rupert Ross, "the process of arriving at . . . decision[s] [is] communal" (27). According to Miller, such an emphasis on consensus building "perfectly reflect[s] the value system of Aboriginal societies, which [place] a premium on mutual support, generosity, and non-interference in the affairs of others" (60–61).

14   In other words, I worry that Driskill's contention that systems of gender are always oppressive might blind us to the vibrant possibilities of gender systems that themselves are liberatory, even as I understand that such systems do not fundamentally preclude the possibility of gender-based oppression and violence. As Métis scholar Emma LaRocque reminds us,

"We know enough about human history that we cannot assume[,] . . . even in those original societies that were structured along matriarchal lines, that matriarchies necessarily prevented men from oppressing women" (qtd. in Anderson, *Recognition* 36–37).

15   In 1985, the federal government passed Bill C-31 with the intention of amending the discriminatory sections of the *Indian Act* pertaining to gender. According to Mi'kmaq scholar Bonita Lawrence, "As a result of the bill, approximately 100,000 Native women and their children have received Indian status. However, although Bill C-31 officially brought the Indian Act into compliance with international human rights standards, it has still managed to maintain divisions among Native people along the basis of gender and blood quantum, largely through not addressing past injustices" (13).

16   I should note, however, that the traditional governance structure of the Haudenosaunee continued to function alongside the imposed band council structure in many communities for decades after the introduction of the *Indian Act,* and in several communities it has been reinstated in recent years. Monture notes, for example, that in Six Nations of the Grand River "the Confederacy Council remained in place until 1924, albeit under the ever-watchful eye of the local Indian Agent on the reserve. Up to that time, the traditional leadership had endured Canadian Confederation in 1867, the introduction of the *Indian Act* in 1876, and an ever-increasing population of Canadian citizens in the most heavily populated region of the country" (17).

17   In the case of the Haudenosaunee, this meant "no longer consider[ing]" the Confederacy to be made up of "sovereign nations" allied with the British, with whom the Crown had "entered into agreements in good faith before and after the [American revolutionary] war," but as collectives of domestic dependent subjects (Monture 17).

18   For elaborations, see Milloy; and Truth and Reconciliation Commission.

19   For a discussion of the pass system, see Williams; for a discussion of centralization, see Paul.

20   I stress again here that, of course, this is not meant to deny the possibility of gender-based violence occurring in Haudenosaunee or other communities prior to settler colonialism.

21   In this way, I argue that "Indigenous masculinity," as perceived by mainstream settler society, actually mirrors the invention of what Scott Morgensen calls "colonial masculinity." Morgensen writes that, "for colonial masculinity to achieve dominance, it had to be invented: European modes of manhood arrived on Indigenous lands, changed as they participated in colonial violence, and became entrenched as methods of settler rule. As creations of conquest, forms of colonial masculinity are not natural, necessary, or permanent, any more than is colonization itself" (39). Settler

imaginings of Indigenous masculinity actually participate in the invention of colonial masculinity through an elaborate hegemony involving both absorption and repudiation.

22   For elaborations of these concepts, see Vizenor.

23   When used in the paragraphs below, these terms should be understood as being in quotation marks to indicate their simulated nature. Quotation marks have been removed, however, to aid readability.

24   I first used the term "masculindians" in 2011 in a book chapter titled "Warriors, Healers, Lovers, and Leaders: Colonial Impositions on Indigenous Male Roles and Responsibilities," which offers an early exploration of many of the ideas grappled with in this chapter. I theorized the concept more fulsomely in 2014 in *Masculindians: Conversations about Indigenous Manhood*, arguing that, although my use of the term "was initially intended merely to identify and critique simulated settler stereotypes about Indigenous men, I've become increasingly convinced of the term's generative potential. It points to what I see as an urgent need to grapple with both Indianness and masculinity, and it does so via an irreverent neologism that resists the pull of gender essentialism, biological determinism, and what Vizenor calls the 'faux science' of 'race.' . . . It recognizes the representational/discursive as inherently interwoven with what Ty P. Kāwika Tengan calls the 'bodies and gender and lands,' all of which 'need to be thought of in relation to one another'" ("Into" 3).

25   One of the few among Catlin's paintings that register social dynamics is the *Dance of the Berdache*," in which the community is invoked to portray the social scorn to which queer or two-spirit people were supposedly subjected. The gender valences of this mocking depiction of non-binary Indigenous figures are telling with regard to Catlin's own entrenchment within settler heteropatriarchy.

26   It is unsurprising that these films emerged in the lead up to the quincentenary of Columbus's arrival in what would come to be known as the Americas, a time when Indigenous organizers and activists were demanding a reckoning with the ongoing violence of settler colonialism, thereby whetting settler appetites for narratives of legitimation that would enable audiences to lament the horrors of colonial history while not seeing themselves implicated in them.

27   I thank Daniel Heath Justice for recommendations regarding the language here.

28   Ernest Thompson Seton was a British Canadian author, artist, and naturalist who founded the Woodcraft Indians in 1902 and was one of the founding members of the Boy Scouts of America in 1910. He was responsible for the incorporation of what he considered to be "Indian" cultural elements into the teachings of the Boy Scouts of America. As a naturalist, Seton was passionately committed to the protection of

wildlife and appeared to demonstrate a similarly paternalistic sympathy for Indigenous Peoples, even as his mentorship of youth involved the appropriation of Indigenous materials.

29   Corrections Canada statistics on Indigenous offenders can be found at http://www.csc-scc.gc.ca/publications/005007-3027-eng.shtml. See also Comack; Henry, "Through"; Innes and Anderson, "Introduction"; Piché; and Reber and Renaud.

30   It is crucial to note that Indigenous women are also disproportionately targeted for violence and premature death within the context of settler colonialism, as the National Inquiry into Missing and Murdered Indigenous Women and Girls and studies such as Allison Hargreaves's *Violence against Indigenous Women: Literature, Activism, Resistance* demonstrate (see Hargreaves). And, though settler society engages in entwined strategies of victim blaming in relation to the experiences of Indigenous women through the language of "at risk" lifestyles and racist dehumanization, a key factor in settler society's ability to continue to extend state and vigilante violence against Indigenous men has been a displacement of causality in which they become not victims but causes of the violence that disproportionately affects their communities. This displacement functions to legitimize the criminalization of Indigenous men while absolving settler Canada from its/our culpability for Indigenous dispossession and dehumanization.

31   Footnote 56 of the RCMP report states that a "verbal exchange occurred in an attempt to get the vehicle to leave the yard"; however, the other victims in the car contend that Boushie was "asleep" (see Narine, "'Normal Crime'"). Clearly, a "verbal exchange" could not take place with a sleeping man, and it is unlikely that a "verbal exchange" between a man holding a gun and a youth in a car would be quiet enough not to wake the victim. My thanks to Jamieson Ryan for this observation.

32   The RCMP report on the incident focused more on property violations than on the murder, thereby displacing roles of victim and victimizer in the public depiction of the case: "Initial investigation has revealed five individuals entered onto private property by vehicle in the rural area and were confronted by property owners who were outside and witnessed their arrival. The occupants of the vehicle were not known to the property owners. A verbal exchange occurred in an attempt to get the vehicle to leave the yard and ultimately a firearm was discharged, striking an occupant in the vehicle. . . . One adult male associated to the property was arrested by police at the scene without incident. Three occupants from the vehicle, including two females (one being a youth) and one adult male[,] were taken into custody as part of a related theft investigation. Another male youth is being sought; his identity is still being confirmed at this time" (qtd. in Nunn 1341). Note the number of

times that the word *property* is used in this description and the lack of culpability implied by the vague statement "a firearm was discharged."

33    "Heteropatriarchy" refers specifically to gender systems emergent through Western history that devalue women and non-heterosexual persons. As such, the term is inaccurate (or at least imprecise) in its application to Indigenous contexts prior to contact, like that depicted in Porter's version of the tale of Aionwahta. However, as Métis scholar Emma LaRocque argues, "We know enough about human history that we cannot assume that all Aboriginal traditions universally respected and honoured women. It should not be assumed," she continues, "even in those original societies that were structured along matriarchal lines, that matriarchies necessarily prevented men from oppressing women. There are indications of male violence and sexism in some Aboriginal societies prior to European contact, and certainly after contact" (qtd. in Anderson, *Recognition* 36–37). Furthermore, as Porter himself notes, the era in which the Peacemaker and Aionwahta lived "was perhaps the darkest, most violent, and hopeless, of our entire history"; it was a time in which "the culture, ceremonies and the peaceful ways of life were almost lost" (274). Significantly, Porter relates this "chaos" to miscommunication within "families," since "people didn't follow their clans," and characterizes it as a time in which "war leaders" did not listen to the "women who were crying all the time" (274). The point is not that "heteropatriarchy" is a completely accurate term for describing the gendered conditions depicted in the story but to recognize that the mistreatment of Haudenosaunee women was likely an aspect of the turmoil that necessitated the creation of the Kaienere'kó:wa, The Great Law of Peace.

## 2. SHAME AND DETERRITORIALIZATION

1    See Assembly of First Nations (42) for a parallel example.

2    This system is connected to class as well as race. The same system that works to empower "pure" women such as nuns and middle- and upper-class girls and women constructs other women as impure and sexually available to all men.

3    By appending the term "ecosystemic," I seek to affirm the interdependence of the human and the other-than-human in specific geographical spaces (while acknowledging human propensities to traverse ecosystems). See Deleuze and Guattari; Liffman; and Tatonetti (144–72).

4    Claire Colebrook refers to territorialization as the "connective forces that allow any form of life to become what it is" and to deterritorialization as the forces that cause any form of life "to become what it is not" (xxii).

5    Robert Arthur Alexie attended Peter Warren Dease Residential School in Fort MacPherson, Anthony Apakark Thrasher attended Aklavik

Roman Catholic Residential School in the Northwest Territories, and Louise Bernice Halfe attended Blue Quills Indian Residential School in Alberta.

6    My focus in this chapter is on those who identify as Indigenous men specifically—with the full recognition that all genders are mutually affecting and affected in a relational manner and that the implied binary between men and women normalized by heteropatriarchy is a colonial intervention. For critical discussions of targeted colonial disruptions of Indigenous women's roles and responsibilities, see Allen; Anderson; and Goeman. For critical discussions of colonial disruptions of Indigenous queer and two-spirit traditions, see Driskill et al. Also, I wish to register the problematics involved in reaching to Neal McLeod's theorizations of Cree worthiness and masculinity given his conviction for domestic assault and the tensions discussed more fulsomely in the introduction to this volume.

7    IRS TRC videos can be found at http://trc.ca/media/trc-video.html.

8    The nuns themselves, of course, were subject to patriarchal discipline within the hierarchical power structure of the Catholic Church and the settler colonial gender system more broadly. The behaviours reported by Thrasher, Knockwood, and Alexie were complexly informed and circumscribed by a settler colonial gender regime that treated the body as both symbolically female and the source of sin. In accordance with this causal structure, the female is configured as the source of evil, and purity becomes contingent on the disavowal of the female. Thus, within the gendered theological structure in which the nuns functioned daily, the female is perceived as being responsible for sin and is hated for arousing sinful thoughts in men who have vowed to remain pure—ideological conditions that undoubtedly affected the anxious and violent actions of the nuns depicted above.

9    Included in this list should also be the attempted erasure of queer, non-binary, and two-spirit histories, which I will discuss more fully in Chapter 3.

10   To elaborate, shame does not merely alienate residential school students from the vibrancy of other gendered experiences. Rather, within what Justice calls "the matrix of settler-inscribed shame," the gendered Indigenous body is reproduced as "abject": "[T]o be subject to patriarchal settler violence is, in this lens, to be a passive recipient and thus inherently feminized, and the Indigenous body is thus rendered inhuman through its association with rapeable femininity, thereby becoming something other than human and thus ultimately incapable of kinship or dignity. Like the land, the Indigenous body, under these conditions, exists in settler imaginations as something entirely to be acted upon, claimed, and violated" (personal communication, 4 June 2020).

11 I borrow the term "rebeautify" from Qwo-Li Driskill, who, in *Asegi Stories: Cherokee Queer and Two Spirit Memory*, writes that, "Against this backdrop of sexual violence and the stories of everything we lost, we sometimes forget that these aren't the only stories. Even now, colonization is only a tiny part of a much larger memory that stretches all the way back. Our stories are also of resistance, humour, love, sex, beauty. And that's why rebeautifying our erotic memory is so vitally important: we need to remember the stories that disrupt colonial violence" (138).

12 More accurately, the imposition of the hierarchized gender binary should be understood as a severing of the child from nation-specific ecologies of gender. It is a divorcing of the male-identified child not just from "the feminine" but also from lived understandings of gender diversity.

13 In the *Oxford Dictionary of Psychology*, Andrew Colman defines the word *dissociation* as the "partial or total disconnection between memories of the past, awareness of identity and of immediate sensations, and control of bodily movements, often resulting from traumatic experiences, intolerable problems, or disturbed relationships." Evidence of trauma's causal role in the instigation of "disconnection" between cognitive registry and "immediate sensations" is amply supplied by articles in *The Journal of Trauma and Dissociation*. See also Fonagy and Target; and Giesbrecht and Merckelbach.

14 Such coerced disavowals of the body occurred among female students as well, as evidenced by performative shaming of menses and similarly maniacal punishments of bedwetting and vomiting. Halfe's poem "Nēpēwisiwin—Shame" from *Burning in This Midnight Dream* portrays a child's visit to confessional within "the plundering school": "I hated another one who never taught me / a girl's moon came every month and I had to / hide this visit, hide my tiny breasts. I hated the woman / who marched the little girl, who peed her bed, in front of all of us" (14). Also see Knockwood's discussion of "sex education" for the female students at Shubenacadie quoted above. My effort here is not to suggest a fundamental difference in colonial attitudes toward Indigenous female and male bodies but to interrogate the particular ramifications of coerced disembodiment for male-identified populations who have endured residential schooling.

15 Such deterritorialization involves the active obfuscation (or compromising) of gendered identity in this context. Young men such as Johnston are coercively prevented from successfully performing masculine roles and responsibilities as they are understood within their own communities, and at the same time they are constructed as being inherently incapable of "achieving" white masculinity within the dominant national milieu. As Justice explained to me in, "it's not just that they're forced to adopt different gender values, but that they're put into a space where they

can only ever be inadequate to sociality as gendered beings regardless of where they are" (personal communication, 4 June 2020).

16 For a detailed discussion of these impositions, see Lawrence. I also discuss these matters in Chapter 1 of this book.

17 Having witnessed the preceding survivors' sharing circle, I stayed in the room to attend the Residential School Walkers' special session at the IRS TRC in Halifax. When I say that the tension between stasis and motion proved to be "unsettling," I am describing my own experience of the session along with my later reflections on it with colleagues and friends also in attendance.

18 The video can be found on YouTube at http://www.youtube.com/watch?v=PrVK1wsraow.

## 3. JOURNEYING BACK TO THE BODY

1 For elaboration on anxieties surrounding the discussion of sex and sexuality in Indigenous North America, see Akiwenzie-Damm ("Erotica"); and Akiwenzie-Damm ("Red Hot"). Also see Driskill et al. ("Introduction").

2 By "ecologies of gender," I mean understandings and experiences of gender embedded in and reliant on specific constellations of territories and places. As I discussed in Chapter 1, it matters whether we conceive of those spaces as battlegrounds on which discrete genders compete over scant resources or fertile, creative landscapes in which diverse genders work to generate resources together. Ecological models, I contend, help us to understand the kinds of gender ideologies that we want to uphold.

3 Driskill's poem acutely diagnoses the affective history of violation that threatens interpersonal intimacy on Turtle Island, suggesting that it is influenced not only by individual experiences of trauma but also by the broader trajectory of territorial dispossession (of which such experiences are often a product and in the services of which individual violations are often conducted). The poem's title draws the reader's attention to the relationships that persist among violations of the body, violations of the land, and the affective experiences of territorial dispossession that constitute violations of both. Mark Rifkin explicates this quality of the poet's work: "Driskill . . . refuses the easy distinction of tenor and vehicle in which embodiment serves as a *metaphor* for territoriality. Instead, s/he draws on the reader's experience of attraction, arousal, and gratification as a means of reframing what Native territoriality *is*. . . . To understand peoplehood, the [poetry] suggests, one needs to grasp the physical immediacy and yearning that characterizes the *reciprocity* of place" ("Erotics" 177). In this way, Driskill confronts colonial ideologies that figure Indigenous lands as empty, feminized, and violable—often through metaphors of North America as virginal land awaiting consum-

mation with the masculine European presence to produce "civility" and "culture"—not by denying connections between the land and the body, but by fleshing them out as genuinely affective relationships that are mutually agentive, intimate, and ongoing rather than unidirectional, exploitative, and marked by a moment of conquest. Driskill's poem, as such, anticipates much of what I wish to argue in this chapter.

4    This question is intended implicitly to register the tension between what might be legible as "queer" masculinities and as "straight" masculinities in a dominant cultural milieu, because the former tend to be overdetermined as a rejection of the latter and coded not as "masculinities" but as a species of effeminacy. Of course, not all queer men emote in ways that align with dominant conceptions of femininity, yet concepts such as tenderness and vulnerability tend to be coded in popular culture as feminine or queer, so I ask, using Scofield's work, what does it mean to move these concepts into the terrain of masculinities? Does the queer content of Scofield's poetry, for example, act as a pedagogy that straight men can use and learn from? I am indebted to Jamieson Ryan for fleshing out these questions and their significance.

5    I employ "colonial masculinities" in the sense elaborated in settler scholar Scott Morgensen's "Cutting to the Roots of Colonial Masculinity."

6    I stress here that Simpson's complex theorizations of Indigenous futures exceed the banal biological replications of procreative heterosexual domesticity. Decolonial love is generative in its myriad expressive possibilities and not simply through heterosexual reproduction (see *As We* Chapters 2, 3, 7, and 8).

7    Simpson writes that, "Within Nishnaabewin, refusal is an appropriate response to oppression, and within this context it is always generative" (33). She notes that "I use kwe as method to refuse and to analyze colonialism as a *structure of processes*, and I've placed the eradication of gender violence as a central project of radical resurgence" (35).

8    Consensual vulnerability is not just the purview of men or of those who identify as masculine but can be enacted by anyone regardless of gender identity. I focus on *masculine* expressions of consensual vulnerability here because such expressions are urgently needed, as I argue below, to unsettle masculine privilege and create conditions of possibility for safe intimacy in contexts informed by settler colonialism.

9    I borrow the phrase "dynamic mutuality" from Rifkin, who argues in his article "The Erotics of Sovereignty" that "'Love' for the land," in Driskill's poetry, "appears as more than an abstract feeling, a broad appreciation for a given locale; 'love' indicates a dynamic mutuality in which they are the land's as much as the land is theirs" (176–77). I find the phrase fruitful for the purposes of this chapter because it articulates a mode of interdependence that, through *dynamism*, is both active and generative

(as opposed to static and parasitic) and that, through *mutuality*, implies consent. Furthermore, given the original context of Rifkin's argument, the phrase exceeds anthropocentrism and thereby recognizes how erotic intimacy is territorially and ecosystemically contextual.

10  Here "cruel nostalgia" hearkens back to the invented "traditions"—critiqued by Hokowhitu as "Indigenous heterosexual patriarchal masculinity" ("Taxonomies")—that have been naturalized in ways that serve to police boundaries of gender and sexuality. As Chris Finley argues, "heteropatriarchy has become so natural in many Native communities that it is internalized and institutionalized as if it were traditional" (34).

11  In *As We Have Always Done*, Simpson demonstrates similar skepticism, registering reluctance to "center resurgence around masculinity, even critical masculinity. I'm interested in working with all genders and ages," she elaborates, "to build nationhoods that refuse to replicate heteropatriarchy in all forms" (52). Here Simpson acknowledges the propensity for masculinity to dominate and displace other positionalities, which Coulthard fears in his call for Indigenous masculinities studies to "vacate. not occupy space that indigenous feminist, queer and trans voices should occupy"; however, in declaring her intention to work with "all genders," Simpson concedes that there is space within resurgence for those who self-identify with masculinity while committing to reclaiming Indigenous strategies for safeguarding against masculinity's will to power.

12  I interpret Justice's comment here as entreating readers to look to art as a means of imagining and generating healthier, pluralist, non-hegemonic, non-dominative Indigenous masculinities that are worthy of claiming.

13  Anishinaabe poet and editor Kateri Akiwenzie-Damm elaborates the need for diverse representations of Indigenous masculinity. Speaking with me in *Masculindians*, she states, "I hope that what you're doing . . ." in facilitating conversations about Indigenous masculinities will have a "ripple effect . . . where my sons are going to be able to find a wider range of depictions of Indigenous men that will maybe inspire them, influence them to some extent, and teach them both in that Nanabozho way of what to do and what not to do—because Nanabozho taught through both his good deeds and his misdeeds. They'll have more to draw on than I think Indigenous men have had in the past few generations" ("Affirming Protectorship" 181).

14  In this sense, I diverge somewhat from Driskill's contentions that "Gender is a logic, and a structural system of oppression, whose sole purpose is to categorize people in order to deploy systemic power and control" and that "Gender is a weapon to force us into clear Eurocentric categories, keep us confined in there, ensure we monitor each other's behavior, and then, while we are distracted, take our lands" (*Asegi Stories* 167). Although I agree unequivocally that this is how simplified, myopic, and hierarchi-

cal understandings of gender have been deployed by settler colonizers in the service of conquest, I do not believe that these are the only ways that gender has functioned or can be conceived—particularly in relation to Indigenous worldviews. As Indigenous feminists and queer and two-spirit theorists have demonstrated, Indigenous nations have done (and, in many cases, still do) gender differently; rich and diverse ideas about gender persist in Indigenous languages, creation stories, political structures, and elsewhere that do not align with heteropatriarchy. See, for example, Simpson's theorization of "kwe as method" from *As We Have Always Done* (27–38), based on gendered understandings from the Anishinaabe worldview not beholden to settler colonial thought. In other words, gender does not simply arrive with the colonizer, and gender is not only what settler colonialism says it is.

15   Here Simpson refers to the popular American television program *Dexter*, which aired on Showtime between 2006 and 2013 and follows a Miami forensics expert who is also a serial killer. Significantly, Dexter disposes of the dead bodies by pushing them off his boat and into the ocean.

16   Morgensen's theorization of "colonial masculinity" is useful here: "[F]or colonial masculinity to achieve dominance, it had to be *invented*: European modes of manhood arrived on Indigenous lands, changed as they participated in colonial violence, and became entrenched as methods of settler rule. As creations of conquest, forms of colonial masculinity are not natural, necessary, or permanent, any more than is colonization itself" (39). The pervasive nature of such violent masculinities, however (particularly in relation to their historical targeting of Indigenous women, queer, and two-spirit bodies), thus conditions the context of anxiety throughout Simpson's story.

17   I discuss such kinship relations elsewhere in this volume through the language of integrity: etienne's integrity is fostered through his integration within ecosystemic and familial networks of belonging.

18   I should also note that etienne's Indigeneity is never confirmed in the narrative.

19   I do not mean to imply that the narrator and etienne are somehow liberated from the broader societal context of heteropatriarchal violence. The story's trajectory is not utopian but resurgent. What's important, however, is that they together create conditions in which their interactions are not beholden to and predetermined by heteropatriarchy, which thereby illuminates a more replete set of possibilities for future gender dynamics that are ever more sovereign.

20   Scofield has stated that, when the lines "my mouth / the lodge where you come / to sweat" first came to him, his initial reaction was "I can't write that because that's taking a sacred ceremony and sexualizing it. And then I started to think . . . the sweat is a sacred purification. It's the womb. It's

the womb of Mother Earth. You're being born and you come out. And what I'm describing is just as much a ceremony, is just as sacred.... And that embodied, that one simple act, embodied an incredible ceremony. It embodied an incredible sacredness, and I took a stand on it and said, 'This is sacred, and this is what *Love Medicine*, this is what these poems are about'" ("Liberation" 219–20).

21    Although the speaker's gender is not identified explicitly in this poem, "Ceremonies" is part of a lyric sequence in *Love Medicine and One Song* that, in the words of Métis scholar Warren Cariou, "describes a love triangle, as the narrator moves between his male lover and his female lover" (v). Poems such as "He Is," "Ôchîm ◆ His Kiss," "My Drum, His Hands," and "His Flute, My Ears" describe in intimate detail the sensuous body of the speaker as it is engaged erotically by the beloved, and poems such as "More Rainberries (The Hand Game)" and "Ceremonies" depict the speaker acting on the male body of the beloved.

22    "More Rainberries," for example, concludes thus:

> my hands, delirious with song
> sway to his drumming,
> rock to each beat swooping
> down, down
> to the muskeg, where
>
> scented rainberries
> fat as frogs
> explode in my mouth,
>
> his deepest warmth
>
> a sweet taste
> painting my lips. (ll. 19–29)

The poem concludes in a ritual of rhythmic pulsation that can be read as culminating in ejaculation, with male orgasm honoured as a transformative ceremony. Yet, with fertile imagery of muskeg, frogs, song, and drumming, such gendered reading does not exhaust the passage's interpretive possibilities.

23    I analyze Sumac's poetry in the introduction to *Carrying the Burden of Peace*.

24    To be fair, given the development of "erotics" within feminist and queer of colour theorizing, a discomfort with masculine erotics is unsurprising. In "Uses of the Erotic: The Erotic as Power," Audre Lorde refers to the erotic as "a resource within each of us that lies in a deeply female and

spiritual place, firmly rooted in the power of our unexpressed or unrecognized feeling." Lorde further distinguishes that "The erotic has often been misnamed by men and used against women. It has been made into the confused, the trivial, the psychotic, the plasticized sensation" (53–54).

25   *Maskwa* is the Cree word for bear. The poem "He Is," which directly precedes "Ôchîm ◆ His Kiss" in the collection, concludes with a similar metaphor:

he is spring bear
ample and lean

his berry tongue quick
sweet from the feasting. (ll. 31–34)

26   I employ the "callout" in the manner theorized by Cherokee citizen scholar Sean Kicummah Teuton, who defines the concept in *Red Land, Red Power: Grounding Knowledge in the American Indian Novel* as the "demand for justice" that occurs when "American Indian scholars awaken politically and begin to put their ideas to work" (161).

## 4. DE(F/V)IANT GENEROSITY: GENDER AND THE GIFT

1   Although mobilizing mothering as a central principle of the gift economy, Vaughan is careful not to essentialize mothering as strictly a biological practice: "This approach in which mothering is seen as one example of an alternative mode of distribution breaks the mold of maternity as limited to the relation between mothers and children only. In fact gift economies, which embody many variations of gift giving beyond exchange, use maternity as a general social principle, for both women and men, for women who are not mothers as well as for men who are not fathers. Breaking the mold of mothering as relating only to women and small children also opens the way for considering gift economies as economies of extended or generalized mothering" (1).

2   Gordon Robinson is Eden Robinson's uncle and the Haisla Nation's first published author.

3   Note that I resist the presumption that various Western worldviews are collapsible as one in the same way that I reject the notion that Indigenous worldviews are commensurate. We should remember that worldviews evolve over time and across territories and are inflected by cultural, spatial, temporal, and communal specificities. That being said, my purpose in this section is to demonstrate how the gift and exchange register differently in the context of particular Indigenous worldviews from the Pacific Northwest (specifically among the Syilx, as represented by the work of Armstrong, and the Haisla, as represented by the work of Robinson) versus the West-

ern worldviews imposed on the northern half of this continent over the past 150 years. The point is that, although both exchange and the gift are ever-present in each context, the integrated elements of worldview cause exchange and the gift to be understood in radically different ways, with significant implications for social relations. My argument in the chapter is that Robinson's literary art gifts readers with provocative suggestions about how Indigenous understandings of the gift can be invigorated, even in contexts conditioned by Western worldviews, and that such invigoration can serve to unsettle the settler colonial apparatus that those worldviews serve to naturalize.

4   Chickasaw legal scholar James (Sákéj) Youngblood Henderson rejects "the concept 'culture' for worldview" because to "use 'culture' is to frag-ment Aboriginal worldviews into artificial concepts. The worldview is a unified vision rather than an individual idea" ("Ayukpachi" 261).

5   Note that I do not wish to collapse the Syilx worldview with Haisla, Heiltsuk, or other Indigenous worldviews, although I recognize along with Joanne Fiske that "The First Nations of the Pacific Northwest share political economic features of the clan/potlatch system: kin corporate groups, territorial divisions, social ranking, and the ceremonial investiture of individuals known as hereditary chiefs and/or noble women and men" (218). I turn to Armstrong's work because it offers a striking and accessible investigation of an Indigenous gift economy from *within* an Indigenous philosophical perspective. I have not located a similar discussion of the potlatch or gift economy from within the Haisla worldview, although such a discussion would undoubtedly be valuable to this chapter. That being said, I stress that Armstrong's article is path-clearing and understudied, and I encourage readers to engage with it, to include it on syllabi, and to share it widely. (At the time of my writing, it is available for free online at http://gift-economy.com/women-and-the-gift-economy/).

6   Given such profound differences in worldview, it's unsurprising that the Syilx language does not use gendered pronouns "like 'he' or 'she.'" Armstrong recalls asking her aunt, "'*How come we don't have that idea?*'" Her aunt replied, "'*Well, it has to do with being a person. . . . If you were to say 'he' or 'she' in our language, you would have to point to their genitals, you would have to point to what's between the legs, and why would you talk about a person and point between their legs? . . . It doesn't make any sense.*' And it doesn't—people are what they do and who they relate to and how they relate to the world" (45).

7   It is important to note that Kuokkanen and Vaughan are not using "matriarchy" as a flipside to "patriarchy," in which women exercise domi-nating power to the exclusion of men's authority. Rather, matriarchy is a different structural logic entirely that works toward liberation from such hierarchies and domination of all kinds.

8   The extraliterary resonance of this depiction is all too clear to Indigenous
    nations of the Pacific Northwest that suffered the Canadian government's
    ban on potlatch ceremonies for over half a century between 1885 and
    1951. The anti-potlatch proclamation was issued in 1883 and passed into
    law in 1885. It reads thus: "Every Indian or other person who engages in
    or assists in celebrating the Indian festival known as the 'potlatch' or in
    the Indian dance 'Tamananawas' is guilty of a misdemeanor, and shall
    be liable to imprisonment" (qtd. in "Potlatch Ban").

9   The emphasis of Robinson's narrator that Wil *chooses* to be in this moment
    offers an intriguing analogy for Cree Residential School Walker Patrick
    Etherington Jr.'s emphasis at the IRS TRC event in Halifax that his 2,200
    kilometre walk is what he has *chosen* to do to honour the resilience of resi-
    dential school survivors, as discussed in Chapter 2. In each case, agency is
    attested and affirmed, even in the face of genocidal policies and practices.

10  I employ the term "futurity" here in a manner that exceeds mere biologi-
    cal continuity into an as-yet-unexperienced present. Rather, taking the
    lead from Dillon's theorization of Indigenous futurisms, I use "futurity"
    to refer not to "the product of a victimized people's wishful ameliora-
    tion of their past, but instead a continuation of a spiritual and cultural
    path that remains unbroken by genocide and war" ("Into" 2). Robinson's
    dystopic present, in this sense, is backward and forward looking, map-
    ping possibilities for decolonial futures. In Dillon's words, Indigenous
    futurisms are "a praxis for healing and balance" (3).

11  As the story ends, Wil "holds himself there, in the boat with his brother,
    his father, his mother. The sun on the water makes pale northern lights
    flicker against everyone's faces, and the smell of the water is clean and
    salty, and the boat's spray is cool against his skin" (546). The reader is
    left with a sense of embodied presence—the image of light reflecting,
    the smell of salt water, and the feel of spray—made possible through
    Wil's ongoing agency even in the context of his plausible death by state
    violence. If we understand the violence of the colonial state as targeting
    gender balance in Indigenous communities by suppressing Indigenous
    women's power, then "Terminal Avenue" reminds us that such disrup-
    tions also damage Indigenous men. What I referred to earlier in this
    book as the false promise of patriarchy is betrayed in Robinson's story
    to target and potentially compromise the humanity of Indigenous men,
    as evidenced by Wil's impending death, the suicide of his father, and
    his brother's decision to don "the robin's egg blue uniform of the great
    enemy," thereby becoming complicit in his own dehumanization as part
    of the colonial machine (542).

12  In her article, Fabre discusses the novel *Monkey Beach* specifically. However,
    the commentary remains apt for "Queen of the North," entwined as it
    is with the novel in both storyline and setting.

13     Residential schooling hangs heavily over the story since it is implied that
       the protagonist's abuser, Uncle Josh, might have been a victim of sexual
       abuse in residential school. The potlatch is not referenced in the story.
14     Karaoke appends a note to the "gift": "It was yours so I killed it" (213).
15     In her book *How Should I Read These? Native Women Writers in Canada*,
       Helen Hoy interrogates adroitly the one-sided nature of this exchange,
       noting how the man seeks to extract consumable information from Ka-
       raoke through a series of increasingly personal questions while denying
       her own agency by ignoring any questions that she asks of him.
16     Karaoke references multiple instances during which she wishes urgently to
       disclose her abuse—to Ronny (189), to her boyfriend Jimmy (200), and to
       her mother (196, 213)—but each time something prevents her from doing
       so. This is not meant to imply that she consents to the legitimacy of the
       system of exchange orchestrated by Uncle Josh. After all, she is appalled
       by the Barbie Doll speedboat—"I unwrapped it slowly, my skin crawling"
       (187)—and she is desperate to get rid of the $250 that he leaves on her
       dresser, careful not to purchase "flashy clothes or nice earrings with [the]
       money" because it "would remind [her] of him" (189). Rather, Karaoke's
       opportunities for intervention in the abuse are actively delimited by mul-
       tiple factors, including her economic dependence and that of her mother,
       and the gender politics of settler heteropatriarchy. Discussing the moment
       when she almost discloses the abuse to Jimmy, Karaoke states, "I wanted
       to tell him. I wanted someone else to know and not have it locked inside
       me. I kept starting and then chickening out. What was the point? He'd
       probably pull away from me in horror, disgusted, revolted" (200).
17     Whereas the toy ought to signify mobility and freedom, in a manner
       akin to the sovereign expressions of Haisla cultural autonomy enacted
       by the father's traditional dance on the speedboat in "Terminal Avenue,"
       the Barbie Doll speedboat comes to signify entrapment for Karaoke. At
       the beginning of the story, she describes a recurring dream in which she
       stands by the shore as her uncle's seiner comes into the channel. "Usually
       I can will myself to move," she says, "but sometimes I'm frozen where I
       stand, waiting for the crew to come ashore" (186). Similarly, at the end of
       the story, Karaoke is described as "stand[ing] on the dock, watching the
       *Queen of the North* disappear" (215). The seeming promise of potentiality
       and movement offered by sea vessels in the story escapes Karaoke, whose
       freedom is circumscribed by the embroiled oppressions of capitalist
       commoditization and settler heteropatriarchy.
18     "In our way," writes Armstrong, "when we have to start asking for
       something, that's when we're agreeing that people are irresponsible.
       Irresponsible in not understanding what we're needing, irresponsible
       in not seeing what's needed, and irresponsible in not having moved our
       resources and our actions to make sure that need isn't there." "Queen of

the North" depicts familial relations compromised by economic conditions that foster the abnegation of responsibility, within a community conditioned by colonialist conquest no longer to "lead [their] lives by giving continuously, never ever thinking about what [they] might get back" (Armstrong 49).

19 As a Dene student noted perceptively in one of my undergraduate classes, even the sexual encounter between Karaoke and her eventual boyfriend Jimmy, which on the surface appears to offer the possibility of sensual reciprocity and romantic union, can be read as assault. Karaoke is too intoxicated to remember the encounter with any clarity, but Jimmy is sober enough to drive the pair deep into the woods, where the sex act occurs. Although the matter is not discussed extensively in the story, it does not appear that Karaoke would have been able to provide consent under these conditions.

20 This is among the reasons that Baudrillard's work is elaborated in the "post-Indian" theorizations of Anishinaabe writer Gerald Vizenor. In discussing the simulation of the "Indian" by ethnographic science, Baudrillard writes that "The Indian thereby driven back into the ghetto, into the glass coffin of virginal forest, becomes the simulation model for all conceivable Indians *before ethnology*. The latter thus allows itself the luxury of being incarnate beyond itself, in the 'brute' reality of these Indians it has entirely reinvented—Savages who are indebted to ethnology for still being Savages: what a turn of events, what a triumph for this science which seemed dedicated to their destruction! Of course, these particular Savages are posthumous: frozen, cryogenised, sterilised, protected *to death*, they have become referential simulacra, and the science itself a pure simulacrum" (15).

21 As Daniel Heath Justice argues, in the "poisonous story" of Indigenous deficiency, "every stumble is seen as evidence of innate deficiency, while any success is read as proof of Indigenous diminishment" (*Why* 3). The deficiency of Indigenous persons is constructed through their simulation *as Indians* within the settler colonial imaginary, which then allows failures to assimilate to be interpreted within the colonial matrix as lesser humanity and successful assimilation to be interpreted as progression beyond Indigeneity. In either case, Indianness is imagined to be doomed.

22 Such stylistic innovations include a chapter section narrated in second person and in reverse, another narrated as aborted Alcoholics Anonymous–style letters of atonement, and an entire chapter narrated as transcripts to lost home videos.

23 Note here the relationship between performative sexuality and violence against women. The postured performance of the porn film is conflated in Jeremy's mind with murder: women as objects of the male gaze, vehicles for the satiation of male desire, and targets of male violence.

24    Note the resonance with sexual violence, economic exchange, and consumption in "Queen of the North."

25    The novel is told in nine chapters, four of which constitute an ostensible temporal present. They are entitled "1st Blood," "2nd Blood," "3rd Blood," and "4th Blood," and all revolve around the kidnapping. Although presented in the past tense, they are told via third-person limited narration, compared with the other chapters of the novel, which elaborate the backstory through various flashbacks in first-person and second-person narration and employ stylistic innovations such as the transcripts to lost videos and the epistolary example of Paulie's letters of atonement. The lone deviation to this structure is Tom's letter to his daughter, Melody, which begins the novel and is positioned temporally after the narrative's main action. Although the letter is written at the time of Tom's departure from the family, the context of its consumption is speculative, for it is intended to be opened after Melody's eighteenth birthday.

26    By infinite regression of indebtedness, I mean the inability to reach a ground zero of balance preceding the tipping of scales to require repayment.

27    Jeremy's response to Tom's orchestration of the car theft constitutes one such form of perverse "repayment." After torturing Tom so savagely that he starts to "believe [he] could die," Jeremy "chat[s] and laugh[s] like [they] went to a movie together, like [they] grabbed a bite to eat," declaring, "'As far as I'm concerned, we're even-Steven'" (153, 102).

28    Significantly, Tom chooses neither to do "nothing" nor to "yell for help." Unsure why it seemed to be "embarrassing" to expose the reality of his situation, he diverts to a third option and shouts "'Fire! . . . Fire!'" (124).

29    Within the logic of Jeremy's gender system, sexual intercourse with a sex worker appears to be hypermasculine because it prioritizes the satiation of male sexual desire untethered to concerns about the sexual desire or even well-being of a female sexual partner. The act mobilizes exchange economics to insulate the male figure from genuine feelings of interpersonal empathy or love beyond attraction, which might be deemed effeminate within this system of thought.

30    In this way, Tom's depiction resonates with the work of Leanne Betasamosake Simpson and Gregory Scofield discussed in Chapter 3.

31    Delineating the heteropatriarchal context of the exchange, the skater kids draw from a misogynist and homophobic vernacular, yelling, "'I'm going to kick you in your hairy cunts!'" and "'Suck me off, motherfucker!'" (48).

32    As Akiwenzie-Damm elaborates, "It's about . . . what it means to be a man and to have power. Because power's not necessarily a negative thing. We all need to be and feel empowered. We all need to assert our own power in different ways, but there have been so many negative examples of power being expressed that as soon as you say 'power,' I think for a lot

of people that means power *over* something. Power to bend something to your will. And that's what concerns me" (182).

33 Such articles include Kit Dobson's "Indigeneity and Diversity in Eden Robinson's Work" and Kristina Fagan and Sam McKegney's "Circling the Question of Nationalism in Native Canadian Literature and Its Study."

## 5. MASCULINITY AND KINSHIP

1 The Tłı̨chǫ Nation of the Dene People is also referred to as Dogrib. In his earlier works, Van Camp consistently referred to himself and his nation as Dogrib and now moves back and forth between the two names, sometimes using both together.

2 The young men tell Mikey "fighting stories from home" in an attempt to "make [him] strong" (32) and "[take] him to the field and [show] him how to punch kick defend himself" (30).

3 One horrific example of this bullying involves Scott trapping Mikey in his room for two hours and yelling, "You like that retard? You're on the third floor retard[.] Why don't you jump? JUMP!" (32).

4 Mikey is described in the story as having "had two complete breakdowns so far," being "on drugs for his screaming," and being "THIS close to killing himself" (30).

5 In *Masculindians*, Van Camp discusses the fascination in his work with the "call to being a protector for your community and for all those little ones who can't defend themselves": "[T]hey say the most precious things in this life are defenceless. So you think of childhood, you think of innocence, you think of trust, you know. You cheat on your wife and then you go home and she doesn't know you cheated but you do. Her love, her faith in you is completely defenceless. Or when a child is molested, that child is completely defenceless. Or when a pet is harmed, you know, when an animal is harmed. Completely defenceless. Friendship is defenceless. There's no defence against what a friend can do to you" ("Into" 187).

6 In "The Night Charles Bukowski Died," I read Mikey as providing a prototype of such alternative expressions of masculinity. When told in the cafeteria, "Ho Mikey yer sitting the wrong way you can't see the babes if you're facing the wall," he replies, "I'm not facing the wall I'm looking out the window behind you," leading the narrator to turn and "for the first time [see] a mountain thrust clear through the clouds," turn toward Mikey "who was smiling," and "[take] a picture with [his] heart" (30). Mikey's motivations and actions here exceed the naturalized behaviours that govern the homosocial dorm community, leading the narrator to reckon with territorial beauty and relationality with a male companion in ways that complicate both gender and kinship.

7    Kanien'keha:ka activist Ellen Gabriel has remarked, for example, that "There's men's roles and there's women's roles, in a Haudenosaunee worldview, and there's no need to read more into it than that" ("Plenary Address").

8    This is not meant to imply that we should be letting imposed and inherited masculinities off the hook, treating them uncritically or, worse, as aspirational inevitabilities. Simpson registers her suspicion of moves to absolve masculinities: "I am not suggesting that we center resurgence around masculinity, even critical masculinity. I'm interested in working with all genders and ages to build nationhoods that refuse to replicate heteropatriarchy in all forms" (*As We* 52).

9    The Slavey (Dhe Cho) and the Dogrib (Tłı̨chǫ) are Dene Nations, along with the Chipewyan (Denesuline), Yellowknives (Akaitcho), and Sahtu (Sahtu'T'ine). In Dogrib orator Vital Thomas's version of the Dogrib creation story, the Dogrib appear to emerge from one or another of the other Dene Nations in the aftermath of a great battle: "At the start there were no Dogribs. There was some kind of war, maybe between the Slaveys and the Chipewyans or Eskimos. We don't know where the woman came from. Anyway, there was a war and everyone was killed except one girl who hid herself" (qtd. in Helm et al. 289).

10    In these ways, this telling of the Dogrib creation story demonstrates how, in Cree scholar Robert Alexander Innes's words, "Traditional stories help us understand how Aboriginal people view and practice their kinship relations" (*Elder Brother and the Law of the People* 42).

11    This is in contrast to Thomas's version of the creation story, recorded by non-Indigenous ethnographer June Helm in *The People of Denendeh*, in which the mother "only caught hold of two boys and one girl . . . [who] never turned into pups again. And that's how the Dogrib people started. Those two boys that she raised were the finest hunters and the bravest fighters and the best medicine men that ever lived" (289–91). In Thomas's version, the communal role of the female member of the trio of first Dogribs is not explicitly commented on, and the qualities that distinguish the two male members are presented in decidedly masculine terms as "hunters," "fighters," and "medicine men."

12    The two pathways are not, of course, mutually exclusive since even the puppies/children who become the first Dogribs give in to the initial impulse to flee, which suggests that the desire for individual freedom, although it must be transcended for the good of the nation or community, is natural.

13    For elaboration of the significance of 1985 in relation to band membership and gender, please see Chapter 1.

14    When asked about a seemingly crucial part of the creation story, Larry concedes, "I don't know. Jed never told me that part" (52).

15  As Kanien'keha:ka Clan Mother Janice Hill Kanonshyonne states, there
is a "need for rites of passage, the need to have ceremony and recognition as boys go from one stage of their life to another. You have to end
them being a baby so they can pass on into their boyhood, and end them
being children so they can pass into their manhood. And if they're not
provided with the teachings they need to do those things and if they're
not provided with the ceremony and the understanding that it's time
for them to move into the next stage of their life, they never move out
of that stage. So we have grown men who are really like babies because
they've never been taught it's time to leave that behind now and move on"
(22–23). And as Stó:lō writer Lee Maracle notes, "If we don't have positive
rituals, which are the ones that keep us going . . . in the family with a sense
of wholeness, then we're going to have mad rituals, rituals that keep the
madness running" ("This" 38). Van Camp adds that, "if you're not getting
that welcome at home, you're going to be looking for it somewhere else,
you know? So many of us, I believe, have lost our rites of passage and I
think that's why so many people hunger to get tattooed, they hunger to
be marked, so they're welcomed into manhood" ("Into" 189).

16  African-American theorist bell hooks illustrates the profound disjuncture
between such contemporary performances of "cool" and the origins of "cool"
in the modern history of black masculinity: "Once upon a time black male
'cool' was defined by the ways in which black men confronted the hardships
of life without allowing their spirits to be ravaged. They took the pain of it
and used it alchemically to turn the pain into gold. That burning process
required high heat. Black male cool was defined by the ability to withstand
the heat and remain centered. It was defined by black male willingness to
confront reality, to face the truth, and bear it not by adopting a false pose
of cool while feeding on fantasy; not by black male denial or by assuming a
'poor me' victim identity. It was defined by individual black males daring
to self-define rather than be defined by others" (147).

17  A scene in which the two young men meet for coffee, for example, plays
out through homoerotic posturing that, I would argue, betrays an un-
dercurrent of attraction that exceeds simple, performative, homosocial
humour. When asked why he decided to call Larry, Johnny says, "'Well,
Lare, if you must know, the Big Kahoona has the strangest urge to hump
the skinniest boy in town!'" And when they are about to depart, Johnny
jokes, "'Take your tongue out of my mouth'" (23). Van Camp wrote an
email to Jane Haladay in which he responded to inquiries from her class
about the homoerotics of the two characters' relationship with "'Johnny
Beck is not gay. He's hetero all the way. I do believe that there is a quiet
love and admiration that happens between men that they never talk about.
We light up when our brothers walk into the room. That's what Larry and
Johnny have, nothing more'" (qtd. in Haladay 80). However, he goes on to

concede the possibility of desires that exceed such licit heteronormativity: "'But that's me talking. If your student sees it and can back it up, who's to say he's not right? It's all about interpretation'" (80).

18   This relationship is not, however, without its pitfalls, and Larry's mother—much like Larry himself in some of his behaviours toward Juliet—demonstrates significant lapses in kinship responsibilities throughout the novel. For example, after her husband's rape of her sleeping sister, Larry's mother reportedly "talked her out of" believing that she had been assaulted even though Larry claims that she "fuckin' knew!" (88); moreover, when Larry is bleeding out his ears after his beating by Jazz and needs care, his mother "steps back" from his outstretched arms with "revulsion in her eyes" (81). Significantly, the coming together of Larry and his mother with Jed in a moment of mutual and collective care at the novel's close registers the mother's ongoing capacity for growth, thereby acknowledging that the adulthood toward which Larry is aspiring is not a fixed state but continues to be replete with possibility.

19   Although the dynamic among Johnny, Larry, and Juliet plays with the homosocial desire theorized by Eve Kosofsky Sedgwick, Juliet claims a marked level of control throughout all of her intimate relations in the novel. She purchases Johnny at the slave auction, she calls Johnny into the bedroom for their inaugural sex act, and she initiates the sexual encounter with Larry. Furthermore, she makes the independent decision to keep her baby.

## NAKED AND DREAMING FORWARD: A CONCLUSION

1   I employ both masculine and gender-neutral pronouns in this section because the speaker does not gender himself/themselves other than to identify as "queer." The revulsion of the "native man" at the round dance appears in the poem to be related not just to queerness but also to queer maleness, insofar as the man's performative disavowal of the speaker's humanity can be read as a violent denial of the man's own capacity for homoerotic desire. The biological sex of the speaker, however, is never identified in the poem.

2   The depiction of the "native man" as also a victim of deterritorialization should not be read as absolving him of his dehumanization of the speaker, which not only attacks the speaker's integrity but indeed fractures the community itself.

3   This fertile language builds upon Stó:lō writer Lee Maracle's self-description in *Masculindians*: "I'm a Wolf Clan, backward and forward visionary. That is my relationship to the whole" ("This" 39).

4   Here I employ the term "represents" in the sense of both depicting and speaking on behalf of.

5    Grant's initial runs are not entirely solitary since his neighbour's dog, Snoopy, becomes something of a running partner; as such, my reference to isolation refers to isolation from the human elements of the Six Nations community. Evidence of his desire for integration into that community can be found in his prayer while burning sweetgrass on the morning after his first run, in which Grant asks the Creator to "bring someone special into [his] life" and prays for Justin's family and his own "long-dead parents."

6    As Janice Hill Kanonhysonne argues, in Haudenosaunee culture, aunts and uncles are vital overseers of child development, responsible for significant elements of a child's maturation. For example, "When a girl becomes a woman, we're taught that it's her aunties who take her away and teach her everything she'll ever need to know about being a woman. . . . And men have that same responsibility with boys" (18). Grant's identification with the role of uncle demonstrates commitment to taking on such responsibilities in a manner that transcends biological affiliation.

# WORKS CITED

Akiwenzie-Damm, Kateri. "Affirming Protectorship." McKegney, ed., pp. 172–83.

——. "Erotica. Indigenous Style." *Without Reservation: Indigenous Erotica*, edited by Kateri Akiwenzie-Damm, Kegedonce Press, 2003, pp. xi–xii.

——. "Red Hot to the Touch: WRi[gh]ting Indigenous Erotic Literature." *Me Sexy: An Exploration of Native Sex and Sexuality*, edited by Drew Hayden Taylor, Douglas and McIntyre, 2008, pp. 109–23.

Alexie, Robert Arthur. *Porcupines and China Dolls*. 2002. Theytus Books, 2009.

Alfred, Taiaiake. *Peace, Power, Righteousness: An Indigenous Manifesto*. Oxford UP, 1999.

——. "Reimagining Warriorhood." McKegney, ed., pp. 76–86.

——. *Wasáse: Indigenous Pathways of Action and Freedom*. Broadview, 2005.

Allen, Paula Gunn. *The Sacred Hoop: Recovering the Feminine in American Indian Traditions*. Beacon, 1986.

*An Act for the Gradual Enfranchisement of Indians, the Better Management of Indian Affairs, and to Extend the Provisions of the Act*. 31st Vic, Chapter 42, SC 1869, c 6.

Anderson, Kim. *A Recognition of Being: Reconstructing Native Womanhood*. Second Story, 2000.

——. "Remembering the Sacredness of Men." McKegney, ed., pp. 87–97.

Archibald-Barber, Jesse Rae, ed. *kisiskáciwan: Voices from Where the River Flows Swiftly*. University of Regina Press, 2018.

Armstrong, Jeannette. "Indigenous Knowledge and Gift Giving: Living in Community." Vaughan, ed., pp. 41–49.

Arnott, Joanne. "Intimate Like Muscle and Bone." McKegney, ed., pp. 194–202.

Assembly of First Nations. *Breaking the Silence: An Interpretive Study of Residential School Impact and Healing as Illustrated by the Stories of First Nations Individuals.* Assembly of First Nations, 2010.

Barrera, Jorge. "Enrolment Suspended after Report Finds UVic Indigenous Governance Program Left Students 'Traumatized.'" *CBC*, 24 Apr. 2018, www.cbc.ca/news/indigenous/university-victoria-indigenous-governance-program-suspended-1.4633889.

Battiste, Marie, ed. *Reclaiming Indigenous Voices and Vision.* UBC P, 2000.

Baudrillard, Jean. *Simulations.* Translated by Paul Foss et al., Semiotext(e), 1983.

Bederman, Gail. *Manliness and Civilization: A Cultural History of Gender and Race in the United States, 1880–1917.* U of Chicago P, 2008.

Belcourt, Billy-Ray. "Can the Other of Native Studies Speak?" *WordPress*, 1 Feb. 2016, decolonization.wordpress.com/2016/02/01/can-the-other-of-native-studies-speak/.

——. "Meditations on Reserve Life, Biosociality, and the Taste of Non-Sovereignty." *Settler Colonial Studies*, vol. 8, no. 1, 2018, pp. 1–15.

——. "Sacred." *This Wound Is a World.* Frontenac House Poetry, 2017, p. 17.

——. "To Be Unbodied." *Canadian Art*, 7 Mar. 2019, canadianart.ca/features/to-be-unbodied/.

Benaway, Gwen. "Decolonial Love: A How-To Guide." *Working It Out Together*, workingitouttogether.com/content/decolonial-love-a-how-to-guide/.

*Black Robe.* Directed by Bruce Beresford, performances by Lothaire Bluteau, Aden Young, Sandrine Holt, and Tantoo Cardinal, Alliance Atlantic, 1991.

Blaeser, Kimberley. "Native Literature: Seeking a Critical Center." *Looking at the Words of Our People: First Nations Analysis of*

*Literature*, edited by Jeannette Armstrong, Theytus Books, 1993, pp. 51–62.

Brant, Beth. "Physical Prayers." *Writing as Witness: Essays and Talk*, Women's Press, 1994, pp. 55–66.

Brant, Clare. "Native Ethics and Rules of Behaviour." *Canadian Journal of Psychiatry*, vol. 35, no. 6, 1990, pp. 534–39.

Campbell, Maria. *Halfbreed*. U of Nebraska P, 1982.

——. "Jacob." Moses and Goldie, eds., pp. 122–29.

Cariou, Warren. "Circles and Triangles: Honouring Indigenous Erotics." Introduction to *Love Medicine and One Song: Sâkih-towin-maskihkiy êkwa pêyak-nikamowin*, by Gregory Scofield, Kegedonce, 2009, pp. i–x.

Cariou, Warren, and Alison Calder. "Changing the Script." McKegney, ed., pp. 125–33.

Catlin, George. "Letter—No. 47." *Letters and Notes on the Manners, Customs and Conditions of North American Indians*, vol. 2, 1841, Dover Publications, 1973, pp. 97–107.

——. *Dance of the Berdash* [oil on canvas], 1835–37. Smithsonian American Art Museum, Washington, DC.

——. *Nót-to-way, a Chief* [oil on canvas], 1835–36. Smithsonian American Art Museum, Washington, DC.

Chrisjohn, Roland, and Sherri Young. *The Circle Game: Shadows and Substance in the Indian Residential School Experience in Canada*. 2006. Theytus Books, 2014.

Clark, David Anthony Tyeeme, and Joane Nagel. "White Men, Red Masks: Appropriations of 'Indian' Manhood in Imagined Wests." *Across the Great Divide: Cultures of Manhood in the American West*, edited by Matthew Basso et al., Routledge, 2001, pp. 109–30.

Colebrook, Claire. *Understanding Deleuze*. Allen and Unwin, 2002.

Coleman, Daniel. *Masculine Migrations: Reading the Postcolonial Male in "New" Canadian Narratives*. U of Toronto P, 1998.

Colman, Andrew. "Dissociation." *A Dictionary of Psychology*, 3rd ed., Oxford UP, 2012.

Coltelli, Laura, ed. *Winged Words: American Indian Writers Speak*. U of Nebraska P, 1990.

Comack, Elizabeth. *Racialized Policing: Aboriginal People's Encounters with the Police.* Fernwood Publishing, 2012.

Coulthard, Glen Sean. *Red Skin, White Masks: Rejecting the Colonial Politics of Recognition.* U of Minnesota P, 2014.

Cree, John. "Welcoming Address." Truth and Reconciliation Commission of Canada Quebec National Event, Montreal, 24 Apr. 2013.

Cromley, Elizabeth. "Masculine/Indian." *Winterthur Portfolio,* vol. 31, no. 4, 1996, pp. 265–80.

CSSSPNQL. *Truth and Reconciliation Walkers Testimonies—Walker #1. YouTube,* uploaded by Compte CSSSPNQL, 8 Sept. 2011, www.youtube.com /watch?v=fuWH-maqV6o.

*Dances with Wolves.* Directed by Kevin Costner, performances by Kevin Costner, Mary McDonnell, Graham Greene, and Rodney Greene, Tig Productions, 1990.

Danforth, Jessica. "Our Bodies, Our Nations." McKegney, ed., pp. 118–24.

Deleuze, Gilles, and Félix Guattari. *A Thousand Plateaus: Capitalism and Schizophrenia.* Translated by Brian Massumi, U of Minnesota P, 1987.

Deloria, Vine Jr. Foreword to *New and Old Voices of Wah'kon-tah: Contemporary Native American Poetry,* edited by Robert K. Dodge and Joseph B. McCullough, International Publishers, 1985, pp. ix–x.

@denerevenge. "[C]ritical indigenous masculinities should vacate not occupy space that indigenous feminist, queer and trans voices should occupy." *Twitter,* 27 Jan. 2016 [Twitter account deleted].

——. "I was more convinced when 'masculinity' was a problem not a solution in our indigenous studies analyses." *Twitter,* 3 Dec. 2015 [Twitter account deleted].

Denny, Antle. "Plenary Presentation." Truth and Reconciliation Commission of Canada Atlantic National Event, Halifax, 26 Oct. 2011.

Dillon, Grace L. "Introduction: Indigenous Futurisms, *Bimaashi biidaas mose, Flying* and *Walking towards You.*" *Extrapolation,* vol. 57, nos. 1–2, 2016, pp. 1–7.

———. "*Miindiwag* and Indigenous Diaspora: Eden Robinson's and Celu Amberstone's Forays into 'Postcolonial' Science Fiction and Fantasy." *Extrapolation*, vol. 48, no. 2, 2007, pp. 219–43.

Dobson, Kit. "Indigeneity and Diversity in Eden Robinson's Work." *Canadian Literature*, vol. 201, 2009, pp. 54–69.

Dodd, Anna, and Emily Fagan. "Professor Taiaiake Alfred Resigns from UVic." *The Martlet*, 7 Mar. 2019, www.martlet.ca/professor-taiaiake-alfred-resigns-from-uvic/.

Driskill, Qwo-Li. *Asegi Stories: Cherokee Queer and Two-Spirit Memory*. U of Arizona P, 2016.

———. "Map of the Americas." *Walking with Ghosts*, Salt Publishing, 2005, pp. 9–11.

———. "Stolen from Our Bodies: First Nations Two-Spirits/Queers and the Journey to a Sovereign Erotic." *SAIL*, vol. 16, no. 2, 2004, pp. 50–64.

Driskill, Qwo-Li, et al. "Introduction." Driskill et al., eds., pp. 1–28.

———. eds. *Queer Indigenous Studies: Critical Interventions in Theory, Politics, and Literature*. U of Arizona P, 2011.

Elliot, Alicia. "We Need to Talk about the Cost of Calling Out Abuse within Marginalized Communities." *CBC*, 17 Nov. 2017, www.cbc.ca/arts/we-need-to-talk-about-the-cost-of-calling-out-abuse-within-marginalized-communities-1.4407893.

Ennamorato, Judith. *Sing the Brave Song*. Raven, 1998.

Etherington, Patrick Jr. "Residential School Walkers Panel." Truth and Reconciliation Commission of Canada Atlantic National Event, Halifax, 26 Oct. 2011.

Fabre, Cara. "'There's a Treatment Centre Where the Residential School Used to Be': Alcoholism, Acculturation, and Barriers to Indigenous Health in Eden Robinson's *Monkey Beach*." *Studies in Canadian Literature*, vol. 38, no. 2, 2013, pp. 126–46.

Fagan, Kristina. "Weesageechak Meets the Weetigo: Storytelling, Humour, and Trauma in the Fiction of Richard Van Camp, Tomson Highway, and Eden Robinson." *Studies in Canadian Literature*, vol. 34, no. 1, 2009, pp. 204–26.

Fagan, Kristina, and Sam McKegney. "Circling the Question of Nationalism in Native Canadian Literature and Its Study."

*Review: Literature and Arts of the Americas*, vol. 41, no. 1, 2008, pp. 31–42.

Finley, Chris. "Decolonizing the Queer Native Body (and Recovering the Native Bull-Dyke): Bringing 'Sexy Back' and Out of Native Studies' Closet." Driskill et al., eds., pp. 31–42.

Fiske, Joanne. *Cis dideen kat: When the Plumes Rise: The Way of the Lake Babine Nation*. UBC P, 2000.

Fonagy, Peter, and Mary Target. "Dissociation and Trauma." *Current Opinion in Psychiatry*, vol. 8, no. 3, 1995, pp. 161–66.

Gabriel, Ellen. "Plenary Address." Truth and Reconciliation Commission of Canada Quebec National Event, Montreal, 25 Apr. 2013.

——. "Those Who Carry the Burden of Peace." *WordPress*, 5 Jan. 2014, sovereignvoices1.wordpress.com/2014/01/05/those-who-carry-the-burden-of-peace/.

Giesbrecht, T., and H. Merckelbach. "The Causal Relationship between Dissociation and Trauma: A Critical Review." *Der Nervenarzt*, vol. 76, no. 1, 2005, p. 20.

Gilley, Brian Joseph. "Two-Spirit Men's Sexual Survivance against the Inequality of Desire." Driskill et al., eds., pp. 123–31.

Goeman, Mishuana. *Mark My Words: Native Women Mapping Our Nations*. U of Minnesota P, 2013.

Goldie, Terry. *Fear and Temptation: The Image of the Indigene in Canadian, Australian, and New Zealand Literatures*. McGill-Queen's UP, 1989.

Goulet, Linda. Interview with the author, 29 May 2012.

Grant, Agnes, ed. *Finding My Talk: How Fourteen Canadian Native Women Reclaimed Their Lives after Residential School*. Fifth House Books, 2004.

Haig-Brown, Celia. *Resistance and Renewal: Surviving the Indian Residential School*. Arsenal Pulp Press, 1988.

Haladay, Jane. "'I Liked It So Much I E-Mailed Him and Told Him': Teaching *The Lesser Blessed* at the University of California." *Studies in American Indian Literatures*, vol. 19, no. 1, 2007, pp. 66–90.

Halfe, Louise Bernice. *Bear Bones and Feathers*. Coteau Books, 1994.

——. *Burning in This Midnight Dream*. Coteau Books, 2016.

——. "A Calm Sensuality." McKegney, ed., pp. 48–55.

——. "Introspection on Violence against Women: We Must All Look Inward to Restore Balance." *Eagle Feather News*, 28 Nov. 2017, www.eaglefeathernews.com/missing/introspection-on-violence-against-women-we-must-all-look-inward-to-restore-balance.

Hargreaves, Allison. *Violence against Indigenous Women: Literature, Activism, Resistance*. Wilfrid Laurier UP, 2017.

Helm, June, Teresa S. Carterette, and Nancy Oestreich Lurie. *The People of Denendeh: Ethnohistory of the Indians of Canada's Northwest Territories*. McGill-Queen's UP, 2000.

Henderson, James (Sákéj) Youngblood. "Ayukpachi: Empowering Aboriginal Thought." Battiste, ed., pp. 248–78.

——. "Postcolonial Ghost Dancing: Diagnosing European Colonialism." Battiste, ed., 57–76.

Henry, Robert. "Social Spaces of Maleness: The Role of Street Gangs in Practising Indigenous Masculinities." Innes and Anderson, eds., 181–96.

Highway, Tomson. *Comparing Mythologies*. U of Ottawa P, 2003.

——. *Kiss of the Fur Queen*. Penguin Random House, 1998.

Hill Kanonhsyonne, Janice C. "Where Are the Men?" McKegney, ed., 16–20.

Hokowhitu, Brendan. "Beyond Masculinities Panel." Gender and Decolonization: A Resurgent Gathering, Queen's U, 27 Mar. 2015.

——. "The Death of Koro Paka: 'Traditional' Māori Patriarchy." *The Contemporary Pacific*, vol. 20, no. 1, 2008, pp. 115–41.

——. "Embodied Masculinity and Sport." McKegney, ed., pp. 98–108.

——. "Māori Rugby and Subversion: Creativity, Domestication, Oppression and Decolonization." *The International Journal of the History of Sport*, vol. 26, no. 16, 2009, pp. 2314–34.

——. "Taxonomies of Indigeneity: Indigenous Heterosexual Patriarchal Masculinity." Innes and Anderson, eds., 80–95.

*Holy Bible* [KJV]. American Bible Society, 1999.

hooks, bell. *We Real Cool: Black Men and Masculinity*. Routledge, 2004.

Houle, Terrance, and Adrian Stimson. "Deeper than a Blood Tie." McKegney, ed., pp. 148–59.

Hoy, Helen. *How Should I Read These? Native Women Writers in Canada.* U of Toronto P, 2001.

"Indigenous Governance Programs." *UVic,* www.uvic.ca/hsd/igov/future-students/index.php.

Innes, Robert Alexander. *Elder Brother and the Law of the People: Contemporary Kinship and Cowessess First Nation.* U of Manitoba P, 2013.

Innes, Robert Alexander, and Kim Anderson. "Introduction: Who's Walking with Our Brothers?" Innes and Anderson, eds., pp. 3–20.

——. eds. *Indigenous Men and Masculinities: Legacies, Identities, Regeneration.* U of Manitoba P, 2015.

Innes, Robert Alexander, Kim Anderson, and Jonathan Swift. "'To Arrive Speaking': Voices from the Bidwewidam Indigenous Masculinities Project." Innes and Anderson, eds., pp. 283–308.

Jackson, Randy. Interview with the author, 7 Nov. 2013.

Jackson II, Ronald L. *Scripting the Black Masculine Body: Identity, Discourse, and Racial Politics in Popular Media.* SUNY P, 2006.

Johnston, Basil. *Indian School Days.* U of Oklahoma P, 1988.

——. "Young Men of Good Will." McKegney, ed., pp. 41–47.

Justice, Daniel Heath. "Fear of a Changeling Moon: A Rather Queer Tale from a Cherokee Hillbilly." *Me Sexy: An Exploration of Native Sex and Sexuality,* edited by Drew Hayden Taylor, Douglas and McIntyre, 2008, pp. 87–108.

——. "Fighting Shame through Love." McKegney, ed., pp. 134–45.

——. "'Go Away, Water!' Kinship Criticism and the Decolonization Imperative." *Reasoning Together: The Native Critics Collective,* edited by Craig S. Womack et al., U of Oklahoma P, 2007, pp. 147–68.

——. *Why Indigenous Literatures Matter.* Wilfrid Laurier UP, 2018.

Keene, Adrienne. "The Problematics of Disingenuous Public Apologies." *Native Appropriations,* 27 Nov. 2017, nativeappropriations.com/2017/11/the-problematics-of-disingenuous-public-apologies.html.

King, Thomas. *Truth & Bright Water.* Harper Flamingo, 1999.

——. *The Truth about Stories: A Native Narrative.* House of Anansi Press, 2003.

Klopotek, Brian. "'I Guess Your Warrior Look Doesn't Work Every Time': Challenging Indian Masculinity in the Cinema." *Across the Great Divide: Cultures of Manhood in the American West*, edited by Matthew Basso et al., Routledge, 2001, pp. 251–73.

Knockwood, Isabelle. *Out of the Depths: The Experiences of Mi'kmaw Children at the Indian Residential School at Shubenacadie, Nova Scotia.* Roseway Publishing, 1992.

Komulainen, Shaney. *Face to Face* [photograph]. The Canadian Press, 1990.

Koosees, Sammy Jr. *Truth and Reconciliation Walk. YouTube*, uploaded by Sammy Koosees, 5 Oct. 2011, www.youtube.com/watch?v=PrVK1wsraow.

Kuokkanen, Rauna. *Reshaping the University: Responsibility, Indigenous Epistemes, and the Logic of the Gift.* UBC P, 2007.

*The Last of the Mohicans.* Directed by Michael Mann, performances by Daniel Day-Lewis, Madeleine Stowe, Russell Means, and Eric Schweig, Morgan Creek Productions, 1992.

Lawrence, Bonita. "Gender, Race, and Regulation of Native Identity in Canada and the United States: An Overview." *Hypatia: A Journal of Feminist Philosophy*, vol. 18, no. 2, 2003, pp. 3–25.

Lederman, Marsha. "Indigenous Anthology Stands by Decision to Include Poet Despite Controversy." *The Globe and Mail*, 12 Oct. 2017, www.theglobeandmail.com/news/british-columbia/indigenous-anthology-stands-by-decision-to-include-poet-despite-controversy/article36559475/.

Lee, Erica Violet. "In Defence of the Wastelands: A Survival Guide." *Guts*, 30 Nov. 2016, gutsmagazine.ca/wastelands/.

———. "Land, Language and Decolonial Love." *Red Rising Magazine*, Nov. 2016, pp. 2–6.

———. "Upheaval." *Moontime Warrior*, 6 June 2017, moontimewarrior.com/ [poem since removed].

Lee, Erica Violet, et al. "An Open Letter to the University of Regina Press, Regarding the *Kisiskáciwan* Anthology." *Tumblr*, 10 Oct. 2017, kisiskaciwan openletter.tumblr.com/post/166265774679/an-open-letter-to-the-university-of-regina-press.

Lee, Lloyd L. *Diné Masculinities: Conceptualizations and Reflections.* Createspace Publishers, 2013.

Lifman, Paul. "Indigenous Territorialities in Mexico and Colombia." Regional Worlds at the U of Chicago, 1998.

Lorde, Audre. "Uses of the Erotic: The Erotic as Power." *Sister Outsider*, 1984, Crossing, 2007, pp. 53–59.

Mann, Barbara Alice. *Iroquoian Women: The Gantowisas*. Peter Lang, 2000.

Maracle, Lee. *I Am Woman: A Native Perspective on Sociology and Feminism*. Press Gang, 1999.

——. "This Is a Vision." McKegney, ed., pp. 30–40.

McKegney, Sam. "Into the Full Grace of the Blood of Men: An Introduction." McKegney, ed., pp. 1–15.

——. *Magic Weapons: Aboriginal Writers Remaking Community after Residential School*. U of Manitoba P, 2007.

——. "Strategies for Ethical Engagement: An Open Letter Concerning Non-Native Scholars of Native Literatures." *Studies in American Indian Literatures*, series 2, vol. 20, no. 4, 2008, pp. 56–67.

——. "Warriors, Healers, Lovers, and Leaders: Colonial Impositions on Indigenous Male Roles and Responsibilities." *Canadian Perspectives on Men and Masculinities: An Interdisciplinary Reader*, edited by Jason A. Laker, Oxford UP, 2012, pp. 241–64.

——. ed. *Masculindians: Conversations about Indigenous Manhood*. U of Manitoba P, 2014.

McKegney, Sam, et al. "Strong Men Stories: A Roundtable on Indigenous Masculinities." Innes and Anderson, eds., pp. 243–65.

McLeod, Neal. *Gabriel's Beach*. Hagios, 2008.

——. "Neal McLeod Open Letter." *WordPress*, 17 Oct. 2017, nealmcleodopenletter.wordpress.com/.

——. *Songs to Kill a Witikow*. Hagios, 2005.

——. "Tending the Fire." McKegney, ed., pp. 204–13.

Messner, Michael A. *Politics of Masculinities: Men in Movements*. Sage Publications, 1997.

Miller, J.R. *Lethal Legacy: Current Native Controversies in Canada*. McClelland and Stewart, 2004.

Milloy, John S. *A National Crime: The Canadian Government and the Residential School System, 1879 to 1986*. U of Manitoba P, 1999.

*Mohawk Midnight Runners*. Directed by Zoe Leigh Hopkins, performances by Ryan Scott Greene, R. Douglas Hutchinson, Cody Lightning, and Jon Proudstar, Big Soul Productions, 2013.

Monture, Rick. *We Share Our Matters: Two Centuries of Writing and Resistance at Six Nations of the Grand River*. U of Manitoba P, 2014.

Monture-Angus, Patricia. *Thunder in My Soul: A Mohawk Woman Speaks*. Fernwood Publishing, 1995.

Morgensen, Scott L. "Cutting to the Roots of Colonial Masculinity." Innes and Anderson, eds., pp. 38–61.

Moses, Daniel David. *Almighty Voice and His Wife*. 1992. Playwrights Canada, 2010.

Moses, Daniel David, and Terry Goldie, eds. *An Anthology of Canadian Native Literature in English*. 3rd ed. Oxford UP, 2005.

Narine, Shari. "Creating Awareness during Walk to National Event." *Windspeaker*, vol. 29, no. 7, 2011, ammsa.com/publications/windspeaker/creating-awareness-during-walk-national-event.

——. "'Normal Crime' Scenario Fuels Racism Accusations in Boushie Shooting." *Windspeaker*, vol. 34, no. 10, 2016, https://www.ammsa.com/publications/windspeaker/'normal-crime'-scenario-fuels-racism-accusations-boushie-shooting.

Neuhaus, Mareike. "Indigenous Rhetorics and Kinship: Towards a Rhetoric of Relational Word Bundles." *The Canadian Journal of Native Studies*, vol. 33, no. 1, 2013, pp. 125–45.

Nixon, Lindsay. "#MeToo and the Secrets Indigenous Women Keep." *The Walrus*, 5 Dec. 2018, https://thewalrus.ca/metoo-and-the-secrets-indigenous-women-keep/.

"Not-to-way, a Chief." *Smithsonian American Art Museum*, https://americanart.si.edu/artwork/not-way-chief-4295.

Nunn, Neil. "Toxic Encounters, Settler Logics of Elimination, and the Future of a Continent." *Antipode*, vol. 50, no. 5, 2018, pp. 1330–48.

Oliver, Vanessa, et al. "'Women Are Supposed to Be the Leaders': Intersections of Gender, Race and Colonisation in HIV Prevention with Indigenous Young People." *Culture, Health and Sexuality*, vol. 17, no. 7, 2015, pp. 906–19.

"Our Vision, Purpose and Mission." 'Aha Kāne, www.ahakane.org/about/our_vision_purpose_mission.

Pasternak, Shiri. "The Fiscal Body of Sovereignty: To 'Make Live' in Indian Country." Settler Colonial Studies, vol. 6, no. 4, 2016, pp. 317–38.

Paul, Daniel. We Were Not the Savages: A Micmac Perspective on the Collision of European and Aboriginal Civilizations. Nimbus Publishers, 1993.

Piché, Allison. "Imprisonment and Indigenous Masculinity: Contesting Hegemonic Masculinity in a Toxic Environment." Innes and Anderson, eds., 2015, pp. 197–213.

Porter, Tom (Sakokweniónkwas). And Grandma Said . . . Iroquois Teachings as Passed Down through the Oral Tradition. Transcribed by Lesley Forrester, Xlibris Corporation, 2008.

"Potlatch Ban." Living Tradition: The Kwa kwaka'wakw Potlatch of the Northwest Coast, umistapotlatch.ca/potlatch_interdire-potlatch_ban-eng.php.

Power, Peter. Mob Rule: Chateauguay Mob Burned Mohawks in Effigy to Protest Blockade of Mercier Bridge [photograph], The Toronto Star, 1990.

Queen's University. "Traditional Territories." Queen's University, Nov. 2015, www.queensu.ca/encyclopedia/t/traditional-territories.

Reber, Suzanne, and Robert Renaud. Starlight Tour: The Last, Lonely Night of Neil Stonechild. Random House, 2005.

"Residential Schools in Canada: Educational Guide." Historica Canada, education.historicacanada.ca/files/103/ResidentialSchools_Printable_Pages.pdf.

Rifkin, Mark. "The Erotics of Sovereignty." Driskill et al., eds., pp. 172–89.

——. When Did Indians Become Straight? Kinship, the History of Sexuality, and Native Sovereignty. Oxford UP, 2011.

Robidoux, Michael A. "Historical Interpretations of First Nations Masculinity and Its Influence on Canada's Sport Heritage." International Journal of the History of Sport, vol. 23, no. 2, 2006, pp. 267–84.

Robinson, Eden. Blood Sports. McClelland and Stewart, 2006.

———. "Queen of the North." *Traplines*, 1996, Vintage Canada, 1998, pp. 183–215.

———. *The Sasquatch at Home: Traditional Protocols and Modern Storytelling*. U of Alberta P, 2011.

———. "Terminal Avenue." Moses and Goldie, eds., pp. 541–46.

Robinson, Gordon. *Tales of Kitamaat*. Northern Sentinel, 1961.

Ross, Rupert. *Dancing with a Ghost: Exploring Aboriginal Reality*. Penguin Canada, 2006.

Rowe, Daniel J. "Taiaiake Alfred Resigns from University of Victoria's Indigenous Governance Program." *Two Row Times*, 6 Mar. 2019, https://tworowtimes.com/news/national/alfred-resigns-from-indigenous-governance-program/.

Scofield, Gregory. "A Liberation through Claiming." McKegney, ed., pp. 213–21.

———. *Love Medicine and One Song: Sâkihtowin-maskihkiy êkwa pêyak-nikamowin*. 1997. Kegedonce, 2009.

Scudeler, June. "'This Song I Am Singing': Gregory Scofield's Interweavings of Métis, Gay, and Jewish Selfhoods." *Studies in Canadian Literature*, vol. 31, no. 1, 2006, pp. 129–45.

Sedgwick, Eve Kosofsky. *Between Men: English Literature and Male Homosocial Desire*. Columbia UP, 1985.

Simpson, Audra. *Political Life across the Borders of Settler States*. Duke UP, 2014.

Simpson, Leanne Betasamosake. *As We Have Always Done: Indigenous Freedom through Radical Resistance*. U of Minnesota P, 2017.

———. *Islands of Decolonial Love*. ARP Books, 2013.

———. "Islands of Decolonial Love: Exploring Love on Occupied Land." Talk at School of Kinesiology and Health, Queen's U, 26 Mar. 2015.

———. "Not Murdered, Not Missing: Rebelling against Colonial Gender Violence." *Leanne Simpson*, www.leannesimpson.ca/writings/not-murdered-not-missing-rebelling-against-colonial-gender-violence.

———. "The Powerful Legacy of the Rotiskenrakéh:te—Those That Carry the Burden of Peace." *Leanne Simpson*, www.leannesimpson.ca/writings/the-powerful-legacy-of-the-rotiskenrakhte-those-that-carry-the-burden-of-peace.

Sinclair, Murray. "Closing Remarks." Truth and Reconciliation Commission of Canada Vancouver Island Regional Event, Victoria, 14 Apr. 2012.

———. "Presentation by the Honorable Mr. Justice Murray Sinclair on the Occasion of Receiving an Honorary Doctorate from the University of Winnipeg Fall Convocation." U of Winnipeg, 16 Oct. 2011.

Sinclair, Niigaanwewidam James. "A Dialogue on the Future of Indigenous Masculinities Studies." McKegney, ed., pp. 223–37.

Sison, Marites N. "A Walk Unlike Any Other." Anglican Journal, 1 Dec. 2011, www.anglicanjournal.com/a-walk-unlike-any-other-10238/.

Smoke, Penny. "The Okihtcitâwak Patrol Group Is Helping Clean Up One of Saskatoon's Toughest Neighbourhoods." CBC, 14 Oct. 2018, https://newsinteractives.cbc.ca/longform/street-warriors.

Starblanket, Gina, and Dallas Hunt. "How the Death of Colten Boushie Became Recast as the Story of a Knight Protecting His Castle." The Globe and Mail, 15 Feb. 2018, https://www.theglobeandmail.com/opinion/how-the-death-of-colten-boushie-became-recast-as-the-story-of-a-knight-protecting-his-castle/article37958746/.

Sumac, Smokii. "'Just Make Me Look Like Aquaman': An Essay on Seeing Myself." Tea and Bannock: Indigenous Women Photographers, Telling Story, Sharing Light, teaandbannock.com/2020/02/11/just-make-me-look-like-aquaman-an-essay-on-seeing-myself-smokii-sumac-guest-blogger/.

———. You Are Enough: Love Poems for the End of the World. Kegedonce, 2018.

Sweet, Timothy. "Masculinity and Self-Performance in the Life of Black Hawk." American Literature, vol. 65, no. 3, 1993, 475–99.

Tatonetti, Lisa. The Queerness of Native American Literature. U of Minnesota P, 2014.

———. Written by the Body: Gender Expansiveness and Indigenous Non-Cis Masculinities. U of Minnesota P, 2021.

Tengan, Ty P. Kāwika. Native Men Remade: Gender and Nation in Contemporary Hawai'i. Duke UP, 2008.

———. "Talking Story, Remaking Community." McKegney, ed., pp. 109–17.

Teuton, Sean Kicummah. *Red Land, Red Power: Grounding Knowledge in the American Indian Novel.* Duke UP, 2008.

Thrasher, Anthony Apakark. *Thrasher . . . Skid Row Eskimo.* Edited by Gerard Deagle and Alan Mettrick, Griffin House, 1976.

Truth and Reconciliation Commission of Canada. *Honouring the Truth, Reconciling for the Future: Summary of the Final Report of the Truth and Reconciliation Commission of Canada.* TRC, 2015.

Tuck, Eve, and K. Wayne Yang. "Decolonization Is Not a Metaphor." *Decolonization: Indigeneity, Education and Society,* vol. 1, no. 1, 2012, pp. 1–40.

Tuffin, Lois. "Tasha Beeds: Survivor, Scholar and Water Walker." *MyKawartha.com,* 29 June 2018, www.mykawartha.com/news-story/8697868-tasha-beeds-survivor-scholar-and-water-walker/.

Union of British Columbia Indian Chiefs. "Justice for Colten: UBCIC Statement of Solidarity." *UBCIC,* 12 Feb. 2018, www.ubcic.bc.ca/justice_for_colten.

Valaskakis, Gail Guthrie. *Indian Country: Essays on Contemporary Native Culture.* Wilfrid Laurier UP, 2005.

Van Camp, Richard. "'I Carve My Stories Every Day': An Interview with Richard Van Camp." With Sylvie Vranckx. *Canadian Literature,* vol. 215, 2012, 70–84.

———. "Into the Tribe of Man." McKegney, ed., pp. 184–93.

———. *The Lesser Blessed.* Douglas and McIntyre, 1996.

———. "The Night Charles Bukowski Died." *Angel Wing Splash Pattern,* Kegedonce, 2002, pp. 30–36.

Vaughan, Genevieve. "Introduction: A Radically Different World-view Is Possible." Vaughan, ed., 1–38.

———. ed. *Women and the Gift Economy: A Radically Different Worldview Is Possible.* Inanna Publications and Education, 2007.

Vedal, Lauren. "Closure or Connection? Healing from Trauma in Richard Van Camp's *The Lesser Blessed.*" *Studies in Canadian Literature,* vol. 38, no. 2, 2013, pp. 106–25.

Vizenor, Gerald. *Manifest Manners: Narratives on Postindian Survivance.* U of Nebraska P, 1999.

"Walkers for Truth and Reconciliation." Truth and Reconciliation Commission of Canada, n.d.

Walsh, Bruce. "Publisher's Response to the Open Letter of October 10 re: *Kisiskâciwan*." *University of Regina Press*, 12 Oct. 2017, uofrpress.ca/News-and-Reviews/2017/Publisher-s-Response-to-the-Open-Letter-of-October-10-re-kisiskaciwan.

——. Response to "We Need to Talk about the Cost of Calling Out Abuse within Marginalized Communities." *CBC*, 23 Nov. 2017, www.cbc.ca/arts/we-need-to-talk-about-the-cost-of-calling-out-abuse-within-marginalized-communities-1.4407893.

Williams, Alex, dir. *The Pass System: Life under Segregation in Canada*. V Tape, 2016.

Willmott, Glenn. *Modernist Goods: Primitivism, the Market, and the Gift*. U of Toronto P, 2008.

Wilson, Carla. "Founder of UVic's Indigenous Governance Program Resigns." *Times Colonist*, 10 Mar. 2019, https://www.timescolonist.com/news/local/founder-of-uvic-s-indigenous-governance-program-resigns-1.23659097.

Wilson, Michael T. "'Saturnalia of Blood': Masculine Self-Control and American Indians in the Frontier Novel." *Studies in American Fiction*, vol. 33, no. 2, 2005, pp. 131–47.

Wilson, Shawn. *Research Is Ceremony: Indigenous Research Methods*. Fernwood Publishing, 2008.

Wright, Ronald. *Stolen Continents: Conquest and Resistance in the Americas*. Penguin Canada, 2003.

# PERMISSIONS

*The publisher has made every effort to source the
copyright holders of these writings.*

Armstrong, Jeannette. "Indigenous Knowledge and Gift Giving: Living in Community." Vaughan, ed. Inanna Publications and Education, 2007.

Belcourt, Billy-Ray. *The Wound is a World*. Frontenac House, 2017. Excerpts reprinted with permission.

Driskill, Qwo-Li. "Map of the Americas." *Walking with Ghosts*, 9–11. Salt Publishing, 2005. Excerpts reprinted with permission.

Halfe, Louise Bernice. Excerpts from "Nitotem," "Valentine Dialogue," "Stones," and "nēpēwisiwin—shame" reprinted with permission of the author.

McKegney, Sam, ed. *Masculinidans: Conversations about Indigenous Manhood*. U of Manitoba P, 2014. Excerpts reprinted courtesy of University of Manitoba Press.

Porter, Tom (Sakokwenió'nkwas). *And Grandma Said . . . Iroquois Teachings as Passed Down through the Oral Tradition*. Transcribed by Lesley Forrester. Xlibris Corporation, 2008. Excerpts reprinted with permission.

Robinson, Eden. Excerpts from *Blood Sports* copyright © 2006 by Eden Robinson. Reprinted by permission of McClelland & Stewart, a division of Penguin Random House Canada Limited.

Scofield, Gregory. Excerpts from "Love Medicine" and "One Song"
reprinted with permission of the author.
Sumac, Smokii. *You Are Enough: Love Poems for the End of the World.*
Kegedonce Press, 2018. Excerpts reprinted with permission.
Van Camp, Richard. *The Lesser Blessed.* Douglas and McIntyre, 1996.
Excerpts reprinted with permission from the publisher.

# INDEX

## A

absentee, as stereotype, 33–35, 39–41

Acadian People, 97

*Act for the Gradual Enfranchisement of Indians*, 23–25

'Aha Kāne men's group, xxi

Aionwahta, 9, 51, 53–54, 56, 170, 178; tale of, xxvii, 50, 52–55

Akiwenzie-Damm, Kateri (Anishinaabe), xii, 102, 136, 143

Aklavik Roman Catholic Residential School, 67

Akwesasne Nation, 36

alcohol/alcoholism, 34, 39, 159

Alexie, Robert Arthur (Gwich'in), 64

Alfred, Taiaiake (Kanien'kcha:ka), xxi–xxii, 1

alienation, 9, 61, 66, 157, 167; from body, 182; from families/communities, 41, 43–44, 77, 81, 156, 160, 167, 177; from kinship, 177

Allen, Paula Gunn, xiv, 2, 104, 110

*Almighty Voice and His Wife*, 1

Anderson, Kim (Cree-Métis), xiv–xv, 2, 30, 46, 93, 104, 114, 185

*And Grandma Said...Iroquois Teachings as Passed Down through the Oral Tradition*, 9

Anishinaabe People, x, 8

anthropocentrism, 95, 97, 113

Archibald-Barber, Jesse (Cree-Métis), xxiv

Armstrong, Jeannette (Syilx), xxix, 117, 119, 122–24, 126, 142, 145

Arnott, Joanne (Métis), 102, 175

*Asegi Stories: Cherokee Queer and Two-Spirit Memory*, 7, 48, 79, 109, 189

Assembly of First Nations, 64–65

assimilation, 9–10, 26–28, 30, 40, 75

*As We Have Always Done: Indigenous Freedom through Radical Resistance*: on dismantling heteropatriarchy, xii, xxiii, 54, 103, 107, 146;

*As We Have Always Done* continued
on Indigenous resurgence/
freedom, xvi, 76, 78, 92, 105;
on respect for Indigenous
bodies/integrity, ix–x, xiii,
xxvii, 2, 53, 55, 126, 176, 181
autonomy, xix, 32, 100, 123,
140, 161, 178, 183, 186; of
individuals, 6, 17, 20, 160;
and responsibility, 176;
restrictive influence on, 166

**B**

balance, 56, 87, 189; along gender
lines, 8, 18–24, 28, 30,
49; and gifting, 127, 134,
138; between group and
individual, 5, 32; and kinship
networks, 16; and power,
13, 29; as radical, xvii, xix
band council system, 24, 50
Barrera, Jorge, xxi
Baudrillard, Jean, 132–33
*Bear Bones and Feathers*, 69, 77, 83
Bederman, Gail, 75
Belcourt, Billy-Ray (Driftpile Cree),
xx, 73, 93–94, 149, 176–79, 187
Benaway, Gwen, 106
Bielawski, Ellen (settler), 154
Bigsky, Melvin, 46
biological determinism, xxviii,
5, 16, 95, 108, 181
biological essentialisms, 91, 110
Bird, Louis (Cree), 173
*Black Robe*, 37, 39
Blaeser, Kimberley
(Anishinaabe), xiii

*Blood Sports:* on debt and violence,
xxix, 139–40; on exchange
economics and gender, 120, 131–
32, 134, 137, 146; on gift exchange,
130, 145; on patriarchy and
masculinity, 143, 152, 159, 162, 169
Blue Quills Indian Residential
School, 69
Bourdieu, Pierre, 122
Boushie, Colten, 46–47
Boy Scouts of America, 39
Brant, Beth (Kanien'keha:ka), x,
xxviii, 104, 110–11, 114
Brant, Clare (Kanien'keha:ka), 6–7, 183
*Breaking the Silence: An Interpretive
Study of Residential School
Impact and Healing as
Illustrated by the Stories of
First Nations Individuals*, 65
Brown Spoon Club, 69
bundles, xii, xvii, xx, xxvi, 6

**C**

Calder, Alison, 186
Campbell, Maria (Métis), 29, 77
Campbell, Tenille (Dene-
Métis), xx, xxxii
Canada, Dominion of: as claiming
Indigenous lands, xiii, xx,
xxvii, 26, 49, 99; as effacing
kinship traditions, 68;
and nation-building, 61;
sovereignty of, 22, 25, 49
capitalism, 48, 59, 171, 183; and
economic disparities, 128, 131,
158; and economic exchange,
xxix, 106, 118, 125; and gender

inequities, 129; and gift
   giving, 122, 126. *See also*
   consumerism/consumption
Cariou, Warren (Métis),
   108, 171, 173, 186
Cartesian dualism, 27, 74–75, 81, 113
Catlin, George, 35–37
Cayuga Nation, 17
ceremonies, 53, 83–84, 90, 113, 125,
   177–78; of initiation, 160; as
   rite of passage, 55; and sex, 99
Chingachgook (fictional
   noble savage), 37, 39
Chippewa People, 37
Chomina (fictional noble
   savage), 37–39
Chrisjohn, Roland, 27, 65
Christianity, 3, 21; Genesis
   creation story, 10, 12–16
Chrystos (Menominee), xxviii, 110
*The Circle Game: Shadows
   and Substance in the
   Indian Residential School
   Experience in Canada,* 65
cis-hetero Indigenous males, xii, xvi,
   xxvi–xxvii, 21, 49, 91, 105, 173
Clan Mother (Iakoiá:nehr), 18–19, 24
Clark, David Anthony Tyeeme, 34
Cloutier, Private Patrick, 42–43
Colebrook, Claire, 2, 61
colonialism/colonization. *See*
   settler colonialism
Comack, Elizabeth, 46
*Comparing Mythologies,* 10
competition: of genders, 105;
   and gift-giving, xxix, 118
condolence, 9, 48, 50, 54–55;

ceremony of, 170, 178
consensus building. *See*
   decision-making
constellation of care, 26, 184–85
consumerism/consumption, 9, 63,
   114, 126–28. *See also* capitalism
Cooper, James Fenimore, 38
cooperation, xxix, 16, 118
Coulthard, Glen (Dene),
   xiii, 29, 93, 106
Cowessess First Nation, 158
Cree, John (Kanien'keha:ka), 80
Cree Nation: culture of, xxiii;
   kinship systems in, 79, 81–82;
   transformation stories of, 108
Cromley, Elizabeth, 41, 74
CSSSPNQL, 80

**D**

dances, 113, 125, 165, 176–78
*Dances with Wolves,* 37, 39
Danforth, Jessica (Oneida), 90
debnimzewin (right), 157
debt. *See* indebtedness
decision-making: autonomy of, 100;
   as consensus-based, 13–14, 19, 24,
   37, 122–23, 143; as sovereign, 119
decolonialism/decolonization, xi,
   xxi–xxii, xxvii, 62, 64, 94, 105,
   178; and activism, 113; and
   love, 92, 106, 170; tools of, 114
dehumanization, 48, 125, 141, 151,
   161, 165; of Indigenous men,
   4, 47, 49, 172; of Indigenous
   women, 70, 102; by settler
   colonialism, xix, 49, 177
Dene People, 160

Denny, Antle, 65

deterritorialization, 2, 4, 43, 61, 129–30, 151, 159; as aim of residential schools, 27, 49, 72, 77, 87; as colonial policy/technology, 9–10, 21, 26, 30–31, 47, 75–76, 90, 92, 175–76; and masculinities, 177–78

Dillon, Grace (Anishinaabe), 125

*Diné Masculinities: Conceptualizations and Reflections,* xv

disembodiment, 74, 92, 109, 113; as colonial technology, 62, 87; as effect of residential schools, 76

disempowerment, 41, 60, 138

disintegration: as coerced, 61, 75; as colonial technology, xix, 2, 27, 87; of Indigenous communities, 28, 30, 49, 187; of personhood, 62, 78, 130

dispossession, of Indigenous lands, 2, 126, 188; as colonial policy/technology, x, 7, 29, 31, 49, 61–62, 90–91, 119, 175; as crime, violence, 38, 94; as expansive, 76, 79

Dogrib Nation, 157, 162, 170; creation story of, 153–54, 156, 159, 165, 167, 169. *See also* Tłı̨chǫ

domination, 16, 32, 44, 52, 102, 118, 146, 161. *See also* masculinities, dominant/dominative

Driskill, Qwo-Li (Cherokee), xxviii, 2, 7, 49, 79, 89–90, 102, 104, 109, 166, 189

Dumont, Dawn (Cree), xxiv, xxvi–xxvii

Duran, Bonnie, xiv

Duran, Eduardo, xiv

duty, sense of, 166, 176, 183; as lost, 157

dynamic mutuality, 15, 28, 31, 92, 104–5, 111, 172, 178

# E

*Elder Brother and the Law of the People: Contemporary Kinship and Cowessess First Nation,* 158

elimination, of Indigenous Peoples, 30–31, 38, 46, 49, 118, 132, 180

Elliott, Alicia (Tuscarora), xx, xxiv

embodied discursive action, xxviii, 62, 78–80, 82–83, 87, 150, 185

embodiment, xxix–xxx, 67, 78, 108–9

empathy, 72, 78; and kinship, 60, 65–66

empowerment, 90, 106, 162, 167, 179; and identities, 160; and masculinity, 157, 171–172; and subjectivities, 81

Ennamorato, Judith, 26

erotics/eroticism, xxviii, xxx–xxxi, 104, 107, 113; as sacred, 166; as Two-Spirit and woman-centred, xxviii, 111

Eskasoni reserve, 27

Etherington Jr., Patrick, 79–81, 83–84, 86–87

Etherington Sr., Patrick, 81

ethic of non-interference, 6–7, 9, 17, 19–20, 29, 32, 49, 52, 54

European/white settlers, xvi, 17, 31, 35, 63, 131, 146; creation stories of, 10; and enlightenment, 74;

expansion of, 37–39, 41, 44; as
having exonerated self-image,
40–41; heteropatriarchy of,
30; and masculinities, 33,
109, 188; political power of,
1, 25, 46; privilege of, 127;
and white supremacy, 59
exchange economics, 117–18,
124–26, 129–30, 132, 146;
and gift economy, 137; and
heteropatriarchy, 131; as
naturalized, 134, 144; and
sexuality as a commodity,
128, 141; as simulacrum, 138
extraction: of resources, 61; as
sexual metaphor, 106, 180

# F

Fabre, Cara, 125
Fagan, Kristina, 160, 170
fellatio, as ceremony, 107
femininity/feminism, xxvii, 93; and
beauty, nurture and healing,
156; creative power of, 15; as
eroticized and exoticized,
127; and gift theory, 118
Finding My Talk, 65
forgiveness, xxv–xxvi, 142; as
coercive tool, 144
freedom: as academic, xxiv,
xxvi; and individual self,
16, 105, 157, 168, 179; and
responsibility, 164, 167, 171

# G

Gabriel, Ellen (Kanien'keha:ka),
xxxi, 8, 15, 20, 43–44, 187

Gabriel's Beach, xxiii, 63
Gantowisas (political woman), 19
gender binaries, xii, xxi, 5, 8–9, 20–21,
28–29, 67, 91, 94, 124, 156, 181
gender dynamics, 25, 60, 64, 96, 100
gender ecologies, 10, 100, 151, 175–77;
as competitive, xxviii, 105–6,
110, 162, 178; decolonizing of, 90,
104, 113; and dynamic mutuality,
15, 92; of Haudenosaunee
culture, 19, 21, 24; interventions/
assaults on, 48, 62, 64, 69, 77
gender/gender systems, xv,
xviii, xxvii, 4, 22, 91, 95,
151, 161; attacks on, 49, 162;
complementarity of, xxviii,
29, 87, 90; dominant regimes
of, 186; and economics, 137,
146; equality/interdependence
among, 16, 37, 104, 106, 129; and
identities, xxx, 10, 17, 49, 55,
109; as manipulated by settler
colonialism, 21, 25; roles and
responsibilities of, 7, 32, 48, 50;
as system of oppression, 7–8, 10
gender knowledges, 25, 95, 104,
118, 137, 146, 149, 179, 189
generosity, xv, xxii, 112, 120,
123; ethic of, 142, 145; as
intimate, 141, 150, 166
genocide, 27, 60, 92, 161;
legacies of, 155
gift, logic of, 134, 137, 143–46, 150, 150.
158, 158, 175; as an ethic, 119,
137; and indebtedness, 120, 122;
meaning of, 126–27;
as resilient, 119, 142;

gift, logic of *continued*
and victimization, 126;
in Western worldviews,
121. *See also* indebtedness;
resilience; victimization
gift economies, xxix, xxxi, 119–22,
124–26, 137, 145; as targeted
for elimination, 118; and
values of gift-giving, 131
gift giving, xxix, 117–18,
126–27, 131, 147
Gilley, Brian Joseph, 104, 110
God-figure, as male, 12–13, 15
Goeman, Mishuana (Seneca), 2, 104
Goffman, Erving, 65
Goldie, Terry, 155
Goulet, Jean-Guy, 160
Goulet, Linda, 77
Grand Council Fire, 17–18
Grant, Agnes, 65
The Great Law of Peace
(Kaienere'kó:wa), 17, 50
Greene, Graham (Oneida), 37
Greene, Ryan Scott, 181
Gwich'in People, 62

# H

Haig-Brown, Celia, 65
Haisla People, 119, 146; gift
economy of, 120, 126, 130,
145; potlatch ceremonies,
121, 125; worldview of, 126
*Halfbreed*, 29
Halfe, Louise Bernice (Cree),
xxiv–xxvi, 62, 69, 71–73,
77–78, 83, 129, 177
Haudenosaunee Confederacy, xxvii,

xxxi, 32, 35, 184, 188; ethics of,
54, 183; gender ecology/systems
of, 8, 18–22, 24; governance
structures in, 17–19, 24, 36, 49–
50, 123; kinship system of, 16–
17, 31, 50; knowledge traditions
of, 8, 24, 180; as matrilineal
and matrilocal, 19, 23–24, 49;
and principle of twinship,
16; roles and responsibilities
in, 9, 18–20; worldview of, 8,
13, 16, 18, 20, 29, 53. *See also*
Iroquois; Kanien'keha:ka;
Mohawk; Onwehón:we
Haudenosaunee creation story,
9–10, 12–13, 19, 48; and
convergence of human and
animal, 14; gender systems
in, 17; power dynamic in, 15
Hawaiian culture, xxi, 184
Heiltsuk culture, 119
Henderson, James (Sákéj)
Youngblood (Chickasaw), 32
Henry, Robert (Métis), xv, 44, 46
heteropatriarchy, xvii–xviii, xx,
29, 55, 119, 137, 142, 150, 171,
178, 186; and Christianity, 3;
dismantling of, xxiii, xxvii,
103, 107, 111; and economic
exchange, 131; gender systems
in, 97, 124, 146, 149; and
hypermasculinity, 130; as
naturalized, 134, 144, 187;
negative impacts of, xi, xix,
xxix, 54, 68, 110, 120, 143,
177; and non-dominative
masculinities, 172; and nuclear

family models, 99; and settler
colonialism, ix–x, xii, 23–24,
30, 48, 52, 91, 93–95, 105, 141,
173; social organization of, 158
Highway, Tomson (Cree), 10
Hokowhitu, Brendan (Ngāti
Pūkenga), xiv–xv,
xxx, 3, 93, 95, 187
hooks, bell, 164, 168
Hopkins, Zoe Leigh
(Kanien'keha:ka-Heiltsuk),
xxx, 179–80, 182–85, 188
Houle, Terrance (Blood and
Saulteaux), 147
Hunt, Dallas (Cree), 47
Hunt, Sarah (Kwakwaka'wakw), 104
Hunter, Robert, 81, 84
Hutchison, R. Douglas, 188
hypermasculinity, xiv, xxi–xxii,
xxvii, 7, 9, 33–34, 42, 48–49, 53,
143; and gendered economy,
165; and heteropatriarchy,
130; as individualistic, 151; and
models of maleness, 74–75;
rubric of, 140; and violence,
xxix; 39–41, 43, 100, 110, 140, 149

## I

*I Am Woman: A Native Perspective
on Sociology and Feminism,* 32
identities, ix, 3, 6–7, 31, 47, 98, 137,
187; as diverse/empowered,
20, 119, 171, 179; as gendered,
xxx, 4, 17, 49, 55, 109; and
masculinity, xx, 91, 93
identity, twinship principle
of, 16, 21, 49

inclusivity, xxi–xxii; ethics of,
155; and genders, xi, 67
indebtedness, 137, 139–40, 154;
and exchange economics,
138, 145; and gifts, 122;
and subordination, 120
*Indian Act* (1876), 9, 21, 29–30,
48–49, 75, 81, 188; as
defining Indigenous identity,
22–24, 158; as imposing
patriarchal systems, 22
Indian Residential Schools Truth
and Reconciliation Commission
of Canada (IRS TRC), xxviii, 8,
26, 28, 65, 78, 80, 86; Atlantic
National Event, 60, 62, 81, 83;
Sharing Circles, 63, 82, 87;
survivor testimonies, 64, 67, 75
*Indian School Days,* 66, 77
Indigenous cultures: creation
stories of, 10; as denigrated
in residential school,
68; extinction of, 35, 38;
features of, 33, 40; and
social structures, 32, 41
Indigenous families/communities,
xxv–xxvi, 114, 187; alienation
from, 41, 43–44, 77, 81, 156, 160,
167, 177; dynamic mutuality of,
28, 30; and the individual, ix,
53, 119, 155; integration into, x,
6, 22, 49, 82, 102, 113, 170, 178,
184; roles and responsibilities
in, 3, 19, 24, 129, 142, 160; and
sense of duty, 157; well-being
of, 7, 20, 175. *See also* kinship
bonds/relations/systems

Indigenous governance systems: and the *Indian Act* and *Enfranchisement Act,* 24; manipulations of, 61; model of leadership, 37; as sovereign, 62, 75–76, 103, 124

Indigenous literatures/literary art, ix, xi, xiii, xxiv, xxvii, 10, 56, 79, 93, 145, 189. *See also* Halfe, L.; Robinson, E.; Scofield, G.; Thrasher, A.; Van Camp, R.

Indigenous masculinities, xvii, xx, xxxii, 63, 107; attributes of, xiii, xvii, 95, 112, 146, 150, 152, 168, 172, 186; colonial limitations on, xxxi, 31, 39, 44, 94, 99, 182, 187–88; concept of, xi, xxi, xxix, 3, 5, 8, 40, 86, 93, 111, 114, 142, 176–77, 188; and dominance, xxviii–xxix, 110, 124, 129, 148–50, 179; models of, xiv, xxix–xxx, 95, 139–40, 151, 157, 159, 161–63, 167, 171; roles and responsibilities of, 5–6, 49, 129, 171; as rubrics for decolonization, ix, xi, 93–94, 114; stereotypes of, ix, 34, 43, 70, 94, 149

Indigenous masculinities studies, xv, xx–xxii, xxx, 93, 95, 114, 179; as celebrating consensual vulnerability, 184; as honouring autonomy and integrity, 183; and honouring bodies, 181; as theorizing roles and responsibilities, 187

*Indigenous Men and Masculinities: Legacies, Identities, Regeneration,* xv, 93

Indigenous men/boys/manhood, 32, 61, 181; as portrayed as violent and criminal, 31, 33, 41, 44, 46–47; roles and responsibilities of, 3, 20, 25, 48, 55, 143, 186; as shamed/disempowered, 4, 30, 41, 48, 60, 62, 74, 105

Indigenous Peoples: futures of, xxvii, 7, 48, 55, 92, 101, 110–11, 171–72, 188; identity of, 1, 32, 47, 154, 160; and kinship, 119, 155; liberation of, 4, 76, 90, 92, 99, 122, 130, 142, 148, 182; oppression of, xxxiii, 44, 76, 105, 120, 132; relationship to the land, xxviii, 2, 43, 76, 79, 82, 92, 95, 105, 154, 161; as removed from their lands, xi, 7, 17, 27, 30, 38, 40, 44, 59, 61, 72, 77, 97, 151; worldviews of, xxviii, 29, 92, 95. *See also* kinship bonds/relations/systems

Indigenous women and girls, xi, xvi, xxvi–xxvii, 101–3, 161; as affected by residential schools, 28, 30; and dangers from colonial masculinities, xxv, 91, 99; dehumanization of, 49, 60, 69–70, 161; power and authority of, 2, 24, 30, 33, 106; violence towards, xxiii–xxiv, 48, 69, 96

Indigenous youth, 68, 76, 82, 155, 167

individualism, xiv, 7, 53–54,
    106, 112, 114, 145–46, 160,
    169, 183; as an identity,
    165; and gift-giving, 118; as
    naturalized, 143–44. *See also*
    masculinities, individualistic
Innes, Robert Alexander (Cree),
    xv, 46, 93, 158, 185
integration, 151, 159, 170, 183;
    into the community,
    x, 5–6, 27, 49, 55, 130;
    interpersonal, xix, 80, 184
integrity, xix, xxxiii, 4–5, 123,
    159, 175; individual, 10,
    49, 55, 183; of the person,
    x–xi, 151, 155, 160, 183
intimacy, x–xi, xvi, xix, xxix, xxxi,
    91, 177–78, 184; blockages
    to, 106; as erotic, 98–101,
    108; generative power of,
    xxviii, 152; and generosity,
    112, 141, 172, 175; as physical/
    interpersonal, xx, 90, 92, 103,
    111; sovereign sites of, 99
Inuvialuit People, 62
Iroquoian People, 16–17, 37; as
    matrilineal and matrilocal, 18
*Iroquoian Women: The Gantowisas,* 15
Iroquois People, kinship
    system of, 18
*Islands of Decolonial Love,* xxxiii,
    95–96, 99, 101, 103
isolation, 156, 160, 170, 172, 183

## J

Jackson, Randy (Anishinaabe),
    xiii, 7, 20, 91, 100, 175

Jackson II, Ronald L., 32
Johnston, Basil (Anishinaabe), 66,
    77, 157, 166, 171, 176, 183
justice: and colonialism, 47, 106;
    and hypermasculinity, 53,
    149; and injustice, 97, 104,
    148; as transformative, xxv
Justice, Daniel Heath (Cherokee), x,
    xxxiii, 5, 7, 76, 117; on kinship,
    154–55, 157, 160, 166, 171; on male
    bodies/masculinities, xviii, 74–75,
    90, 94, 104, 106, 112, 129, 180, 182;
    on sexual shame/sexuality, 59,
    173; and stories on Indigenous
    self, 4, 48, 56; on warriorhood, 87

## K

Kanawake Nation, 36
Kanehsatake People, 42
Kanien'keha:ka Nation, 17, 22–23,
    43–45; law of (Kaianere'kó:wa),
    9, 18; warrior flag, 82
Kanonhsyonne Hill, Janice,
    1, 15, 19–20, 50, 55
Kautz, Ben, 47
Keene, Adrienne (Cherokee), xxii
Keepness, Shane (Saulteaux), xv
Kicking Bird (fictional noble
    savage), 37, 39
Kina Gchi Nishnaabeg-ogamig
    (ecology of intimacy), 105
King, Thomas (Cherokee), 10
Kinistino, Night (Cree),
    xxiv, xxvi–xxvii
kinship bonds/relations/
    systems, 54, 60–61, 97, 99,
    107, 161–62, 164, 177, 185;

kinship bonds/relations/systems
   *continued*, as a communal
   value, 14, 18, 154–56, 158,
   169–70; ethics of, 152, 155, 158,
   169; in Indigenous families/
   communities, 23, 62, 130,
   157; as intergenerational
   and multi-gendered, 43; and
   masculinity, 157, 171; rights
   and responsibilities of, xxx,
   76–77, 87, 156–57, 166–67,
   170–71, 173; as targeted for
   destruction by colonialism/
   residential schools, xxviii, 2,
   44, 62, 65–66, 68, 72, 78, 130;
   through storytelling, 151–52, 155
Kioke, James, 81, 83
*kisiskâciwan: Indigenous Voices*
   *from Where the River Flows*
   *Swiftly,* xxiv–xxv
Klopotek, Brian (Choctaw),
   xxx, 33, 74, 132
Knapaysweet, Joey, 46
Knight, Lindsay (Cree),
   xxiv, xxvi–xxvii
Knockwood, Isabelle
   (Mi'kmaq), 65, 67
Komulainen, Shaney, 42–43
Koosees Jr., Samuel, 81, 83–84
Kou-chibou-guac National Park, 97
Kuokkanen, Rauna (Sami), xxix,
   117–19, 121–22, 124, 126, 145–46

**L**

LaChance, Leo, 46
Laforgue, Father, 37–39

Larocque, Bradley, Anishinaabe
   Warrior, 42–43
Larocque, Private Patrick, 44
*The Last of the Mohicans,* 37–39, 53
Law of the People, kinship
   patterns in, 158
Lawrence, Bonita (Mi'kmaq),
   22, 30, 105
Lederman, Marsha, xxv
Lee, Erica Violet (Cree),
   xxiv–xxvii, 101, 103–4
Lee, Lloyd L. (Diné), xv
*The Lesser Blessed,* xxx, 149–50,
   153, 155, 158, 160–161,
   164, 168–69, 170–73
*Letters and Notes on the Manners,*
   *Customs and Conditions of*
   *North American Indians,* 35
Lewis, Daniel Day, 38
LGBTQ persons. *See* queer/trans/
   two-spirit persons
liberation. *See* freedom
Lightning, Cody (Cree), 179, 188
Longman, Nickita (Saulteaux),
   xxiv, xxvi–xxvii
Lorde, Audre, 32
*Love Medicine and One Song:*
   *Sâkihtowin-maskihkiy*
   *êkwa pêyak-nikamowin,*
   xii, 89, 107, 111, 113

**M**

Macdonald, John A., 26, 28, 30
*Magic Weapons: Aboriginal Writers*
   *Remaking Community after*
   *Residential School,* 68, 79

male bodies/maleness, ix, xi, 91, 95,
114, 182, 187; denigration of,
69, 71, 75, 87, 110; as diverse,
179–80; and embodied
subjectivities, 109, 112;
hypermasculine models
of, 106; as racialized and
sexually aberrant, 75, 90;
roles and responsibilities of,
158; as sacred space, 107–8;
sexuality of, xxviii, 105, 107,
161; and violence, 30, 74, 180
Maliseet People, 27
Mann, Barbara Alice, 15–17, 19
Maoli People, 62
Māori People, xiv, 62, 74
Maracle, Lee (Stó:lō), 2,
6–7, 22, 32, 104
marginalization, and
oppression, 131, 140
masculindians, 33–34, 39, 43, 187–88;
stereotypes of, 40, 132
*Masculindians: Conversations
about Indigenous Manhood,*
xiv–xv, xvii, xxiii, 6, 90
masculinities: as colonial, xvi, xxxi,
91–92, 94, 96–97, 99–100,
103, 109, 180; as dominant/
dominative, xvi–xvii, xxvii, 94,
110, 124, 130, 137, 140, 149, 172,
179; as individualistic, 43, 122,
130, 140, 162, 166–67, 170–72
Mauss, Marcel, 121–22, 144
Mays, Kyle T. (Saganaw
Anishinaabe-Black), xxii
McAdam, Sylvia (Cree),

xxiv, xxvi–xxvii
McKegney, Sam, 59, 90,
112, 171, 173, 184
McLeod, Neal (Cree-Swedish),
xxiii–xxiv, xxvi, 63
Means, Russell (Lakota), 38
Medicine Man, 35
medicines, xii, xvii, xx, 92, 103,
107, 113, 156–57, 167, 170
Messner, Michael, 168
Métis People, 154
Mi'kmaq Grand Council, 65
Mi'kmaq People, 27, 62, 65, 97
Miller, J.R., 17–19
Milloy, John S., 27
misogyny, xxii, 110, 136
*Mohawk Midnight Runners,* xxx,
179–81, 183, 185–86, 188
Mohawk warrior: effigies as
burned by racists, 44–45;
as hypermasculine, 9
Monture, Rick (Kanien'keha:ka),
9, 13, 22
Monture-Angus, Patricia
(Kanien'keha:ka), 33
Moose Cree First Nation, 79
Morgensen, Scott, xv–xvi,
4, 94–95, 188
mortification, permanent, 65–66
Moses, Daniel David (Delaware), 1
mouth, 129, 141; as associated with
individual desire, 126; as
metaphorical sweat lodge,
107; and sexual release, 161
muskrat (anò:kien), 11, 15

# N

Nagel, Joane, 34

*Native Men Remade: Gender and Nation in Contemporary Hawai'i*, xv, xxviii, 62, 80, 86, 185

natural world, as under human control in Genesis, 14

Naytowhow, Colin (Cree), 82, 187

Neuhaus, Mareike, 151

nitotem (intimacy, openness), 77

"Nitotem" (poem), 62, 71, 73, 75–77, 83, 177

Nixon, Lindsay (Cree-Métis-Saulteaux), xx, xxii, xxv–xxvi

non-interference, ethic of, 6–7, 9, 17, 19–20, 29, 32, 49, 52, 54

North West Mounted Police, 30

*Nót-to-way, a Chief,* 35–36

nuclear family models, 99, 132, 134–36, 168; naturalized as dominant, 169

Nunn, Neil (settler), 31, 46–47

# O

Oka Land Reclamation of 1990, 42–44

Okihcitâwak Street Patrol, 81

okihcitâwak (worthy men), 63, 81–82, 187

Oliver, Vanessa, 102

Oneida Nation, 17

Onondaga Nation, 17, 50

Onwehón:we Peoples, 44

oppression, xii, 105, 110; and capitalist exchanges, 119; and gender, 7–8, 10, 21; and marginalization, 131, 140; as naturalized, 145; and toxic masculinity, 148

# P

Pacific Northwest Indigenous worldviews, 158

Pasternak, Shiri, 31

patriarchy, 61, 112, 168. *See also* heteropatriarchy

Peacemaker, 50, 53

Piché, Alison, 46

*Porcupines and China Dolls,* 64

Porter (Sakokwenión:kwas), Tom (Kanien'keha:ka), xxvii, 9–10, 13, 15, 17–20, 23, 48–50, 52–53, 55

potlatch systems: as banned, 126; ceremonies of, 121, 124–25; and settler governments, 118–20

protectorship, 43, 142–43

Proudstar, Jon, 188

# Q

Québécois nationalism, 44

queer and two-spirit theory, xv, xxvii–xxviii, 7, 91, 109–10, 177

*The Queerness of Native American Literature,* 109

queer/trans/two-spirit persons, xi, xiii, xvi, xxi, xxvii, 21, 93–94, 107, 111; as affected by colonial policy, 28, 30; as devalued, 49; dispossession of, 91; violence towards, xxiv, 103; vulnerability of, 101

# R

race/racism, x, 23, 44, 90, 153–54; as disempowering, 41; and gender, 2, 25, 75; and inferiority, 75; as masculine, 33, 132; and shaming, 91; and violence, 38, 75

rape, 59–60, 78, 139, 141, 161

Reber, Susanne, 46

reciprocity, 16, 76, 105, 129, 178

reconciliation, within the survivors' families, 78–79

*Red Rising Magazine,* 103

reintegration, 82, 178

Renaud, Robert, 46

residential school system, xxviii, 9, 21, 26–28, 30, 49, 76, 90, 126, 188; as causing alienation, 66, 68, 77, 82; dysfunctional gender dynamics at, 29, 64, 135; as genocidal program, 60–61; and intergenerational legacies of abuse, 72, 78, 80; and kinship/sibling relations, 60, 151; policies of, 60–61, 81; and shame, 73–75, 87, 160–161; survivors/survivor testimonies, xxviii, 60, 62–65, 75, 77–78, 80, 86–87; violence in, 65, 71–72, 74–75, 78, 87, 128

Residential School Walkers, xxviii, 62, 82, 84–85; as embodied discursive action, 79–80; and empowered subjectivities, 81; and reterritorializing acts, 79, 83

resilience, 21, 82, 180; of gift logic, 118–19; of masculinist heteronormity, 172

*Resistance and Renewal,* 65

resurgence, of Indigenous Peoples, xiii, xvi, 79, 92, 101, 103, 113, 178; collective models for, 50, 54; and hypermasculinity, xxi, xxvii, 150; and masculinities, 91, 111

reterritorialization, 9, 54, 62, 79, 178; as radical, xxviii, 62, 78, 82

Rifkin, Mark, 15, 61–62, 68, 114, 169

Robinson, Eden (Haisla-Heiltsuk): on effects of colonial rule, 124, 126, 135–36, 144, 151–152; on gender and economics, xxix, 119–20, 125, 127–28, 130–32, 146; on masculinities, 129, 140–41, 143, 159, 162

Robinson, Gordon (Haisla), 121

Ross, Rupert, 6

Rotiskenrakéh:te ethics, 187

Royal Canadian Mounted Police, 30, 47

# S

Sachem (Chief) (Roiá:nehr), 18–19, 24

*The Sacred Hoop: Recovering the Feminine in American Indian Traditions,* 110

safety, xxii, 100, 143, 157; of community, xxvi, xxxi, 44, 187; of women, girls, queer, and two-spirit persons, xxv, 106

*The Sasquatch at Home:*
   *Traditional Protocols and*
   *Modern Storytelling,* 119
savage, noble: as stereotype,
   33–34, 37–41
Schellenberg, August
   (Kanien'keha:ka), 37
Scofield, Gregory (Cree-Métis),
   xii, xvii, xxviii, 89–90, 104,
   106–14, 129, 166, 171, 182, 184
Scott, Duncan Campbell, 27, 30
Scudeler, June (Métis), 107
Sedgwick, Eve Kosofsky, 52
Sehóti (my people), 154
self-determination, 54, 105
Seneca Nation, 17
sensuality, xviii, 67, 90–91, 112; and
   embodiment, 111; and intimacy,
   xix, xxx, 102, 170, 172–73
Seton, Ernest Thompson, 39
settler colonialism, xvii, xix, xxviii,
   17, 40, 55, 59, 74, 132, 134;
   as destroying Indigenous
   nationhoods, xi, xxiii, xxvii,
   9, 32, 49, 99; deterritorializing
   assault of, 1–2, 8, 31, 43–44,
   47–48, 104, 124, 175–77;
   gendered systems of, xxviii,
   4, 9, 15, 64, 92, 98, 175, 178;
   and masculinities, xii–xiii,
   xvi, 64, 75, 93–95, 97, 99–100,
   103, 180, 182, 188; negative
   characteristics/effects of, ix,
   21, 59, 71, 100–101, 103, 114, 171,
   187; power of, 8, 40, 106–7;
   as sustained by capitalism,
   126; technologies/policies

of, x, 7, 10, 26, 38, 61–62,
   74–75, 86, 90, 106, 160; tools
   for healing, 111; and violence,
   50, 79, 91, 94, 101, 103, 161
sexuality: as ceremony, 90; and
   colonial dispossession, 126;
   and desire, xviii, 67, 109–10,
   173; and domination, 139; and
   exchange systems, 141; and
   intimacy/relationships, 71, 102,
   129, 140, 173; and shame, 59, 62,
   67; and violence, 90, 135, 161
shame, of the body, 71, 73, 75,
   77, 90, 110, 114, 161; as
   debilitating, 86; as racialized,
   91; and sexuality, 59, 62, 67;
   and social engineering, 68
Shubenacadie Indian Residential
   School, 65, 67
Shubenacadie reserve, 27
Simpson, Audra
   (Kanien'keha:ka), 3, 9
Simpson, Leanne Betasamosake
   (Michi Saagiig Nishnaabeg):
   on decolonial love, 95, 102,
   104–5, 113–14; on gender
   dynamics, xxi, xxviii, 96, 98,
   106; on Indigenous bodies and
   lives of meaning, ix–x, xxvii,
   53–55, 59, 76, 78, 176, 181, 184;
   on Indigenous masculinities,
   xii, xxiii, xxxiii, 91, 95, 97, 99,
   107, 110–11, 129; on Indigenous
   resurgence, xvi, 101, 103; on
   protectorship, 43; on settler
   colonialism, xi, 92, 100, 126,
   146; on territoriality, 2, 48

simulacra: and heteropatriarchy, 134, 138; precession of, 132, 134, 136

*Simulations,* 132

Sinclair, James (Niigaanwewidem) (Anishinaabe), 180–81

Sinclair, Justice Murray (Anishinaabe), 64, 78

Sison, Marites N., 81

Six Nations Territory, 36, 179, 181–82, 185; as maintaining their culture, 22

Sky Woman (Atsi'tsiaká:ion), 10–15, 19, 48–49; creation story, xxvii, 10, 20

Sky World (Karonhià:ke), 11–13, 15

Smithsonian American Art Museum, 36

Smoke, Penny, 82, 187

social engineering, 75, 131, 135, 140, 188; as colonial technology, x, xxvii, 30, 68, 74, 79; through residential schools, 27–28, 66, 76, 87. *See also* assimilation; residential school system

social organization, 10, 17, 122, 158, 169, 186

*Songs to Kill a Wîhtikow,* xxiii

St. Peter Claver's Indian Residential School, 66

Stanley, Gerald, 46–48

Starblanket, Gina (Cree-Saulteaux), 47

stereotypes: of cowboys and Indians, 150; of Indigenous masculinities, ix, 33–34, 37, 39–43, 70, 94, 132, 149–50, 187; of violence, xxx, 43, 47

Stonechild, Neil, 46

storytelling, xii, 4–5, 154, 189; as used to develop kinship network, 151–52, 155

Studi, Wes (Cherokee), 39

Styres, Jon, 46

subjective corporeality, agentive, 109

subordination, 22, 27, 120, 138, 144

suicide, 80–81, 159, 161, 171, 181

Sumac, Smokii (Ktunaxa), xvi–xx, xxxi–xxxii, 110

Sutherland, Erin (Métis), xv

sweat lodge, 107–8

Sweet, Timothy, 3, 48

Swift, Jonathan, 93, 185

Syilx Nation: and consensus building, 143; gift economy of, 122–24, 126, 145

## T

Tatonetti, Lisa, xv, 104, 109–10, 114

Tengan, Ty P. Kāwika (Kanaka Māoli), xiv, xxviii, 62, 79–80, 86, 150, 184–85

territoriality, 2, 8, 48, 61, 82, 92, 175

Tłįchǫ Nation, 153, 160, 167; creation story of, 151; culture of, 166; kinship system, 151, 158–159; Traditional Territory of, 158

Thrasher, Anthony Apakark (Inuvialuit), 29, 66–68

transition, FTM (female-to-male), xvi, xix, 110

trans persons. *See* queer/trans/two-spirit persons

trauma, multiple, 60, 66, 151–53; and disembodiment, 72, 74;

trauma, multiple *continued*
ethical witnessing of, 64; as
intergenerational, 126; legacies
of, 75; memories of, 101–2
Trent University, xxiii
*The Truth about Stories: A*
*Native Narrative*, 10
Tuck, Eve (Unangax̂), 104, 155
Tuffin, Lois, xxiii
Tuscarora People, 17
two-spirit persons. *See* queer/
trans/two-spirit persons
Tyendinaga Nation/Mohawk
Territory, 19, 36

**U**

Union of British Columbia
Indian Chiefs, 47
University of Regina Press
(URP), xxiv
University of Victoria: Indigenous
Governance Program, xxi
University of Winnipeg, 78

**V**

Valaskakis, Gail Guthrie
(Chippewa), xxx, 42
Van Camp, Richard (Tłı̨chǫ), xxix,
153, 164, 168, 173, 179; and
gender, 156; and just violence,
148–49; and kinship relations,
xxx, 147, 151–52, 155, 169; and
masculinity, 150, 171, 180
Vaughan, Genevieve, 117–18,
121–22, 124, 168
Vedal, Lauren, 170, 172–73
victimization, 64, 96; by

Canadian government, 97,
99; through gift-giving, 126;
of women and girls, 102
violence, xiv, xxix, 40, 43, 47, 75, 139,
159, 163; and accountability,
xxv; cycle of, xxiv, 72, 162,
167; as gender-based, xxiii–
xxiv, xxvii, 48, 50, 52–53,
59, 90–91, 106, 180; as just,
147–49; as lateral, 105, 129;
and masculinity, xvi, xxx,
130, 136, 143, 156, 170–71, 187;
as patriarchal/colonial, 31,
73, 94, 134, 189; as racialized,
38; as transactional, 145
Vizenor, Gerald (Anishinaabe),
32, 44, 132, 177
Vranckx, Sylvie, 149
vulnerability, xii, xxvi, xxviii–xxx,
90, 111, 175, 179, 183; as agentive,
113, 129; as consensual, 92,
95, 98–101, 108, 112, 184–85;
to exploitation, 128–29; fear
of, 102; of masculinities,
97; as openness, 171

**W**

wâhkôtowin (Cree kinship), 77, 79
*Walking with Ghosts*, 89
Walsh, Bruce, xxiv, xxvi
Ward, Sakej (Mi'kmaq), 1, 3, 48
warrior, bloodthirsty, as
stereotype, 33–35, 39–42
warrior (rotiskenrakéh:te)/
warriorhood, xxx–xxxi,
1, 33–34, 44, 82–83, 87,
187; as reimagined, 188;

as responsibility, xxxiii;
Westernized notion of, 7
*Wasáse: Indigenous Pathways of Action and Freedom*, 1
Water World, 11–13
Western worldview, 121, 124
*When Did Indians Become Straight? Kinship, the History of Sexuality, and Native Sovereignty*, 61–62, 68, 114
Whiskeychan, Frances, 81
Whitehead, Joshua (Oji-Cree), xx
white people/settlers. *See* European/white settlers
white supremacy, 50
*Why Indigenous Literatures Matter*, 4–5, 48, 56, 117

wîhtikow (Cree cannibal beast), xxiii
Willmott, Glenn, 122, 144
Wilson, Carla, xxi
Wilson, Michael, 41
Wilson, Shawn (Cree), 154, 160
*Women and the Gift Economy*, 122
Woodcraft Indians, 39
*Written by the Body: Gender Expansiveness and Indigenous and Non-Cis Masculinities*, 114

# Y

Yang, K. Wayne, 155
*You Are Enough: Love Poems for the End of the World*, xvi–xvii, xix, 110
Young, Sherri, 27, 65